EXCEL

gurus gone wild

by

Bill Jelen

*with 112K contributors
and 6,156,123 guests*

HOLY MACRO! BOOKS

PO Box 82, Uniontown, OH 44685

Printed in USA by Malloy

First Printing: March 2009

Author: Bill Jelen

Technical Editor: Bob Umlas

Editor: Kitty Wilson

Interior Design: Fine Grains (India) Private Limited, New Delhi, India

Cover Design: Shannon Mattiza, 6Ft4 Productions

Published by: Holy Macro! Books, 13386 Judy Ave, PO Box 82, Uniontown OH 44685

Distributed by Independent Publishers Group

ISBN 978-1-932802-40-5

Library of Congress Control Number: 2008923727

ABOUT THE AUTHOR

Bill Jelen is the host of MrExcel.com and the author of 24 books. But this book was really written by thousands of people who contributed to the MrExcel.com message board or who have spoken up at one of my Power Excel seminars with a cool trick. In many cases, new ideas at the board happen through a collaborative process – someone asks a question, others answer, others build on that answer, Someone posts something simply amazing, more people build on the amazing concept, and then a whole bunch of really talented Excel gurus will offer kudos for a really slick solution. If you are one of the people who have participated in this process, this this book is also written by you.

About the MrExcel Message Board: While MrExcel.com debuted on November 21, 2008, the message board did not debut until 2009. Using a script from Matt's Script Archive, the original message board was born. Bill wrote, "you can still keep sending your questions to me via e-mail, or you can post them at the message board. And, if you happen to be at the message board and see an easy question, give that person an answer." He figured it would be sort of like the take-a-penny, leave-a-penny cup that you see by the cash register. In the early months, Ivan Moala, Dave and Cecilia became frequent regulars at the board. Today, over 100,000 people have signed up as members, there are many hundreds of regulars, and six million unique visitors pass through the site annually. The community at the MrExcel.com message board continues to provide answers to 30,000 questions a year. In fact, with 365,000 answers archived, it is likely that the answer to nearly any Excel question has already been posted.

ACKNOWLEDGMENTS

Thank you to the entire community at the MrExcel.com message board. This includes everyone who has posted a question, suggested an answer and those who lurk without posting.

MrExcel.com was started in 1998. Over the years, a number of folks have been on the payroll and helped grow the site: Anne Troy. Mala Singh. Juan Pablo Gonzalez. Tracy Syrstad. Suat Ozgur. Far more people volunteer and keep the community humming. Kristy Sharpe,

Greg Truby, Nate Oliver, Paddy Davies, Richard Schollar, Chris Smith, Suat Ozgur, Zack Barresse, Ivan Moala, Joe4, all volunteer as admins and moderators.

Thanks to the pioneers – the first regulars, back when it might take 4 hours before Ivan Moala, Dave from Oz or Cecilia from the Pacific Northwest would check in with an answer.

Mala Singh of XLSoft Consulting wrote the speedometer and macroeconomic supply curve add-ins and does all of our engineering projects (see examples at http://www.mrexcel.com/graphics.shtml). Mala pitched in to help write up some topics in this book. Thanks to Mala for helping to get the book to press.

Aladin Akyurek is the king of Ctrl+Shift+Enter formulas. Like everyone else, I usually have to run his formulas through the Auditor Toolbar's Evaluate Formula feature before I can figure out how it is working, but they always impress. Aladin's tireless formula examples have raised many to the level of Excel guru.

This list could fill an entire book, but thanks to the folks who answer a lot of questions: Norie, Aladin Akyurek, Andrew Poulsom, Smitty, Jindon, Erik.Van.Geit, Richardschollar, Vog, Jonmo1, Von Pookie, Paddyd, Joe4, Barry Houdini, Juan Pablo González, Mark W., Yogi Anand, HOTPEPPER, Peter_Sss, Just_Jon, Zack Barresse, Nateo, Fairwinds, Tusharm, Tom Urtis, Greg Truby, Sydneygeek, Brian From Maui, Joe Was, Lenze, Oaktree, Halface, Domenic, Brianb, Glennuk, Datsmart, Donkeyote, Nimrod, Tom Schreiner, Rorya, Mikerickson, Pgc01, NBVC, Acw, Onlyadrafter, Andrew Fergus, Daniels012, Tommygun, Tazguy37, Steveo591, Ivan F Moala, Schielrn, Texasalynn, Fazza, Barry Katcher, Lewiy, Alexander Barnes, Phantom1975, Damon Ostrander, DRJ, Ralpha, Domski, Mark O'Brien, Tactps, Stanleydgromjr, Mudface, Richie(UK), Starl, Parry, Al_B_Cnu, Cbrine, Jack In The UK, Todd Bardoni, Jon Von Der Heyden, Gerald Higgins, Iridium, Jon Peltier, Dougstroud, Seti, Thenooch, Stormseed, Jaafar Tribak, Dk, PA HS Teacher, Xlgibbs, Xld, Anne Troy, Ravishankar, Dave3009, Hatman, Jimboy, Barrie Davidson, Venkat1926, Krishnakumar, Njimack, Jay Petrulis, Vicrauch, Iliace, P Sitaram, Gates Is Antichrist, Oorang, XL-Dennis, Shajueasow, Markandrews, RAM, Santeria, SIXTH SENSE, Giacomo, Chris Davison,

Eliw, IML, Nbrcrunch, Cornflakegirl, Agihcam, Itr674, Dave Hawley, Mike Blackman, Sweater_Vests_Rock, Derek, Dominicb, Shades, Travis, Corticus, Brew, Plettieri, Dave Patton, Hawaiian Harry, Iggydarsa, Glaswegian, Bat17, Boller, Al Chara, Brian.Wethington, Colo, Ekim, Mortgageman, Jim May, Russell Hauf, Babycody, Yee388, Btadams, Mdmilner, Ktab, Howard, Mrkowz, Kskinne, Mickg, Gord, Earlyd, Pekkavee, Ian Mac, Kenneth Hobson, Verluc, Fergus, Willr, CT Witter, Davers, Ndendrinos, Arthurbr, Ajm, Sal Paradise, Thorpyuk, Staticbob, Pauljj, Dbmathis, Brettvba, Chitosunday, Pcc, ADAMC, PATSYS, Ponsy Nob., Ponsonby, Sykes, Martinee, Justinlabenne, Bubbis Thedog, Shippey121, Harvey, Excelr8r, Yard, Sssb2000

I appreciate the people from the MrExcel community whom I've had the opportunity to meet over the years. It is always cool to discuss Excel tricks over lunch or dinner. I'll miss a few, but Tracy, Juan Pablo, NateO, Greg Truby, Smitty, Richard, Jon, Bryony, Russ, Mel, Aaron, Brian from Maui, Matt aka Oaktree, Jay Petrulis, Tushar, Chip Pearson, Duane Aubin, Asaad Alli, Freddy Fuentes and a dozen more who I aren't popping into my head at this moment.

Thanks to the guys on the Excel team who I know on a first name basis. Dave, Chad, Charlie, Joe, - your dedication to the world's best spreadsheet is appreciated. I also appreciate that you always answer my e-mails when I have a bizarre Excel question or oddity.

Thanks to my friends; facebook friends, Facebook fans, Twitter followers, podcast viewers, friends from the old TechTV, readers who write in with ideas, anyone wearing an Excel Master pin, those who reaches for a MrExcel book when they have a problem, people who come to my seminars in places like Springfield Missouri, Columbus Indiana, and Madison Wisconsin (at least one cool tip in this book came from those cities and more).

At the office, thanks to Lora White for keeping things running and editing the podcasts and thanks to my sister Barb Jelen who packed and shipped this book to you.

Thanks to my family. Josh, Zeke, and Mary Ellen.

DEDICATION

Dedicated to every person who has ever answered a question at the MrExcel Message Board.

FOREWORD

This book was born in a British pub.

I was in England in 2007 to perform a couple more Power Excel Seminars. The night before the seminar in Southampton, a group of people from the MrExcel Message board got together for dinner. Russ Cockings, Bryony Stewart-Seume, Richard Schollar, Jon Von Der Hayden and Mel Smith were talking about some amazing tricks that they've seen at the board when someone, probably either Jon or Richard comments that their MrExcel favorites list was a veritable reference guide to Excel and VBA. These are very smart people who know a whole lot about Excel. You have to wonder what types of things would impress this group enough to cause them to add it to their favorites list.

You can check out that favorites list at http://www.mrexcel.com/favorites.html. You will find amazing ideas as you browse those topics. Yes, some are niche topics and many are arcane. However, if you use Excel all day, it is pretty wild to find someone who was able to coax the impossible out of our favorite spreadsheet.

To say that this book is a niche book is an understatement. I am not out to reach the masses with this book. Topics in this book are arcane. A person who uses Excel for 2000 hours per year might need to use any given topic once every 20,000 years. It is probably 1 tenth of one percent of the people using Excel will find any of this stuff fascinating. If you happen to be one of these people, then this book is for you. For the other 99.9%, take this book back to the bookstore and exchange it for Learn Excel 97-2010 from MrExcel or Pivot Table Data Crunching.

For the first two sections of this book, my general requirement for inclusion was that the topic had to be amazing to either me or favorited by a number of MrExcel MVP's. Some things came from the MrExcel Message Board, others came up during my Excel seminars. In the third section, I go through some basics to get you comfortable with Excel VBA and then launch into some amazing VBA utility macros. The appendix is an Excel function reference, with suggested uses for 120 of the 362 functions.

If you want to try out a technique, the files used in the production of the book are available for download at http://www.mrexcel.com/gurufiles.html.

Contents

SECTION 1 - FORMULAS

SECTION 2 - TECHNIQUES

SECTION 3 - MACROS

PART 1

FORMULAS

Find the First Non-Blank Value in a Row

Challenge: You want to build a formula to return the first non-blank cell in a row. Perhaps columns B:K reflect data at various points in time. Due to the sampling methodology, certain items are checked infrequently.

Solution: In Figure 1, the formula in A4 is:

```
=INDEX(C4:K4,1,MATCH(1,INDEX(1-ISBLANK(C4:K4),1,0),0))
```

Although this formula deals with an array of cells, it ultimately returns a single value, so you do not need to use Ctrl+Shift+Enter when entering this formula.

`=INDEX(C3:K3,1,MATCH(1,INDEX(1-ISBLANK(C3:K3),1,0),0))`

	A	B	C	D	E	F	G	H	I	J	K
1	1st Non-Blank		Data Range								
2	1					1					
3	5				5						
4	4					4		7		6	
5	7		7	6	7	8	9				
6	8								8		
7	7					7					
8	5						5				
9	1							1			
10	8								8		
11	1									1	
12	#N/A										

Figure 1. You find the first non-blank cell in each row of C2:K12 and return that value in column A.

Breaking It Down: Let's start from the inside. The `ISBLANK` function returns `TRUE` when a cell is blank and `FALSE` when a cell is non-blank. Look at the row of data in `C4:K4`. The `ISBLANK(C4:K4)` portion of the formula will return:

`{TRUE,TRUE,FALSE,TRUE,TRUE,FALSE,TRUE,FALSE,TRUE}`

Notice that this array is subtracted from 1. When you try to use `TRUE` and `FALSE` values in a mathematical formula, a `TRUE` value is treated as a 1, and a `FALSE` value is treated as a 0. By specifying `1-ISBLANK(C4:K4)`, you can convert the array of `TRUE`/`FALSE` values to 1s and 0s. Each `TRUE` value in the

ISBLANK function changes to a 0. Each FALSE value changes to a 1. Thus, the array becomes:

{0,0,1,0,0,1,0,1,0}

The formula fragment 1-ISBLANK(C4:K4) specifies an array that is 1 row by 9 columns. However, you need Excel to expect an array, and it won't expect an array based on this formula fragment. Usually, the INDEX function returns a single value, but if you specify 0 for the column parameter, the INDEX function returns an array of values. The fragment INDEX(1-ISBLANK(C4:K4),1,0) asks for row 1 of the previous result to be returned as an array. Here's the result:

Part I

{0,0,1,0,0,1,0,1,0}

The MATCH function looks for a certain value in a one-dimensional array and returns the relative position of the first found value. =MATCH(1,Array,0) asks Excel to find the position number in the array that first contains a 1. The MATCH function is the piece of the formula that identifies which column contains the first non-blank cell. When you ask the MATCH function to find the first 1 in the array of 0s and 1s, it returns a 3 to indicate that the first non-blank cell in C4:K4 occurs in the third cell, or E4:

Formula fragment: MATCH(1,INDEX(1-ISBLANK(C4:K4),1,0),0)

Sub-result: MATCH(1, {0,0,1,0,0,1,0,1,0},0)

Result: 3

At this point, you know that the third column of C4:K4 contains the first non-blank value. From here, it is a simple matter of using an INDEX function to return the value in that non-blank cell. =INDEX(Array,1,3) returns the value from row 1, column 3 of an array:

Formula fragment: =INDEX(C4:K4,1,MATCH(1,INDEX(1-ISBLANK(C4:K4),1,0),0))

Sub-result: =INDEX(C4:K4,1,3)

Result: 4

Additional Details: If none of the cells are non-blank, the formula returns an #N/A error.

Alternate Strategy: Subtracting the ISBLANK result from 1 does a good job of converting TRUE/FALSE values to 0s and 1s. You could skip this step, but then you would have to look for FALSE as the first argument of the MATCH function:

=INDEX(C4:K4,1,MATCH(FALSE,INDEX(ISBLANK(C4:K4),1,0),0))

Summary: The formula to return the first non-blank cell in a row starts with a simple ISBLANK function. Using INDEX to coax the string of results into an array allows this portion of the formula to be used as the lookup array of the MATCH function.

Source: http://www.mrexcel.com/forum/showthread.php?t=53223

CALCULATE WORKDAYS FOR 5-, 6-, AND 7-DAY WORKWEEKS

Challenge: Calculate how many workdays fall between two dates. Excel's NETWORKDAYS function does this if you happen to work the five days between Monday and Friday inclusive. This topic will show you how to perform the calculation for a company that works 5, 6, or 7 days a week.

Background: The NETWORKDAYS function calculates the number of workdays between two dates, inclusive of the beginning and ending dates. You specify the earlier date as the first argument, the later date as the second argument, and optionally an array of holidays as the third argument. In Figure 2, cell C3 calculates only 5 workdays because February 16, 2009, is a holiday. This is a cool function, but if you happen to work Monday through Saturday, it will not calculate correctly for you.

C3			f_x	=NETWORKDAYS(A3,B3,$E$2:$E$11)		
	A	**B**	**C**	**D**	**E**	**F**
1	Project Start	Project Due	Workdays		Holidays	
2	Tue, Jan 20, 09	Tue, Jan 27, 09	6		1/1/2009	
3	Tue, Feb 10, 09	Tue, Feb 17, 09	5		1/19/2009	
4	Fri, Jul 10, 09	Mon, Jul 13, 09	2		2/16/2009	
5	Fri, Jan 2, 09	Thu, Dec 31, 09	251		5/25/2009	
6					7/3/2009	
7					9/7/2009	
8					10/12/2009	
9					11/11/2009	
10					11/26/2009	
11					12/25/2009	

Figure 2. Traditionally, NETWORKDAYS assumes a Monday–through–Friday workweek.

Setup: Define a range named Holidays to refer to the range of holidays.

Solution: The formula in C3 is:

```
=SUMPRODUCT(--(COUNTIF(Holidays,ROW(INDIRECT(A3&":"&B3)))
=0),--(WEEKDAY(ROW(INDIRECT(A3&":"&B3)),3)<6))
```

Although this formula deals with an array of cells, it ultimately returns a single value, so you do not need to use Ctrl+Shift+Enter when entering this formula.

Breaking It Down: The formula seeks to check two things. First, it checks whether any of the days within the date range are in the holiday list. Second, it checks to see which of the dates in the date range are Monday-through-Saturday dates.

You need a quick way to compare every date from A3 to B3 to the holiday list. In the current example, this encompasses only 8 days, but down in row 5, you have more than 300 days.

The formula makes use of the fact that an Excel date is stored as a serial number. Although cell A3 displays February 10, 2009, Excel actually stores the date as 39854. (To prove this to yourself, press Ctrl+` to enter Show Formulas mode. Press Ctrl+` to return to Normal mode.)

It is convenient that Excel dates in the modern era are in the 39,000–41,000 range, well within the 65,536 rows available in Excel 97-2003. The date corresponding to 65,536 is June 5, 2079, so this formula will easily continue to work for the next 70 years. (And if you haven't upgraded to Excel 2007 by 2079, well, you have a tenacious IT department.)

Excel starts evaluating this formula with the first INDIRECT function. The arguments inside INDIRECT build an address that concatenates the serial number for the date in A3 with the serial number for the date in B3. As you can see in the sub-result, you end up with a range that points to rows 39854:39861:

Formula fragment: INDIRECT(A3&":"&B3)

Sub-result: INDIRECT("39854:39861")

Normally, you would see something like "A2:IU2" as the argument for INDIRECT. However, if you have ever used the POINT method of entering a formula and gone from column A to the last column, you will recognize that =SUM(2:2) is equivalent to =SUM(A2:IV2) in Excel 2003 and =SUM(A2:XFD2) in Excel 2007.

The first step of the formula is to build a reference that is one row tall for each date between the start and end dates.

Next, the formula returns the ROW function for each row in that range. In the case of the dates in A3 and A4, the formula returns an array of eight row numbers (in this case, {39854;39855;39856;…;39861}). This is a clever way of returning the numbers from the first date to the last date. In row 5, the ROW function returns an array of 364 numbers:

Formula fragment: ROW(INDIRECT(A3&":"&B3))

Sub-result: {39854;39855;39856;39857;39858;39859;39860;39861}

Now you can compare the holiday list to the range of dates. `=COUNTIF(Holidays,sub-result)` counts how many times each holiday is in the range of dates. In this case, you expect the function to return a 1 if a holiday is found in the range of dates and a 0 if the holiday is not found. Because you want to count only the non-holiday dates, the formula compares the `COUNTIF` result to find the dates where the holiday `COUNTIF` is 0:

Formula fragment: `--COUNTIF(Holidays,ROW(INDIRECT(A3&":"&B3)))=0`

Result: `{1;1;1;1;1;1;0;1;1}`

For every date in the date range, the `COUNTIF` formula asks, "Are any of the company holidays equal to this particular date?" Figure 3 illustrates what is happening in the first half of the formula. Column E represents the values returned by the `ROW` function. Column F uses `COUNTIF` to see if any of the company holidays are equal to the value in column E. For example, in E3, none of the holidays are equal to 39855, so `COUNTIF` returns 0. However, in F8, the formula finds that one company holiday is equivalent to 39860, so `COUNTIF` returns 1.

In column G, you test whether the result of the `COUNTIF` is 1. If it is, the `TRUE` says to count this day.

In column H, the minus-minus formula converts each `TRUE` value in column G to 1 and each `FALSE` value in column G to 0.

In Figure 3, cells H2:H9 represent the virtual results of the first half of the formula, which finds the dates that are not holidays.

`=COUNTIF(I$2:I$11,E3)`

	E	F	G	H	I
1	Date	CountIf	CountIf=0	--G	Holidays
2	39854	0	TRUE	1	1/1/2009
3	39855	0	TRUE	1	1/19/2009
4	39856	0	TRUE	1	2/16/2009
5	39857	0	TRUE	1	5/25/2009
6	39858	0	TRUE	1	7/3/2009
7	39859	0	TRUE	1	9/7/2009
8	39860	1	FALSE	0	10/12/2009
9	39861	0	TRUE	1	11/11/2009
10					11/26/2009
11					12/25/2009

Figure 3. The first half of the formula counts days that are not holidays.

The second half of the formula uses the WEEKDAY function to find which dates are not Sundays. The WEEKDAY function can return three different sets of results, depending on the value passed as the Return_Type argument. Figure 4 show the values returned for various Return_Type arguments. In order to isolate Monday through Saturday, you could check to see if the WEEKDAY function with a Return_Type of 1 is greater than 1. You could check to see if the WEEKDAY function with a Return_Type of 2 is less than 7. You could check to see if the WEEKDAY function with a Return_Type of 3 is less than 6. All these methods are equivalent.

Part I

=WEEKDAY($A3,B$2)

	A	B	C	D	E
1		Return_Type ------>			
2		1	2	3	
3	Sun, Feb 8, 09	1	7	6	
4	Mon, Feb 9, 09	2	1	0	
5	Tue, Feb 10, 09	3	2	1	
6	Wed, Feb 11, 09	4	3	2	
7	Thu, Feb 12, 09	5	4	3	
8	Fri, Feb 13, 09	6	5	4	
9	Sat, Feb 14, 09	7	6	5	
10					
11		1	Sunday = 1, Saturday = 7		
12		2	Monday=1, Sunday = 7		
13		3	Monday=0, Sunday=6		
14					

Figure 4. The WEEKDAY function can return 1, 7, or 6 for Sundays.

The second half of the formula uses many of the tricks from the first half. The INDIRECT function returns a range of rows. The ROW function converts those rows to row numbers that happen to correspond to the range of dates. The WEEKDAY(,3) function then converts those dates to values from 0 to 6, where 6 is equivalent to Sunday. The virtual result of the WEEKDAY function is shown in column L of Figure 5. The formula compares the WEEKDAY result to see if it is less than 6. This virtual result is shown in column M of Figure 5. Finally, a double minus converts the TRUE/FALSE values to 0s and 1s, as shown in column N. Basically, this says that we are working every day in the range, except for N7, which is a Sunday.

Formula fragment: `--(WEEKDAY(ROW(INDIRECT(A3&":"&B3)),3)<6)`

Result: `{1;1;1;1;1;1;0;1}`

L3		▼		*fx*	=WEEKDAY(K3,3)	
	K	L	M	N	O	P
1	Date	Weekday(3)	L<6	Not Sunday		H*N
2	39854	1	TRUE	1		1
3	39855	2	TRUE	1		1
4	39856	3	TRUE	1		1
5	39857	4	TRUE	1		1
6	39858	5	TRUE	1		1
7	39859	6	FALSE	0		0
8	39860	0	TRUE	1		0
9	39861	1	TRUE	1		1
10				Total		6

Figure 5. The 1s in column N mean the date is not a Sunday.

Finally, SUMPRODUCT multiplies the Not Holiday array by the Not Sunday array. When both arrays contain a 1, we have a workday. When either the Not Holiday array has a 0 (as in row 8) or the Not Sunday array has a 0 (as in row 7), the result is a 0. The final result is shown in the SUM function in P10: There are 6 workdays between the two dates.

As with most array solutions, this one formula manages to do a large number of sub-calculations to achieve a single result.

Additional Details: What if you work 7 days a week but want to exclude company holidays? The formula is simpler:

=SUMPRODUCT(--(COUNTIF(Holidays,ROW(INDIRECT(A2&":"&B2)))=0))

The problem becomes trickier if days in the middle of the week are the days off. Say that you have a part-time employee who works Monday, Wednesday, and Friday. The Not Sunday portion of the formula now needs to check for 3 specific weekdays. Note that the Return_Type 2 version of the WEEKDAY function never returns a 0. Because this version of the WEEKDAY function returns digits 1 through 7, you can use it as the first argument in the CHOOSE function to specify which days are workdays. Using =CHOOSE(WEEKDAY(Some Date,2),1,0,1,0,1,0,0) would be a way of assigning 1s to Monday, Wednesday, and Friday.

Because CHOOSE does not usually return an array, you have to enter the following formula, using Ctrl+Shift+Enter:

=SUMPRODUCT(--(COUNTIF(Holidays,ROW(INDIRECT(A3&":"&B3)))=0),--(CHOOSE(WEEKDAY(ROW(INDIRECT(A3&":"&B3)),2),1,0,1,0,1,0,0)))

Summary: This topic introduces the concept of creating a huge array from two simple values. For example, =ROW(INDIRECT("1:10000")) generates a 10,000-cell array filled with the numbers from 1 to 10,000. You can use this concept to test many dates while only specifying a starting and ending point, thus solving the NETWORKDAYS problem for any type of workweek.

Source: http://www.mrexcel.com/forum/showthread.php?t=69761

STORE HOLIDAYS
IN A NAMED RANGE

Part I

Challenge: The NETWORKDAYS and WORKDAY functions can take a list of company holidays as the third argument. If you store the list of holidays in AZ1: AZ10, there is a chance that someone will inadvertently delete a row, so you want to move the range of company holidays to a named range.

Solution: There is an easy way to convert the range of holidays to a named range. Follow these steps:

1. Type your company holidays as a column of dates in E1:E10.

2. In a blank cell, type =E1:E10. Do not press Enter. Instead, press the F9 key. Excel calculates the formula and returns an array of date serial numbers, as shown in Figure 6. Notice that everything after the equals sign is already selected.

3. Press Ctrl+C to copy the array to the Clipboard.

4. Press Esc to exit Formula Edit mode. The formula disappears.

5. Visit the Name dialog box. (In Excel 97-2003, select Insert, Name, Define. In Excel 2007, select Formulas, Define Name.)

6. Type Holidays as the name.

7. In the Refers To box, clear the current text. Type an equals sign. Press Ctrl+V to paste the array of dates to the box. Click OK.

E	F	G	H	I	J	K	L	M
1/1/2009								
1/19/2009								
2/16/2009		={39814;39832;39860;39958;39997;40063;40098;40128;40143;40172}						
5/25/2009								
7/3/2009								
9/7/2009								
10/12/2009								
11/11/2009								
11/26/2009								
12/25/2009								

Figure 6. Press F9, and Excel converts the range reference to an array of serial numbers.

Now you can use the named range `Holidays` as the third argument of the `WORKDAY` and `NETWORKDAYS` functions.

Gotcha: While these names work fine with `WORKDAY` and `NETWORKDAYS`, they fail in complex array formulas.

Summary: You can convert a range of dates to a named array to simplify the use of the `WORKDAY` and `NETWORKDAYS` functions.

SUM EVERY OTHER ROW OR EVERY THIRD ROW

Challenge: In Figure 7, someone set up a worksheet with dollars in rows 2, 4, 6, 8, and so on and percentages in rows 3, 5, 7, 9, and so on. You want to sum only the dollars, which are stored in the even rows. While you're at it, you'd like to know how to sum the odd rows or every third row.

Solution: There are a lot of possible approaches to this problem, some of which require you to figure out which rows to sum.

- To sum the odd rows: `=SUMPRODUCT(MOD(ROW(3:100),2),(C3:C100))`

- To sum the even rows: `=SUMPRODUCT(--(MOD(ROW(2:99),2)=0),(C2:C99))` or `=SUMPRODUCT(MOD(ROW(1:98),2),(C2:C99))`

- To sum every third row (2, 5, 8, etc.): `=SUMPRODUCT(--(MOD(ROW(2:148),3)=2),(C2:C148))`. See Figure 8

C100		f_x	=SUMPRODUCT(--(MOD(ROW(A2:A99),2)=0),(C2:C99))		
	A	B	C	D	E	F
1	Customer	Info	Q1	Q2	Q3	Q4
93	Wonderful Briefcase Supply	GP %	49%	51%	46%	48%
94	Wonderful Glass Corporation	Dollars	14266	15842	10897	19081
95	Wonderful Glass Corporation	GP %	49%	53%	45%	47%
96	Wonderful Jewelry Company	Dollars	13274	14183	12042	11075
97	Wonderful Jewelry Company	GP %	48%	54%	50%	52%
98	Wonderful Scooter Corporation	Dollars	17934	19855	11155	15019
99	Wonderful Scooter Corporation	GP %	48%	46%	52%	40%
100			713681	767432	720601	733809

Figure 7. You want to sum the even rows.

Summing the Odd Rows

Think back to when you were just learning division. If you had the problem 38 divided by 5, you would write that the answer is 7 with a remainder of 3. Excel provides the MOD function to return the remainder in a division problem. —For example, =MOD(7,2) calculates 7 divided by 2 and returns 1 as the remainder. The remainder of an odd number divided by 2 is 1. It is 0 for all even numbers. You can therefore use MOD to assign a 1 to each odd-numbered row and a 0 to each even-numbered row.

The problem is simple if you want only the odd rows. You can use an array of 1s and 0s in SUMPRODUCT. Multiplying the range C3:C100 by the result of the MOD function (an array of alternating 1s and 0s) results in every other number being added up.

Summing the Even Rows

The MOD(ROW(),2) function returns 1 for an odd row, and it returns 0 for an even-numbered row. Therefore, if the result of the MOD function is 0, you know you're working with an even-numbered row. Using MOD(ROW(),2)=0 will return an array of TRUE and FALSE values. You can then use the double minus sign to convert the TRUE/FALSE values to 1/0 values.

A simpler but less intuitive solution is to adjust the MOD argument so that it is one row behind the sum range. If you hope to grab the even rows from C2:C99, you can specify a range for the ROW function that starts one row above the real range. Use MOD(ROW(1:98),2) to ensure that the first value MOD returns is 1, followed by 0, 1, 0, 1, and so on.

Summing Every Third Row

Figure 8 shows a situation in which cost rows have been added. In this case, you would like to sum every third row—rows 2, 5, 8, etc. If you use =MOD(Row,3), you get 1 for rows 1, 4, and 7. You get 2 for rows 2, 5, and 8. You get 0 for rows 3, 6, and 9. To sum only the sales rows, you need to test if the result of the MOD function is a 2. Since this test will return True/False values, use the double minus to convert the True/False values to 1/0 values. So the formula becomes:

=SUMPRODUCT(--(MOD(ROW(2:148),3)=2),(C2:C148))

C149	▼	fx =SUMPRODUCT(--(MOD(ROW(2:148),3)=2),(C2:C148))			
	A	B	C	D	E	F
1	Customer	Info	Q1	Q2	Q3	Q4
142	Wonderful Glass Corporation	GP %	49%	53%	45%	47%
143	Wonderful Jewelry Company	Dollars	13,274	14,183	12,042	11,075
144	Wonderful Jewelry Company	Cost	6,902	6,524	6,021	5,316
145	Wonderful Jewelry Company	GP %	48%	54%	50%	52%
146	Wonderful Scooter Corporation	Dollars	17,934	19,855	11,155	15,019
147	Wonderful Scooter Corporation	Cost	9,326	10,722	5,354	9,011
148	Wonderful Scooter Corporation	GP %	48%	46%	52%	40%
149			713,681	767,432	720,601	733,809

Figure 8. You want to sum every third row.

Part
I

Alternate Strategy: While all the solutions presented so far are going to amaze your co-workers, they are all inherently dangerous. If someone inserts a new row in the worksheet, the MOD functions won't work as you want them to.

It was not stated in the original problem, but if the worksheet really has a column B that identifies Dollars and GP%, then it would be safer to use a SUMIF function to sum the dollar amounts:

```
=SUMIF($B2:$B99,"Dollars",C2:C99)
```

This formula instructs Excel to look through B2:B99. If the value in that row says "Dollars", Excel adds up the corresponding value from column C. With this solution, there is no worry that dollars on even rows will accidentally shift to odd rows.

Summary: While you can guru-out with SUMPRODUCT solutions galore, the simplest solution might be to use SUMIF.

Source: http://www.mrexcel.com/forum/showthread.php?t=232025

WHY THE MINUS MINUS?
COERCE NUMBERS FROM TRUE/FALSE

Challenge: While IF and other functions that expect logical tests can easily convert TRUE and FALSE values to 1s and 0s, the SUMPRODUCT function cannot do this. Why do you sometimes use a minus minus in SUMPRODUCT?

In Figure 9, for example, the SUMPRODUCT formula to calculate a 2% bonus for sales above \$20,000 and with GP% above 50% fails:

```
=SUMPRODUCT((C4:C14>20000),(D4:D14>0.5),C4:C14)*0.02
```

If you simply build a SUMPRODUCT formula with your criteria and the numeric field, you end up with calculations such as TRUE * TRUE * 21000, which SUMPRODUCT incorrectly evaluates to 0.

=SUMPRODUCT((C4:C14>20000),(D4:D14>0.5),C4:C14)*0.02						
	A	B	C	D	E	F
1	Pay a Bonus if Revenue is > 20000 and Profit % is > 50%.					
2						
3	Invoice	Rep	Revenue	GP%		Bonus
4	1010	Fred	24011	49.1%		0
5	1011	Bob	20489	48.8%		0
6	1012	Joey	19040	48.4%		0
7	1013	Joey	21000	55.0%		1
8	1014	Bob	19898	49.4%		0
9	1015	Bob	21818	50.5%		1
10	1016	Bob	19324	51.0%		0
11	1017	Bob	22207	50.7%		1
12	1018	Bob	18642	48.1%		0
13	1019	Fred	21602	48.3%		0
14	1020	Fred	22902	51.6%		1
15						
16		Bonus:	0			
17						

Figure 9. You would think Excel's Boolean logic rules could handle this.

In Figure 10, the first term of SUMPRODUCT has been evaluated. You see the array TRUE ; TRUE , ...

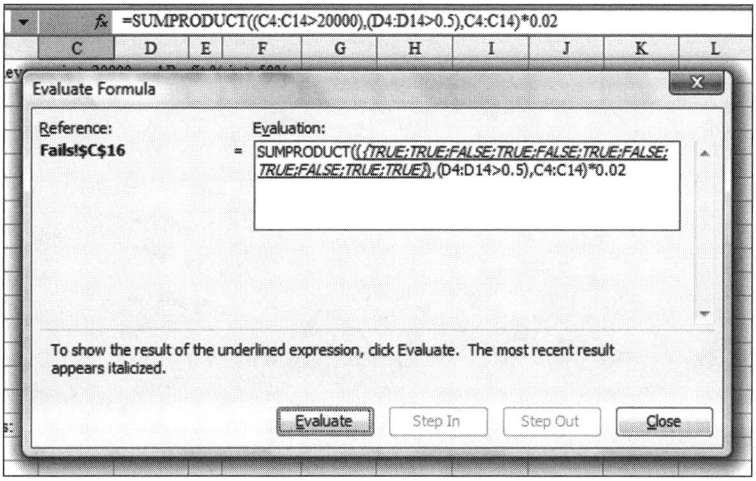

Figure 10. The SUMPRODUCT function does not deal well with TRUE * TRUE * a number.

Solution: You need a way to convert the TRUE/FALSE values to 1/0 values. Excel gurus use the minus minus in order to coerce Excel to change an array of TRUE/FALSE values to 1s and 0s:

`-- (C4:C14>20000)`

As shown in Figure 11, this formula does the trick:

`=SUMPRODUCT (-- (C4:C14>20000) ,-- (D4:D14>0.5) ,C4:C14) *0.02`

=SUMPRODUCT(--(C4:C14>20000),--(D4:D14>0.5),C4:C14)*0.02

	A	B	C	D	E	F
1	Pay a Bonus if Revenue is > 20000 and Profit % is > 50%.					
2						
3	Invoice	Rep	Revenue	GP%		
4	1010	Fred	24011	49.1%		
5	1011	Bob	20489	48.8%		
6	1012	Joey	19040	48.4%		
7	1013	Joey	21000	55.0%		
8	1014	Bob	19898	49.4%		
9	1015	Bob	21818	50.5%		
10	1016	Bob	19324	51.0%		
11	1017	Bob	22207	50.7%		
12	1018	Bob	18642	48.1%		
13	1019	Fred	21602	48.3%		
14	1020	Fred	22902	51.6%		
15						
16		Bonus:	1758.54			

Figure 11. By using minus minus, you convert the TRUE/FALSE to 1/0, and the formula works.

Alternate Strategy: In fact, all the following operations also convert an array of TRUE/FALSE to an array of 1/0:

```
N(C4:C14>20000)
1*(C4:C14>20000)
(C4:C14>20000)+0
(C4:C14>20000)^0
```

You could multiply the criteria terms together, replace the comma with an asterisk, and let Excel perform all the logical tests. The formula to calculate the bonus would be:

```
=SUMPRODUCT((C4:C14>20000)*(D4:D14>0.5),C4:C14)*0.02
```

This syntax allows you to combine AND and OR logic. Say that you want to pay the bonus if both conditions are met or if the rep is Joey. You would add some parentheses and indicate that the bonus is also paid when the rep is Joey:

```
=SUMPRODUCT(((C4:C14>20000)*(D4:D14>0.5))+(B4:
B14="Joey"),C4:C14)*0.02
```

Figure 12 shows a formula that conditionally sums based on two AND and one OR criteria.

=SUMPRODUCT((((C4:C14>20000)*(D4:D14>0.5))+(B4:B14="Joey"),C4:C14)*0.02							
	A	**B**	**C**	**D**	**E**	**F**	**G**	**H**
1	Pay a Bonus if Revenue is > 20000 and Profit % is > 50%, or if Rep="Joey"							
2								
3	Invoice	Rep	Revenue	GP%				
4	1010	Fred	24011	49.1%				
5	1011	Bob	20489	48.8%				
6	1012	Joey	19040	48.4%				
7	1013	Joey	21000	55.0%				
8	1014	Bob	19898	49.4%				
9	1015	Bob	21818	50.5%				
10	1016	Bob	19324	51.0%				
11	1017	Bob	22207	50.7%				
12	1018	Bob	18642	48.1%				
13	1019	Fred	21602	48.3%				
14	1020	Fred	22902	51.6%				
15								
16		Bonus:	2559.34					
17								

Figure 12. You can build the Boolean logic as one term of the SUMPRODUCT function.

Summary: To use logical tests in SUMPRODUCT, you can convert the TRUE/FALSE values to 1/0 values by using minus minus or other methods described in this topic.

Source: http://www.mrexcel.com/forum/showthread.php?t=221125 and http://www.mrexcel.com/forum/showthread.php?t=128907

INTRODUCING THE BORING USE OF SUMPRODUCT

Challenge: Your IT department sends you a file with unit price and quantity sold. You need to calculate total revenue. You usually add a new column and total that column, but there must be a way to total the 5,000 line items with only one formula.

Solution: There is an Excel function designed to solve this very problem. The SUMPRODUCT function takes two or more similar-shaped ranges, multiplies them together, and sums the results.

Part I

In Figure 13, the range C4:C5003 contains quantities. Cells D4:D5003 contain unit prices. The formula =SUMPRODUCT(C4:C5003,D4:D5003) performs 5,000 multiplications and adds up the results. For example, Excel finds that C4*D4 is 57,473.95, and C5*D5 is 31,488.30. This process continues for all the cells in the array. Finally, Excel sums the individual multiplication results and returns the answer 181,056,129.80.

=SUMPRODUCT(C4:C5003,D4:D5003)			
	A	**B**	**C**	**D**
1				181,056,129.80
2				
3	Item	Acct	Qty	UnitPrice
4	N456	A1104	661	86.95
5	T919	A8063	354	88.95
6	N456	A6905	464	86.95
7	U993	A3508	520	96.95

Figure 13.   SUMPRODUCT can do many intermediate multiplications and sum the results.

Additional Details: You can specify up to 30 similar-shaped arrays as arguments for SUMPRODUCT (255 arrays in Excel 2007)

Summary: SUMPRODUCT can multiply two or more arrays and sum the results.

UNDERSTAND BOOLEAN LOGIC: FALSE IS ZERO; AND IS *,OR IS + AND EVERYTHING ELSE IS TRUE

Challenge: You want to become a guru at Excel formulas. To master conditional computing formulas, you need to understand Boolean logic facts.

Background: For a brief time, I was planning on being an electrical engineer. While most of the Notre Dame electrical engineering curriculum and I did not get along, my favorite class was logic design. I learned how to reduce many decisions down to a series of wires, electricity, and tiny chips that could perform AND, OR, and NAND operations. I learned how to use Karnaugh maps to reduce a circuit down to the minimal number of chips. It was fascinating stuff, and it translates amazingly well to writing criteria in Excel.

With integrated circuits, a circuit is either on or off. On means TRUE, or 1. Off means FALSE, or 0. The table on the left is the truth table for a simple AND operation. While one approach is to memorize these rules, you can also convert a problem to a simple mathematical calculation, as in the table on the right, which converts TRUE to 1, converts FALSE to 0, and multiplies the two values. Notice that the results in A and B in the left table are equivalent to the results in A*B in the right table.

Boolean Values				Digital Values		
Condition A	Condition B	A and B		Condition A	Condition B	A*B
FALSE	FALSE	FALSE		0	0	0
FALSE	TRUE	FALSE		0	1	0
TRUE	TRUE	TRUE		1	1	1
TRUE	FALSE	FALSE		1	0	0

With integrated circuits, an OR gate accepts two or more incoming wires. If any of the incoming wires are on, the output wire is on. Again, you can memorize the facts in the table on the left below, or you can simply change the TRUE to 1, the FALSE to 0, and the OR sign to a plus sign, as in the table on the right. If the result is 1 or greater, the entire problem is TRUE.

Boolean Values				Digital Values		
Condition A	Condition B	A or B		Condition A	Condition B	A+B
FALSE	FALSE	FALSE		0	0	0
FALSE	TRUE	TRUE		0	1	1
TRUE	TRUE	TRUE		1	1	2
TRUE	FALSE	TRUE		1	0	1

Part I

Solution: How does this talk of integrated circuits apply to Excel? When you build IF functions that require multiple logical tests, you frequently string together many AND, OR, and NOT functions to achieve a result. These formulas can get unduly complex, and you can use Boolean logic facts to simplify them.

Let's say that you need to design a formula to calculate a 2% bonus. The bonus is paid if revenue is > 20,000 and gross profit percentage is > 50%. The bonus is also paid whenever the sales rep name is Joey. (Joey is the boss's son.)

If you only needed to see whether the revenue is greater than 20,000, the formula would be:

```
=IF(C4>20000,0.02*C4,0)
```

When you add in the additional condition that GP% needs to be > 50%, the formula is:

```
=IF(AND(C4>20000,D4>0.5),0.02*C4,0)
```

Add in the wrinkle that Joey always get paid, and you have:

```
=IF(OR(AND(C4>20000,D4>0.5),B4="Joey"),0.02*C4,0)
```

=IF(A2,TRUE,FALSE)				
	A	**B**	**C**	**D**
1	Value			
2	-1234	TRUE	=IF(A2,TRUE,FALSE)	
3	-1	TRUE		
4	0	FALSE		
5	1	TRUE		
6	2468	TRUE		
7				
8				

Figure 14. A nonzero number used as a logical test is TRUE

Any time a formula calls for a logical test, you can include a calculation that generates a number. If the resulting number is 0, the logical test is FALSE. If the resulting number is anything else, the logical test is TRUE. In Figure 14, column A contains several numbers. Column B tests whether column A is TRUE or FALSE. You can see that all positive and negative numbers are TRUE, and the 0 in A4 is considered FALSE.

Using the Excel logic rules, you can restate any AND function by simply multiplying the logical tests together. To do so, you surround each logical test in parentheses. For example, you could rewrite:=AND(C4>20000,D4>0.5) as:

=(C4>20000)*(D4>0.5)

In Figure 15, column E shows the results of the latter formula.

F4			▼		fx =(C4>20000)*(D4>0.5)	
	A	B	C	D	E	F
1	Pay a Bonus if Revenue is > 20000 and Profit % is > 50%.					
2						
3	Invoice	Rep	Revenue	GP%		Bonus
4	1010	Fred	24011	49.1%		0
5	1011	Bob	20489	48.8%		0
6	1012	Joey	19040	48.4%		0
7	1013	Joey	21000	55.0%		1
8	1014	Bob	19898	49.4%		0
9	1015	Bob	21818	50.5%		1
10	1016	Bob	19324	51.0%		0
11	1017	Bob	22207	50.7%		1
12	1018	Bob	18642	48.1%		0
13	1019	Fred	21602	48.3%		0
14	1020	Fred	22902	51.6%		1

Figure 15. If your operation is AND, multiply the various logical tests together.

The result of this calculation is always 0 or 1. It is 0 when the bonus should not be paid, and it is 1 when the bonus should be paid. Thus, if all your terms need to be joined by an AND, you can simply multiply the terms by the bonus calculation:

=(C4>20000)*(D4>0.5)*0.02*C4

Figure 16 shows the results of this calculation.

=(C7>20000)*(D7>0.5)*0.02*C7

	A	B	C	D	E	F	
1	Pay a Bonus if Revenue is > 20000 and Profit % is > 50%.						
2							
3	Invoice	Rep	Revenue	GP%		Bonus	
4	1010	Fred	24011	49.1%		0	
5	1011	Bob	20489	48.8%		0	
6	1012	Joey	19040	48.4%		0	
7	1013	Joey	21000	55.0%		420	
8	1014	Bob	19898	49.4%		0	
9	1015	Bob	21818	50.5%		436.36	
10	1016	Bob	19324	51.0%		0	
11	1017	Bob	22207	50.7%		444.14	
12	1018	Bob	18642	48.1%		0	
13	1019	Fred	21602	48.3%		0	
14	1020	Fred	22902	51.6%		458.04	

Figure 16. You can multiply the bonus calculation by the results of your AND operations.

Excel's Boolean logic rules run into some problems when you introduce OR operations.

When you convert an OR to an addition operation, there is a chance that the result might be > 1. Figure 17 shows this. You can restate this formula:

```
=IF(OR(AND(C4>20000,D4>0.5),B4="Joey"),0.02*C4,0)
```

as:

```
=((C7>20000)*(D7>0.5))+(B7="Joey")
```

In row 7, Joey actually qualifies for a regular bonus, so the result of the logical test is 2. It would be incorrect to multiply the revenue by 2%. (Actually, Joey's dad might like this idea....) Any time you have an OR in the equation, you have to convert the result to TRUE or FALSE, or 0 or 1. Either of these formulas would calculate the bonus correctly:

```
=IF((C4>20000)*(D4>0.5)+(B4="Joey"),TRUE,FALSE)*C4*0.02
```

```
=IF((C4>20000)*(D4>0.5)+(B4="Joey"),1,0)*C4*0.02
```

=(C7>20000)*(D7>0.5)+(B7="Joey")								

	A	B	C	D	E	F	G	H
1	Pay a Bonus if Revenue is > 20000, Profit % is > 50%. Or, pay a bonus is the Rep is Joey							
2								
3	Invoice	Rep	Revenue	GP%		Bonus		
4	1010	Fred	24011	49.1%		0		
5	1011	Bob	20489	48.8%		0		
6	1012	Joey	19040	48.4%		1		
7	1013	Joey	21000	55.0%		2		
8	1014	Bob	19898	49.4%		0		
9	1015	Bob	21818	50.5%		1		
10	1016	Bob	19324	51.0%		0		
11	1017	Bob	22207	50.7%		1		
12	1018	Bob	18642	48.1%		0		
13	1019	Fred	21602	48.3%		0		
14	1020	Fred	22902	51.6%		1		

Figure 17. You can convert OR functions to addition and test whether the result is TRUE.

Summary: Understanding the Boolean logic facts can simplify your IF calculations. Remember that FALSE is 0, AND is *, OR is +, and everything else is TRUE.

USE GET.CELL TO HIGHLIGHT NON-FORMULA CELLS

Challenge: You want to highlight all the cells on a worksheet that do not contain formulas.

Solution: Before VBA, macros were written in an old macro language now known as XLM. That language offered a GET.CELL function, which provides far more information than the current CELL function. In fact, GET.CELL can tell you more than five dozen different attributes of a cell.

GET.CELL is cool, but there is one gotcha. You cannot enter this function directly in a cell. You have to define a name to hold the function and then refer to the name in the cell. For example, to find out whether cell A1 contains a formula, you use =GET.CELL(48,Sheet1!A1). However, you need something more generic than this for the conditional formatting formula. Using =INDIRECT("RC",False) is a handy way to refer to the cell in which the formula exists. Thus, the formula to tell if the current cell contains a formula is:

```
=GET.CELL(48,INDIRECT("RC",False))
```

To make use of this formula, follow these steps in Excel 2003:

1. To define a new name, select Insert, Name Define and use a suitable name, such as `HasFormula`. In the Refers To box, type `=GET.CELL(48,INDIR ECT("RC",FALSE))`, as shown in Figure 18. Click Add. Click OK. You use the Define Name dialog to define a name in Excel 2003.

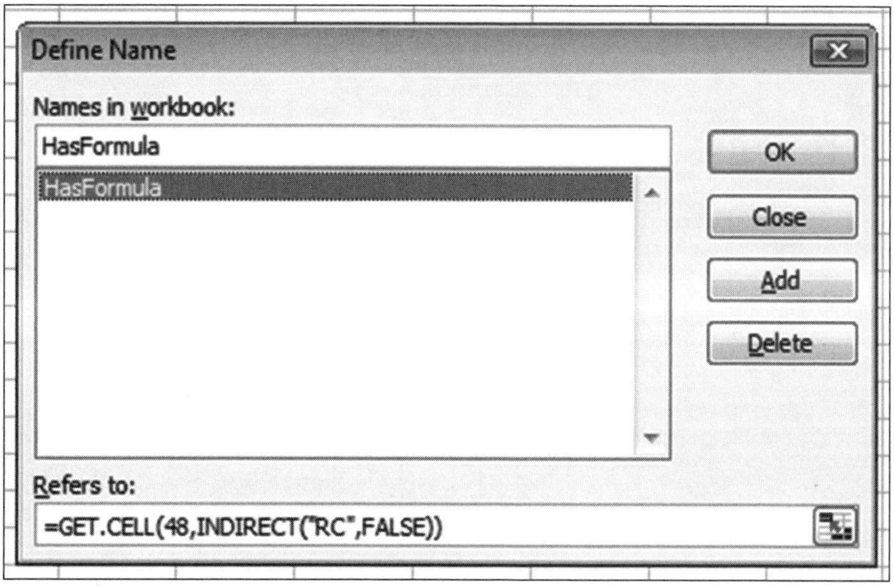

Figure 18. You use the Define Name dialog to define a name in Excel 2003.

2. Select a range of cells.

3. Select Format, Conditional Formatting. Change the first dropdown to Formula Is. Type `=HASFORMULA`, as shown in Figure 19. Click the Format button and choose a format for the cell. Click OK.

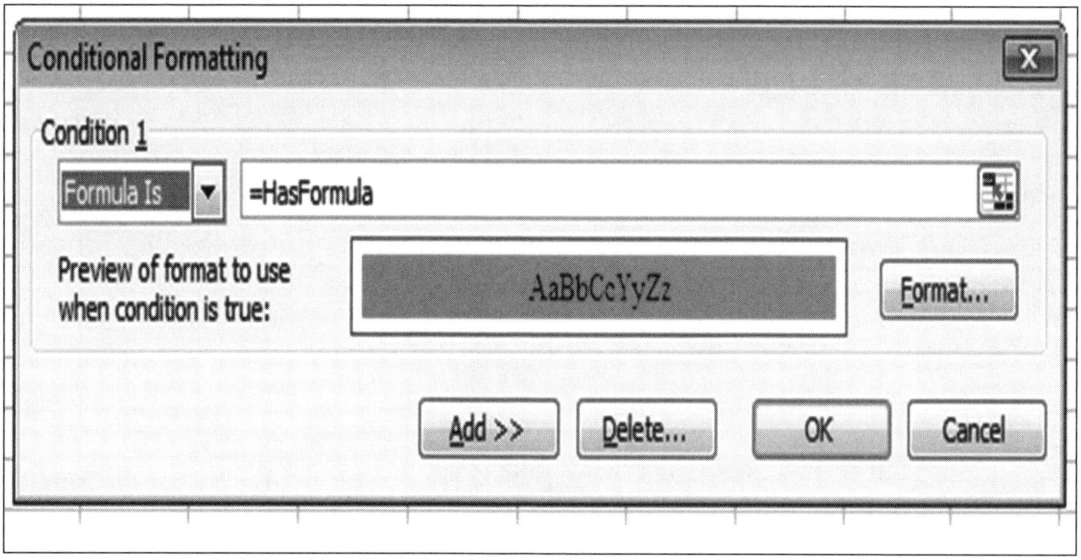

Figure 19. You can use the relatively obscure Formula Is version of conditional formatting.

To make use of this formula, follow these steps in Excel 2007:

1. To define a new name, select Formulas, Name Manager, New and use a suitable name, such as `HasFormula`. In the Refers To box, type `=GET.CELL(48,INDIRECT("RC",FALSE))`, as shown in Figure 20. Click OK. Click Close. You use the New Name dialog to define a name in Excel 2007.

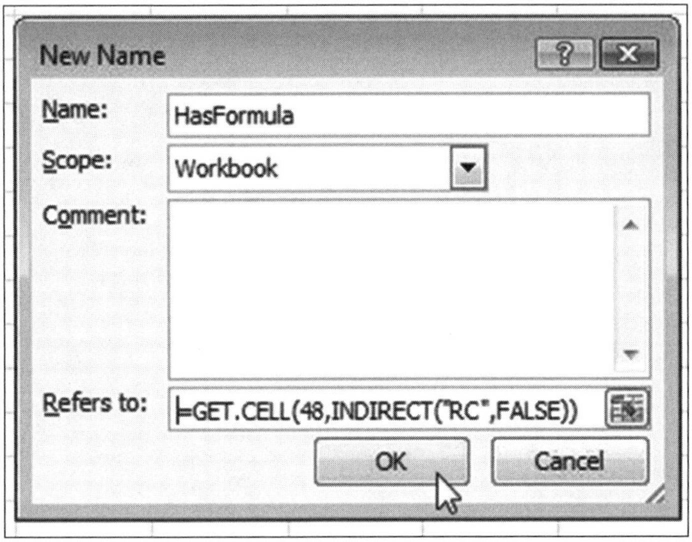

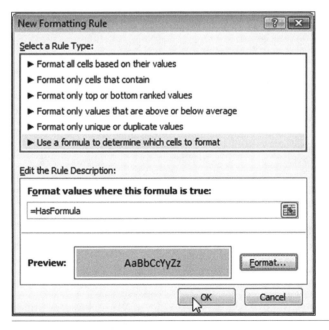

Figure 20. You use the New Name dialog to define a name in Excel 2007.

2. Select the cells to which you want to apply the conditional formatting.

3. Select Home, Conditional Formatting, New Rule. Choose Use a Formula to Determine Which Cells to Format. In the lower half of the dialog type `=HASFORMULA`, as shown in Figure 21. Click the Format button and choose a format for the cell. Click OK.

Figure 21. You use the New Formatting Rule dialog to set up conditional formatting in Excel 2007.

To highlight every cell that does not contain a formula, use =NOT(HasFormula) in the conditional formatting dialog.

Massive Gotcha: You cannot copy any cells that contain this formula to a different worksheet without risking an Excel crash.

Breaking It Down: While most people typically use A1-style references, the R1C1-style reference works better in the INDIRECT function. Normally, an R1C1-style reference points to another cell. For example, =RC[-2] refers to the current row and two cells to the left of the current cell. =R[10]C[3] refers to 10 rows below and 3 columns to the right of the current cell. An R1C1 formula without any modifiers, =RC, refers to the current cell. This is a case where an R1C1 formula is far simpler than the equivalent A1 formula, =ADDRESS(ROW(),COLUMN(),4).

Part I

Alternate Strategy: The advantage of using the method described above is that the formatting will automatically update whenever someone changes a cell to contain either a formula or a constant. If you simply need to get a snapshot of which cells contain formulas, follow these steps:

1. Select all cells by pressing Ctrl+A.
2. Press Ctrl+G to display the Go To dialog.
3. Click the Special button in the lower-left corner of the Go To dialog.
4. In the Go To Special dialog, choose Formulas and click OK.
5. Choose a color from the Paint Bucket icon.

Additional Details: The complete list of GET.CELL arguments follows. Note that in some cases, functionality has changed significantly, and the argument may no longer return valid values.

Argument	Returns
1	Absolute reference of the upper-left cell in reference, as text in the current workspace reference style (usually A1 style, but it might be R1C1 style if someone has chosen R1C1 style in their Excel Options dialog).
2	Row number of the top cell in the reference.
3	Column number of the leftmost cell in the reference.
4	Same as TYPE(reference).
5	Contents of the reference.
6	Formula in the reference, as text, in either A1 or R1C1 style, depending on the workspace setting.
7	Number format of the cell, as text (for example, "m/d/yy" or "General").
8	Number indicating the cell's horizontal alignment:
	1 = General
	2 = Left

	3 = Center
	4 = Right
	5 = Fill
	6 = Justify
	7 = Center across cells
9	Number indicating the left-border style assigned to the cell:
	0 = No border
	1 = Thin line
	2 = Medium line
	3 = Dashed line
	4 = Dotted line
	5 = Thick line
	6 = Double line
	7 = Hairline
10	Number indicating the right-border style assigned to the cell. See argument 9 for descriptions of the numbers returned.
11	Number indicating the top-border style assigned to the cell. See argument 9 for descriptions of the numbers returned.
12	Number indicating the bottom-border style assigned to the cell. See argument 9 for descriptions of the numbers returned.
13	Number from 0 to 18, indicating the pattern of the selected cell, as displayed in the Patterns tab of the Format Cells dialog box, which appears when you choose the Cells command from the Format menu. If no pattern is selected, returns 0.
14	If the cell is locked, returns TRUE; otherwise, returns FALSE.
15	If the cell's formula is hidden, returns TRUE; otherwise, returns FALSE.
16	A two-item horizontal array containing the width of the active cell and a logical value that indicates whether the cell's width is set to change as the standard width changes (TRUE) or is a custom width (FALSE).
17	Row height of cell, in points.
18	Name of font, as text.
19	Size of font, in points.
20	If all the characters in the cell, or only the first character, are bold, returns TRUE; otherwise, returns FALSE.
21	If all the characters in the cell, or only the first character, are italic, returns TRUE; otherwise, returns FALSE.
22	If all the characters in the cell, or only the first character, are underlined, returns TRUE; otherwise, returns FALSE.
23	If all the characters in the cell, or only the first character, are struck through, returns TRUE; otherwise, returns FALSE.
24	Font color of the first character in the cell, as a number in the range 1 to 56. If font color is automatic, returns 0.

25	If all the characters in the cell, or only the first character, are outlined, returns TRUE; otherwise, returns FALSE. Outline font format is not supported by Microsoft Excel for Windows.
26	If all the characters in the cell, or only the first character, are shadowed, returns TRUE; otherwise, returns FALSE. Shadow font format is not supported by Microsoft Excel for Windows.
27	Number indicating whether a manual page break occurs at the cell:
	0 = No break
	1 = Row
	2 = Column
	3 = Both row and column
28	Row level (outline).
29	Column level (outline).
30	If the row containing the active cell is a summary row, returns TRUE; otherwise, returns FALSE.
31	If the column containing the active cell is a summary column, returns TRUE; otherwise, returns FALSE.
32	Name of the workbook and sheet containing the cell. If the window contains only a single sheet that has the same name as the workbook, without its extension, returns only the name of the book, in the form BOOK1.XLS. Otherwise, returns the name of the sheet, in the form [Book1]Sheet1.
33	If the cell is formatted to wrap, returns TRUE; otherwise, returns FALSE.
34	Left-border color, as a number in the range 1 to 56. If color is automatic, returns 0.
35	Right-border color, as a number in the range 1 to 56. If color is automatic, returns 0.
36	Top-border color, as a number in the range 1 to 56. If color is automatic, returns 0.
37	Bottom-border color, as a number in the range 1 to 56. If color is automatic, returns 0.
38	Shade foreground color, as a number in the range 1 to 56. If color is automatic, returns 0.
39	Shade background color, as a number in the range 1 to 56. If color is automatic, returns 0.
40	Style of the cell, as text.
41	Returns the formula in the active cell without translating it. (This is useful for international macro sheets.)
42	The horizontal distance, measured in points, from the left edge of the active window to the left edge of the cell. May be a negative number if the window is scrolled beyond the cell.
43	The vertical distance, measured in points, from the top edge of the active window to the top edge of the cell. May be a negative number if the window is scrolled beyond the cell.

Part I

44	The horizontal distance, measured in points, from the left edge of the active window to the right edge of the cell. May be a negative number if the window is scrolled beyond the cell.
45	The vertical distance, measured in points, from the top edge of the active window to the bottom edge of the cell. May be a negative number if the window is scrolled beyond the cell.
46	If the cell contains a text note, returns TRUE; otherwise, returns FALSE.
47	If the cell contains a sound note, returns TRUE; otherwise, returns FALSE.
48	If the cells contains a formula, returns TRUE; if a constant, returns FALSE.
49	If the cell is part of an array, returns TRUE; otherwise, returns FALSE.
50	Number indicating the cell's vertical alignment:
	1 = Top
	2 = Center
	3 = Bottom
	4 = Justified
51	Number indicating the cell's vertical orientation:
	0 = Horizontal
	1 = Vertical
	2 = Upward
	3 = Downward
52	The cell prefix (or text alignment) character, or empty text ("") if the cell does not contain one.
53	Contents of the cell as it is currently displayed, as text, including any additional numbers or symbols resulting from the cell's formatting.
54	Returns the name of the PivotTable view containing the active cell.
55	Returns the position of a cell within the PivotTable view.
56	Returns the name of the field containing the active cell reference if inside a PivotTable view.
57	Returns TRUE if all the characters in the cell, or only the first character, are formatted with a superscript font; otherwise, returns FALSE.
58	Returns the font style as text of all the characters in the cell, or only the first character, as displayed in the Font tab of the Format Cells dialog box (for example, "Bold Italic".)
59	Returns the number for the underline style:
	1 = None
	2 = Single
	3 = Double
	4 = Single accounting
	5 = Double accounting

60	Returns TRUE if all the characters in the cell, or only the first character, are formatted with a subscript font; otherwise, returns FALSE.
61	Returns the name of the PivotTable item for the active cell, as text.
62	Returns the name of the workbook and the current sheet, in the form `[book1]sheet1`.
63	Returns the fill (background) color of the cell.
64	Returns the pattern (foreground) color of the cell.
65	Returns TRUE if the Add Indent alignment option is on (Far East versions of Microsoft Excel only); otherwise, returns FALSE.
66	Returns the book name of the workbook containing the cell in the form `BOOK1.XLS`.

Part I

Summary: You can use `GET.CELL` to return more information than is available by using the `CELL` function. You can then use conditional formatting to highlight every cell that does not contain a formula.

Source: http://www.mrexcel.com/archive2/18800/21312.htm

REFER TO A CELL WHOSE ADDRESS VARIES, BASED ON A CALCULATION

Challenge: You need to refer to a cell, but the cell address varies, based on a calculation.

Solution: The `INDIRECT` function takes an argument that looks like a cell reference and returns the value in that reference.

In Figure 22, the formula in row 2 asks for the `INDIRECT` of the cell immediately above the formula. So, in D2, the formula tells Excel to get the `INDIRECT` of cell D1. Cell D1 has a valid cell address of C9. The formula returns the current value from cell C9, which is 17.

D2	▼	*fx* =INDIRECT(D1)		
	A	B	C	D	E
1		Which cell do you want?		C9	B7
2		Value in that cell:		17	10
3					
4		1	2	3	
5		4	5	6	
6		7	8	9	
7		10	11	12	
8		13	14	15	
9		16	17	18	

Figure 22. You can use the `INDIRECT` function to specify a cell address, and Excel returns the value at that address.

Additional Details: In Lotus 1-2-3, this function was the @@ ("at-at") function.

Additional Details: The argument for INDIRECT can be a named range. You could create an ad hoc reporting engine by using named ranges and INDIRECT.

In Figure 23, a named range has been set up for each column in a report.

	Revenues			*fx*	193517	
	A	B	C	D	E	F
1	Dept	Revenues	COGS	GP	Expenses	EBITA
2	A001	193517	89598	103919	92554	11365
3	A002	123498	59032	64466	58912	5554
4	A003	169167	76294	92873	67972	24901
5	A004	308596	146583	162013	79337	82676
6	A005	138470	63281	75189	96847	-21658
7	A006	443301	211898	231403	94936	136467
8	A007	142757	66382	76375	91932	-15557
9	A008	219188	100388	118800	52375	66425
10	A009	497412	233784	263628	60490	203138

Figure 23. You can set up a named range for each column.

Tip: See page 76 for a method to quickly create many range names.

Cell C12 in Figure 24 contains a validation dropdown list that allows a person to choose any of the headings in A1:F1 (Figure 24).

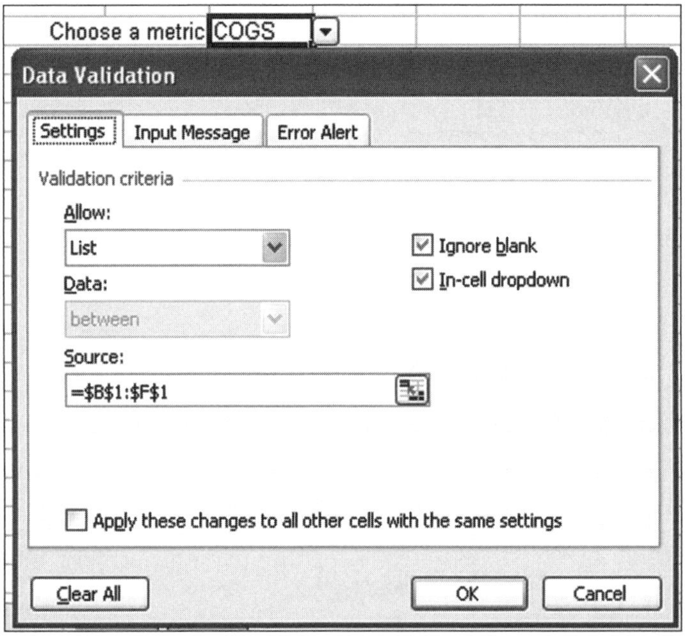

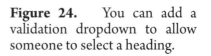

Figure 24. You can add a validation dropdown to allow someone to select a heading.

The formula in B13 uses concatenation to build a proper label for the cell. The formula could be:

```
="Total "&C12 or =CONCATENATE("Total ",C12)
```

The formula in C13 asks for the SUM of the INDIRECT of the name in C12. In Figure 25, C12 contains the word COGS. Because COGS is defined as C2: C10, Excel sums the range C2:C10 and returns the answer as the result of the formula.

C13		f_x =SUM(INDIRECT(C12))			
	A	B	C	D	E	F
1	Dept	Revenues	COGS	GP	Expenses	EBITA
2	A001	193517	89598	103919	92554	11365
3	A002	123498	59032	64466	58912	5554
4	A003	169167	76294	92873	67972	24901
5	A004	308596	146583	162013	79337	82676
6	A005	138470	63281	75189	96847	-21658
7	A006	443301	211898	231403	94936	136467
8	A007	142757	66382	76375	91932	-15557
9	A008	219188	100388	118800	52375	66425
10	A009	497412	233784	263628	60490	203138
11						
12		Choose a metric	COGS			
13		Total COGS	1047240			

Figure 25. The INDIRECT formula returns all the values in a named range.

When someone chooses a new metric from cell C12, the INDIRECT formula sums a different column. Figure 26 shows the total expenses.

A	B	C	D	E	F
Dept	Revenues	COGS	GP	Expenses	EBITA
A001	193517	89598	103919	92554	11365
A002	123498	59032	64466	58912	5554
A003	169167	76294	92873	67972	24901
A004	308596	146583	162013	79337	82676
A005	138470	63281	75189	96847	-21658
A006	443301	211898	231403	94936	136467
A007	142757	66382	76375	91932	-15557
A008	219188	100388	118800	52375	66425
A009	497412	233784	263628	60490	203138
	Choose a metric	Expenses			
	Total Expenses	695355			
				Sum=695355	

Figure 26. When you change the metric in C12, the formula totals a different column. The total in the status bar in the lower right verifies that the formula is working.

Additional Details: The argument for INDIRECT can be calculated on the fly. In Figure 27, cell C3 concatenates a column letter from C1 and a row number from C2, and it returns a value from B8.

	C3	▾	fx =INDIRECT(C1&C2)			
	A	B	C	D	E	F
1	Random Column:	B		=CHAR(randbetween(65,68))		
2	Random Row:	8		=randbetween(6,12)		
3	Value at intersect:	52		=INDIRECT(C1&C2)		
4						
5						
6	43	78	74	79		
7	49	82	55	88		
8	78	52	89	70		
9	41	87	83	66		
10	45	91	82	58		
11	76	65	60	66		
12	55	78	51	77		

Figure 27. Here, the reference is concatenated from values in other cells.

Summary: The INDIRECT function allows you to calculate from where to pull a value.

POINT TO ANOTHER WORKSHEET WITH INDIRECT

Challenge: You need to grab cell B4 from one of many worksheets. You have to determine which worksheet, based on a cell label or a calculation, and you're wondering if INDIRECT can point to another worksheet.

Setup: INDIRECT can point to another worksheet. However, it requires special handling if the worksheet name contains spaces or a date.

If a worksheet has a space in the name, you must build the reference to the worksheet by using apostrophes around the worksheet name, followed by an exclamation point and then the cell address. For example:

```
='Income Statement'!B2
```

If the worksheet name contains no spaces, you can leave out the apostrophes:

```
=Revenue!B2
```

However, if you have a mix of worksheet names that may or may not contain a space, you might as well plan on including the apostrophes.

Solution: Figure 28 shows six branch worksheets. Each has data in column B. The goal is to write a formula in row 4 that will pull data from column B of the various worksheets, based on the labels in row 3. The formula in cell G4 in Figure 28 works fine for row 4:

```
=INDIRECT("'"&G$3&"'!"&"B4")
```

Note: This formula includes the extra hassle of using apostrophes, even though only one of the worksheets, Eden Prairie, contains a space.

Part
I

G4				*fx* =INDIRECT("'"&G$3&"'!"&"B4")		
	A	B	C	D	E	F	G
1	Sales Summary						
2							
3		Atlanta	Boston	Chicago	Dallas	Eden Prairie	Fargo
4	Sales $	1555	1186	2567	1977	1736	1235
5	Sales Units						
6	# Transactions						
7	Labor Hours						
8	UPT						

◄ ► ►I \ **Main** / Atlanta / Boston / Chicago / Dallas / Eden Prairie / Fargo /

Figure 28. These INDIRECT function points to a variable worksheet.

However, the problem with the formula in G4 is that it is hard-coded to grab data from B4, so it cannot automatically copy to rows 5 through 7. To allow the formula to grab data from other rows, you can use the CELL function or the ADDRESS function. Both of these methods work. You can be up and running using CELL in a matter of seconds, but ADDRESS might ultimately be easier, once you understand the nuances of using it.

=CELL("address",$B4) returns the text $B$4. This is perfect for inserting in the INDIRECT function. The dollar sign before the B makes sure that the formula points to column B on each worksheet. The lack of a dollar sign before the 4 in $B4 allows the formula to point to row 5, 6, 7, and so on as you copy down. In Figure 29, the formula in cell C5 is:

```
=INDIRECT("'"&C$3&"'!"&CELL("address",$B5))
```

This formula can be copied throughout the table.

C5		*fx* =INDIRECT("'"&C$3&"'!"&CELL("address",$B5))			
	A	B	C	D	E
1	Sales Summary				
2					
3		Atlanta	Boston	Chicago	Dallas	Ede
4	Sales $	1555	1186	2567	1977
5	Sales Units	29	18	37	32
6	# Transactions	13	8	13	11
7	Labor Hours	24	24	32	24

Figure 29. Adding CELL allows you to copy one formula throughout the table.

You can use the ADDRESS function instead of the CELL function. In its simplest form, =ADDRESS(Row,Column) returns a cell address. For example, =ADDRESS(5, 2) returns the text $B$5. Initially, it might seem more complex to write =ADDRESS(ROW(),2) instead of using CELL in order to refer to column B in the current row. However, ADDRESS offers three additional optional arguments:

Note: The third and fourth arguments do not help you in this topic, but you have to learn them so that you can get to the fifth argument.

- The third argument controls whether and where dollar signs appear in the address. Here is an easy way to remember how this argument works:. The number in the argument corresponds to how many times you press the F4 key to achieve the combination of dollar signs:

  » =ADDRESS(5,2,1) gives you $B$5.

  » =ADDRESS(5,2,2) locks only the row (B$5).

  » =ADDRESS(5,2,3) locks only the column ($B5).

  » =ADDRESS(5,2,4) locks nothing (=B5).

- The fourth argument controls whether you get an A1-style reference or an R1C1-reference:

  » =ADDRESS(5,2,1,1) return the A1-style reference $B$5.

  » =ADDRESS(5,2,1,0) return the R1C1 reference R5C2.

- The fifth argument can accept a sheet name. In this case, Microsoft examines the sheet name and figures out whether you need apostrophes:

  » =ADDRESS(5,2,4,1,"Atlanta") returns Atlanta!B5.

  » =ADDRESS(5,2,4,1,"Eden Prairie") returns 'Eden Prairie'!B5.

Note: You don't really have to remember how the third and fourth arguments work. If you simply use =ADDRESS(5,2,,,"Atlanta"), Excel returns Atlanta!$B$5.

The version of ADDRESS with the fifth argument returns text that can be used in the INDIRECT function. In Figure 30, the formula in cell D6 is:

=INDIRECT(ADDRESS(ROW(),2,4,1,D$3))

The first argument in ADDRESS is ROW(), which ensures that Excel grabs the row where the formula is. The second argument is hard-coded to a 2 to make sure you always get column B. The third and fourth arguments return a relative A1-style reference. The fifth argument contains only a dollar sign before the row to make sure you always get a sheet name from row 3, but the column can change as the formula is copied.

D6		f_x	=INDIRECT(ADDRESS(ROW(),2,4,1,D$3))	
	A	B	C	D	E
1	Sales Summary				
2					
3		Atlanta	Boston	Chicago	Dallas
4	Sales $	1555	1186	2567	1977
5	Sales Units	29	18	37	32
6	# Transactions	13	8	13	11
7	Labor Hours	24	24	32	24

Figure 30. Using ADDRESS is a bit more complicated than using CELL, but it involves a shorter formula.

Part
I

Additional Details: There is a version of INDIRECT that works with R1C1-style references because there are times when using R1C1 is actually easier. So far, all the examples of INDIRECT have used only a single argument. Leaving off the second argument:

=INDIRECT("B4")

or specifying TRUE as the second argument:

=INDIRECT("B4",TRUE)

tells Excel to interpret the reference as an A1-style reference. Using FALSE as the second argument:

=INDIRECT("RC",False)

tells Excel to interpret the reference as an R1C1 reference.

The reference =RC points to the current row and the current column. Including a number after the R or C creates an absolute reference to a particular row or column. =RC2 is the R1C1 method for referring to column B of this row. If you use R1C1, you don't have to worry about using CELL or ADDRESS. In Figure 31, the formula used in C7 is:

=INDIRECT("'"&C$3&"'!RC2",FALSE)

This formula can be copied throughout the table. Note that you do not have to switch the worksheet to R1C1 style in order to use this formula.

C7		f_x	=INDIRECT(""&C$3&"!RC2",FALSE)	
	A	B	C	D	E
1	Sales Summary				
2					
3		Atlanta	Boston	Chicago	Dallas
4	Sales $	1555	1186	2567	1977
5	Sales Units	29	18	37	32
6	# Transactions	13	8	13	11
7	Labor Hours	24	24	32	24

Figure 31. R1C1 style is not popular, but it certainly makes this formula easier to write.

Summary: With a little extra thought, you can use INDIRECT to point to another worksheet.

GET DATA FROM ANOTHER WORKSHEET BY USING INDIRECT

Challenge: You have 31 daily worksheets in a workbook, 1 for each day of the month. A cell on the summary worksheet contains a date. You want to use the date cell in INDIRECT to grab data from a certain day's worksheet, but the formula always returns a #REF! error.

In Figure 32, cell E3 contains a date. You've used the custom number format MMM D YYYY to ensure that the date in E3 looks like the worksheet name. The formula returns an error.

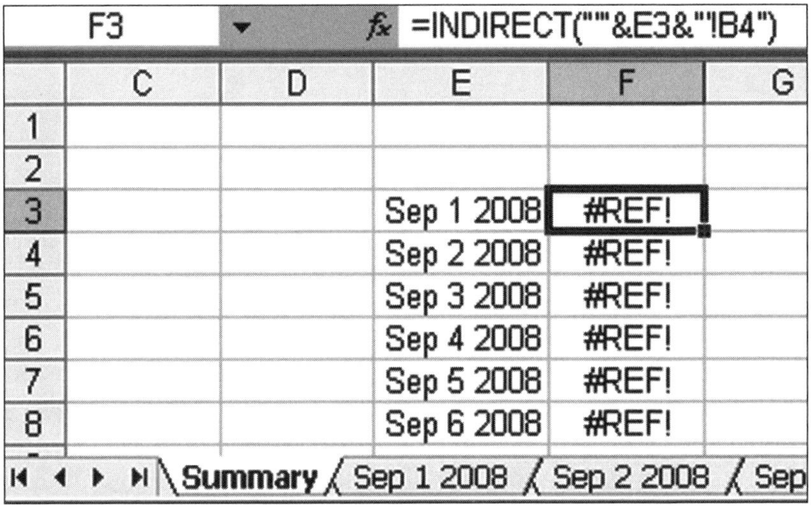

Figure 32. Using INDIRECT based on a date doesn't seem to work.

Background: No matter how you format cell E3, Excel converts the date back to a serial number when it is used in INDIRECT. You might hope for a reference like 'Sep 1 2008'!B4 but instead get ='39692'!B4. Figure 33 shows the formula after you use Evaluate Formula. 39692 is how Excel actually stores the date September 1, 2008, on a Windows PC.

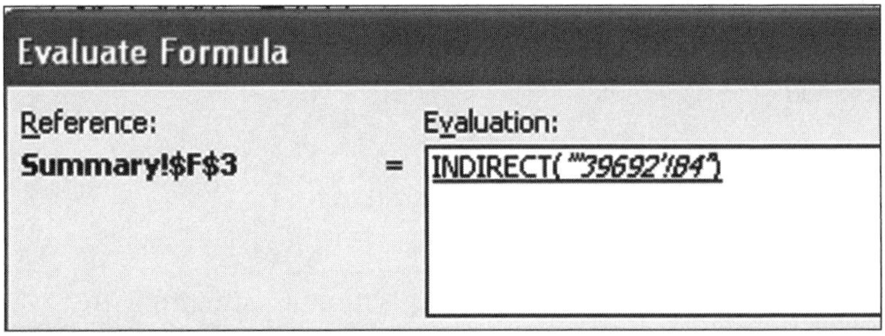

Figure 33. The reference fails because Excel changes the date back to a serial number.

Solution: You need to specify the correct custom number format by using the TEXT function. In Figure 34, the formula is =INDIRECT("'"&TEXT(A3, "mmm d yyyy")&"'!B4"). This builds a reference such as 'Sep 1 2008'!B4.

=INDIRECT("'"&TEXT(A3,"mmm d yyyy")&"'!B4")

	A	B	C	D
1				
2	Date	Sales		
3	9/1/2008	1555		
4	9/2/2008	1186		
5	9/3/2008	1736		
6	9/4/2008	2094		
7	9/5/2008	2157		
8	9/6/2008	2567		

|◄ ◄ ► ►| \ **Summary** / Sep 1 2008 / Sep 2 2008 ,

Figure 34. You use the TEXT function to convert the date to text that looks like a date.

The second argument of the TEXT function coerces the date to match the style of the worksheet name. If someone built a worksheet with a name such as Sep-1, the formula would be:

=INDIRECT("'"&TEXT(A3,"mmm-d")&"'!B4")

If your worksheets are named 9-1, the formula would be:

=INDIRECT("'"&TEXT(A3,"m-d")&"'!B4")

If you are lucky enough that your worksheets are simply named 1, 2, 3, and so on, you can use =INDIRECT(DAY(A3)&"!B4"), as shown in Figure 35.

=INDIRECT(DAY(A3)&"!B4")

	A	B	C
1			
2	Date	Sales	
3	9/1/2008	1555	
4	9/2/2008	1186	
5	9/3/2008	1736	
6	9/4/2008	2094	
7	9/5/2008	2157	
8	9/6/2008	2567	

|◄ ◄ ► ►| \ **Summary** / 1 / 2 / 3 / 4 /

Figure 35. In this case, TEXT can be replaced with DAY.

Part I

Gotcha: Formulas built with `INDIRECT` are particularly susceptible to generating `#REF!` errors if someone changes a worksheet name. Say that you have the `=3!B4`. If you change the name of the worksheet from 3 to Sep 3, the formula automatically changes to `='Sep 3'!B4`. However, when you start using `INDIRECT`, the formula fails when someone changes the name of the worksheet. If you use `INDIRECT`, you need to convince people not to change the worksheet names or protect the workbook.

Summary: A date used in `INDIRECT` always changes back to the date serial number. You need to use other functions to force the date to appear in the proper format.

USE INDIRECT TO GET A DATA FROM A MULTI-CELL RANGE

Challenge: As described in several other topics, `INDIRECT` is pretty cool for grabbing a value from a cell. Can `INDIRECT` point to a multi-cell range and be used in a `VLOOKUP` or `SUMIF` function?

Solution: You can build an `INDIRECT` function that points to a range. The range might be used as the lookup table in a `VLOOKUP` or as a range in `SUMIF` or `COUNTIF`.

In Figure 36, the formula pulls data from the worksheets specified in row 4.

The second argument in the `SUMIF` function looks for records that match a certain date from column A.

Note: Because each worksheet might have a different number of records, I chose to have each range extend to 300. This is a number that is sufficiently larger than the number of transactions on any sheet. The formula in cell B5 is:

```
=SUMIF(INDIRECT(B$4&"!A2:A300"),$A5,INDIRECT(B$4&"!C2:C300"))
```

=SUMIF(INDIRECT(D$4&"!A2:A300"),$A5,INDIRECT(D$4&"!C2:C300"))						
	A	B	C	D	E	F	G
4		Store1	Store2	Store3	Store4	Store5	Store6
5	1/1/2009	194	434	611	154	521	124
6	1/2/2009	1082	410	155	107	284	605
7	1/3/2009	903	338	137	985	1745	1937
8	1/4/2009	530	856	1018	373	780	673
9	1/5/2009	642	312	1257	700	695	462
10	1/6/2009	219	70	808	233	805	682
11	1/7/2009	581	1649	394	67	657	2615
12	1/8/2009	361	206	1151	1232	216	117

Figure 36. Each `INDIRECT` points to a rectangular range on the other worksheet.

Summary: You can use `INDIRECT` to grab data from a multi-cell range.

ALWAYS POINT TO CELL B10

Challenge: You want to create a formula that always points to cell B10. Normally, if you have a formula that points to B10 or even $B$10, the formula changes if you cut and paste B10 or if you insert or delete rows above row 10.

In Figure 37, a formula in D1 checks to see if a value is in cell B10. In Figure 38, even after items are deleted from rows 6, 8, and 9, the formula still reports an item in B10, even though cell B10 is empty. This is because the formula has changed to point to B7 in Figure 38.

D1		fx	=IF(NOT(ISBLANK(B10)),"GFI Emergency!","")		
	A	B	C	D	E	F
1	GhostFighters Inc.			GFI Emergency!		
2	Unresolved call log					
3						
4	Time Logged	Incident				
5	5:44 AM	Haunting at 123 Main				
6	6:41 AM	Apparition on Broadway				
7	7:24 AM	Paranormal activity on State				
8	12:34 PM	Macintosh with a virus				
9	5:28 PM	Rattling Chains at 4821 Lake Street				
10	8:25 PM	Cold chill at Civic Theatre				
11	9:37 PM	Crying baby heard in attic of 748 Broad Vista				

Figure 37. This formula points to B10

D1		fx	=IF(NOT(ISBLANK(B7)),"GFI
	A	B	C	D
1	GhostFighters Inc.			GFI Emergency!
2	Unresolved call log			
3				
4	Time Logged	Incident		
5	5:44 AM	Haunting at 123 Main		
6	7:24 AM	Paranormal activity on State		
7	8:25 PM	Cold chill at Civic Theatre		
8	9:37 PM	Crying baby heard in attic of 748 Broad V		

Figure 38. The reference moves to B7 if you delete three rows above B10.

Solution: You can use `INDIRECT("B10")` to ensure that the formula always points to cell B10. Even if you delete or insert rows, and even if you cut B10 and paste to B99, your formula will always point to B10 (Figure 39).

=IF(NOT(ISBLANK(INDIRECT("B10"))),		
C	D	E
	GFI Emergency!	

Figure 39. `INDIRECT("B10")` tells Excel to always look in cell B10.

Gotcha: If you are a fan of formula auditing, note that the Trace Dependents and Trace Precedents commands do not recognize the relationship between cell B10 and the formula in Figure 39. If you use Trace Dependents from cell B10, Excel will report that there are no dependents.

Summary: To force a formula to always point to cell B10, you can use `INDIRECT("B10")`.

USE NATURAL LANGUAGE FORMULAS WITHOUT USING NATURAL LANGUAGE FORMULAS

Challenge: Excel 2003 offers relatively obscure natural language formulas, but they were removed from Excel 2007. The table nomenclature in Excel 2007 isn't as easy to use.

Solution: To solve this problem, you can use the intersection character in your `SUM` function. Everyone knows that `=SUM(A2:A10)` sums the nine-cell range from A2 through A10. Most people realize that `=SUM(A1,A3,A5,A7,A9)` adds up the five cells specified. However, very few people understand that the space character is actually an intersection operator when used in a `SUM` function!

Say that you have the worksheet shown in Figure 40. As discussed in "Quickly Create Many Range Names" on page 76, you can add range names by using these steps:

1. Select the range A1:F13.

2. Use Insert, Name, Create (in Excel 2003) or Formulas, Create from Selection (in Excel 2007).

3. In the Create Names or Create Names from Selection dialog, select Top Row and Left Column. Click OK. Excel creates names for the 12 cities in column A. For example, the name Louisville applies to cells B13:F13. Excel

also creates five range names for the headings in row 1. For example, the GP range refers to D2:D13.

You can now easily sum a range by using =SUM(Sales) or =SUM(Atlanta,Charlotte). However, if you include a space between the named ranges, Excel includes only the cells at the intersection of the two ranges. The formula =SUM(Boston COGS) finds the one cell at the intersection of the Boston range (B3:F3) and the COGS range (C2:C13). Only one cell is in common between these two ranges, so the result is the 88,351 found in cell C3.

Part
I

C17			f_x =SUM(Boston COGS)		
A	B	C	D	E	F
1		Sales	COGS	GP	Expenses	Income
2 Atlanta	114,945	52,530	62,415	22,299	40,116
3 Boston	183,681	88,351	95,330	23,674	71,657
4 Charlotte	153,487	70,144	83,343	23,070	60,274
5 Dallas	124,998	59,874	65,124	22,500	42,624
6 Eden Prarie	187,889	91,314	96,575	23,758	72,817
7 Fargo	114,700	55,056	59,644	22,294	37,350
8 Galveston	141,324	67,553	73,771	22,826	50,945
9 Homer	164,235	76,369	87,866	23,285	64,581
10 Islip	149,636	69,581	80,055	22,993	57,063
11 Jacksonville	166,847	78,585	88,262	23,337	64,925
12 Kansas City	118,117	56,932	61,185	22,362	38,822
13 Louisville	199,441	95,931	103,510	23,989	79,521
14					
15		462,692 =SUM(Boston)			
16		862,219 =SUM(COGS)			
17		88,351 =SUM(Boston COGS)			

Figure 40. Excel creates five named ranges in this selection.

Summary: When you use a space between arguments in a SUM function, Excel returns only the intersection of the ranges.

SUM A CELL THROUGH SEVERAL WORKSHEETS

Challenge: You have 12 identical worksheets, one for each month. You would like to summarize each worksheet. Is there a better way than using =Jan!B4 +Feb!B4+Mar!B4+Apr!B4...?

Solution: You can use a 3-D formula such as =SUM(Jan:Dec!B4), as shown in Figure 41.

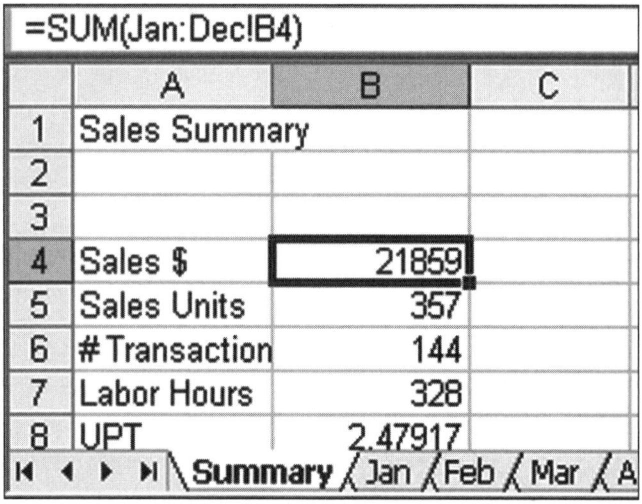

=SUM(Jan:Dec!B4)

	A	B	C
1	Sales Summary		
2			
3			
4	Sales $	21859	
5	Sales Units	357	
6	# Transaction	144	
7	Labor Hours	328	
8	UPT	2.47917	

◄ ◄ ► ►┃ \ **Summary** ╱ Jan ╱ Feb ╱ Mar ╱ A

Late-breaking Tip: To add up cell B4 on all the worksheets with Sales in the sheet name, type =SUM('*Sales'!B4) and press Enter.

Figure 41. A 3-D formula adds up all instances of B4 on the 12 sheets from Jan through Dec.

If the first or last worksheet contains a space in the name, you have to use apostrophes around the pair of worksheet names: =SUM('Jan 2009:Dec 2009'!B4).

You can easily copy this formula to other cells on the summary worksheet.

Gotcha: Do not drag the summary worksheet to appear after the Jan worksheet, or you will set up a circular reference.

Additional Details: It is possible to set up a named range that refers to a 3-D range. Here is an interesting way to set up a named range:

1. Go to cell B4 on the Jan worksheet.
2. Select Insert, Name, Define.
3. The Refers To box contains =Jan!B4. Click in the box. Hold down the Shift key. Click on the Dec worksheet. The Refers To box changes to =Jan:Dec!B4.

Summary: A 3-D formula can sum a specific cell on several worksheets.

SUM VISIBLE ROWS

Challenge: A SUM function totals all the cells in a range, whether they are hidden or not. You want to sum only the visible rows.

Solution: You can use the SUBTOTAL function instead of SUM. The formula you need is slightly different, depending on how you hid the rows.

If rows are hidden by using Format, Row, Hide, you use:

=SUBTOTAL(109,E2:E564)

This is an unusual use for SUBTOTAL. Normally, SUBTOTAL is used to force Excel to ignore other SUBTOTAL cells within a range. SUBTOTAL can perform any of 11 operations. The first parameter indicates Average (1), Count (2), CountA (3), Max (4), Min (5), Product (6), StdDev (7), StdDevP (8), Sum (9), Var (10), or VarP (11). When you add 100 to this parameter, Excel includes only visible cells in the result.

In Figure 42, you can see that the result of the SUM in row 565 and the result of the SUBTOTAL (9, in row 567 are identical. When you switch to SUBTOTAL (109, in row 566, Excel total only the visible cells in the range.

Part I

E566			ƒx =SUBTOTAL(109,E2:E564)				
A	B	C	D	E	F	G	H
1 Region	**Product**	**Date**	**Customer**	**Quantity**	**Revenue**	**COGS**	**Profit**
2 Central	DEF	6/25/2004	AIG	200	4060	1968	2092
30 East	XYZ	8/22/2004	AT&T	600	15006	6132	8874
72 West	XYZ	5/3/2004	Bank of America	800	19288	8176	11112
78 Central	DEF	2/27/2004	Chevron	900	20610	8856	11754
564 West	XYZ	10/3/2004	Wal-Mart	500	12760	5110	7650
565			SUM:	313900	6707812	2978394	3729418
566			SUBTOTAL(109:	3000	71724	30242	41482
567			SUBTOTAL(9:	313900	6707812	2978394	3729418

Figure 42. The 100 series of SUBTOTAL functions sum, average, and count only the visible rows.

Gotcha: There is an error in Excel Help. The Help topic says that the 100 series parameters sum only visible cells. This is true only of cells that are in hidden rows. If your data is hidden due to hiding a column, Excel still includes those cells (Figure 43).

H2						ƒx =SUBTOTAL(109,C2:F2)
A	B	C	E	G	H	
1 Region	**Customer**	**Q1**	**Q3**	**SUM**	**SUBTOTAL(109,**	
2 Central	AIG	200	215	890	890	
3 East	Chevron	600	678	2640	2640	
4 West	Thales	800	788	3292	3292	
5 West	IEEE	800	791	3244	3244	
6 Central	AT&T	500	498	1899	1899	

Figure 43. The formula fails to ignore cells hidden using hidden columns.

Additional Details: There is an unusual exception to the behavior of the SUBTOTAL function. When your rows have been hidden by any of the Filter commands (Advanced Filter, AutoFilter, or Filter), Excel includes only the visible rows in a SUBTOTAL (9, function. There is no need to use the 109 version. In Figure 44, Advanced Filter is used to find only the AT&T records for two products. The regular SUBTOTAL with an argument of 9 works fine to sum only the visible rows.

E570		▼	*fx* =SUBTOTAL(9,E6:E568)		

	D	E	F	G	H
1	Criteria Range:		Product	Customer	
2			ABC	AT&T	
3			DEF	AT&T	
4					
5	Customer	Quantity	Revenue	COGS	Profit
33	AT&T	600	14154	5904	8250
40	AT&T	800	15488	6776	8712
41	AT&T	700	13412	5929	7483
42	AT&T	300	6018	2952	3066
43	AT&T	800	16936	7872	9064
44	AT&T	800	17056	7872	9184
45	AT&T	300	6522	2952	3570
569					
570	SUBTOTAL(9:	15700	325167	144350	180817

Figure 44. You don't have to use 109 if your rows are hidden as the result of a filter.

Why even mention this strange anomaly? Because there is a little-known shortcut key to sum the visible rows as the result of a filter. Try these steps:

1. Choose one cell in your data set.

2. From the Excel 2003 menu, choose Data, Filter, AutoFilter. From the Excel 2007 ribbon, choose Data, Filter. Excel adds dropdowns to each heading.

3. Open the Customer dropdown. In Excel 2003, choose one customer. In Excel 2007, uncheck Select All and then choose one customer.

4. Move the cell pointer to a cell immediately below the filtered data. Choose a cell below one or all of the numeric columns.

5. Press Alt+= or click the AutoSum icon. Instead of using a SUM function, Excel uses =SUBTOTAL (9, which totals only the rows selected by the filter (Figure 45).

E565		▼	*fx* =SUBTOTAL(9,E2:E564)				

	C	D	E	F	G	H
1	Date	Customer ▼	Quant ▼	Reven ▼	CO(▼	Pr(▼
78	2/27/2004	Chevron	900	20610	8856	11754
79	3/16/2004	Chevron	400	8116	3388	4728
80	7/30/2004	Chevron	1000	18290	8470	9820
81	10/13/2004	Chevron	300	7032	3066	3966
565			2600	54048	23780	30268

Figure 45. Pressing Alt+= fills in the SUBTOTAL functions in the selection.

Tip: After adding the formulas shown in Figure 45, insert two blank rows above row 1. Cut the formulas in the total row and paste to the new row 1. After you do this, your ad hoc totals are always visible near the headings.

Summary: You can use variations of the SUBTOTAL function to ignore hidden rows.

LEARN R1C1 REFERENCES

Part I

Challenge: R1C1 cell referencing comes in handy in several situations, such as in VBA, when you're using INDIRECT, and with conditional formatting. It isn't hard to learn.

Background: VisiCalc introduced the A1 naming style for cells. Lotus 1-2-3 used the same system. With the Multiplan product, Excel used a system in which columns were numbered. The cell that you and I know as D10 would have been referred to as R10C4 in Multiplan (for row 10, column 4).

During the spreadsheet wars, Microsoft realized that most of the world was used to A1 referencing, and to compete, it would have to pretend that Excel used A1 references. Of course, Excel only pretends to use A1. It really uses R1C1 behind the scenes. If you don't believe me, in Excel 2003 select Tools, Options, Generaal, R1C1 style as shown in Figure 46. In Excel 2007, use Office Icon, Excel Options, Formulas, Working with Formulas, R1C1 Reference Style..

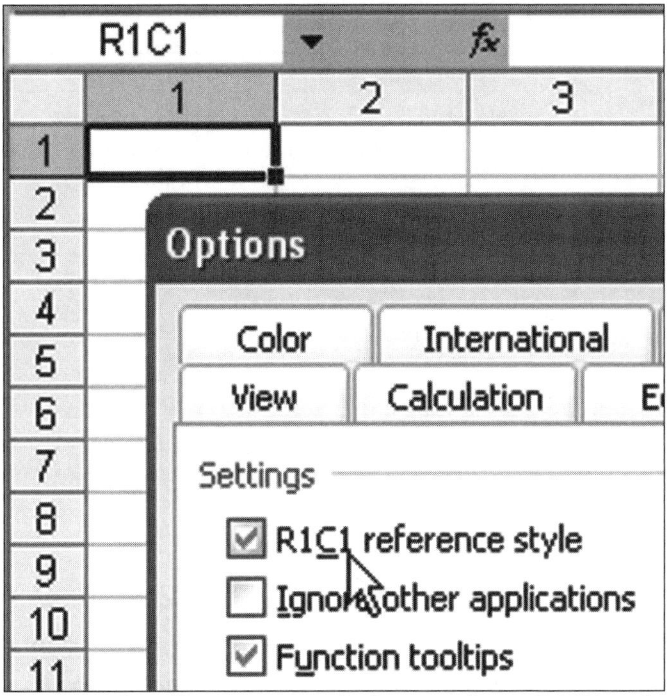

Figure 46.   You are one click away from R1C1-style spreadsheets.

Note that I am not suggesting that you switch over to R1C1 references. That would be as crazy as suggesting that Microsoft replace the familiar File, Edit, View, Insert, Format, Tools, Data, Window, and Help with a new user interface. Instead, I am suggesting that you understand the reference style because there are times when it is easier to use R1C1 than A1 (as with INDIRECT or VBA).

Solution: An R1C1-style reference contains the letter R and the letter C. Without any modifiers, the R means "the same row where this formula is entered," and the C means "the same column where the formula is entered."

The simplest R1C1 reference is =RC. If you are in cell C10 and enter =RC, you are referring to cell C10. (This would also cause a circular reference error.)

When you follow the R or the C with a number in square brackets, you are referring to a cell that is some number of cells away. For example =RC[-1] in C10 refers to B10. =R[10]C in C10 refers to C20. You can modify both the row and column. For example, =R[1]C[1] in C10 refers to D11.

Note: For rows, positive numbers move down the worksheet. Negative numbers move up the spreadsheet. For columns, positive numbers move to the right on the worksheet. Negative numbers move to the left on the worksheet.

If you want to build a formula to calculate GP% in column I, you have to divide this row's column H by this row's column F. This is a bit of a hassle to do, and the formula is different in each row (Figure 47).

	F	G	H	I
	Revenue	COGS	Profit	GP%
1				
2	22810	10220	12590	=H2/F2
3	2257	984	1273	=H3/F3
4	18552	7872	10680	=H4/F4
5	9152	4088	5064	=H5/F5
6	21730	9840	11890	=H6/F6
7	8456	3388	5068	=H7/F7
8	16416	6776	9640	=H8/F8
9	21438	9198	12240	=H9/F9
10	6267	2541	3726	=H10/F10

Figure 47. With A1 references, the formula in each cell is different.

Think about the formula you use to do this in R1C1 style. You want this row, one column to the left divided by this row, 3 columns to the left. You can use exactly the same formula, no matter which row you are in: All the formulas in Figure 48 are =RC[-1]/RC[-3]. This is pretty cool.

R4C9 ▼	*fx* =RC[-1]/RC[-3]		
6	**7**	**8**	**9**
1 Revenue	COGS	Profit	GP%
2 22810	10220	12590	=RC[-1]/RC[-3]
3 2257	984	1273	=RC[-1]/RC[-3]
4 18552	7872	10680	=RC[-1]/RC[-3]
5 9152	4088	5064	=RC[-1]/RC[-3]
6 21730	9840	11890	=RC[-1]/RC[-3]
7 8456	3388	5068	=RC[-1]/RC[-3]

Figure 48. With R1C1, the formula is the same in each cell.

How about absolute references? In Figure 49, the formula =F2*$M$1 ensures that you always use the tax rate in cell M1. To specify an absolute reference using R1C1, you leave off the square brackets. Cell $M$1 is the 13th column of row 1, so by using R1C13, you always point to M1.

J	K	L	M
		Sales Tax	Tax Rate 0.07
=F2*$M$1			
=F3*$M$1			
=F4*$M$1			
=F5*$M$1			
=F6*$M$1			
=F7*$M$1			
=F8*$M$1			
=F9*$M$1			

Figure 49. Absolute references in A1 style require dollar signs.

In Figure 50, the formula becomes =RC[-4]*R1C13.

10	**11**	**12**	**13**
	Sales Tax	Tax Rate 0.07	
=RC[-4]*R1C13			
=RC[-4]*R1C13			
=RC[-4]*R1C13			
=RC[-4]*R1C13			
=RC[-4]*R1C13			
=RC[-4]*R1C13			

Figure 50. To specify an absolute value in R1C1, you omit the square brackets. The number now refers to a specific row and column number.

Summary: R1C1-style referencing is not hard to learn and enables easier use of INDIRECT.

Part

I

RANDOM NUMBERS WITHOUT DUPLICATES

Challenge: You want to generate random numbers between 1 and 100 without any duplicates. Excel offers the functions `RAND()` and `RANDBETWEEN()`, but both of them are likely to generate duplicates, and you frequently need to generate a series of random numbers without duplicates.

Background: I frequently use a three-column method to solve this problem, but `PGC01` posted an impressive formula to handle this problem.

To understand the formula, you have to understand how the `SMALL` function works. Typically, `SMALL` returns the kth-smallest value in an array. For example, `=SMALL({60,10,20,30,40,50},3)` returns 30, as 30 is the third-smallest number in the list.

If the array specified as the first argument contains anything non-numeric, those entries are ignored. `=SMALL({60,10,FALSE,30,40,50},3)` returns 40 because the 20 has been replaced by `FALSE`.

Solution: `PGC01`'s formula builds an array of the unused numbers in the range and then selects from those numbers.

To illustrate, consider Figure 51.

	A	B	C	D	E	F	G	H	I	J	K	L
1	Generate Random Numbers 1 through 10 without repeats.											
2												
3		Start		Start		Start		Start		Start		Start
4		1		1		4		1		6		2
5		7		4		9		9		3		5
6		4		3		7		3		8		9
7		6		2		6		5		7		8
8		3		10		10		4		5		7
9		2		6		2		2		4		1
10		5		9		5		8		2		6
11		9		7		8		10		10		3
12		8		8		3		6		9		4
13		10		5		1		7		1		10

Figure 51. Formulas generate six sets of the numbers, 1 to 10, randomly sequenced.

In figure 51, the array formula in cell B9 is:

```
=SMALL(IF(COUNTIF(B$3:B8,ROW($1:$10))<>1,ROW($1:$10)),1+I
NT(RAND()*(10-ROW()+ROW(B$4))))
```

Excel starts evaluating this formula with the COUNTIF function. ROW($1:$10) generates an array of the numbers, 1, 2, 3,...10. The COUNTIF function tells Excel to look through the numbers generated so far in B$3:B8 and count how many are equal to 1. This answer is either going to be 1 or 0. Because 1 already occurs in the range, the COUNTIF will be 1. But, for the number 2, the answer will be 0 because a 2 has not been chosen yet.

Figure 52 shows what is happening in the IF(COUNTIF()) portion of the formula:

	A	B	C	D	E	F	G	H
1	Generate Random Numbers 1 through 10 without repeats.							
2								
3		Start		...IF(COUNTIF(B$3:B8,ROW($1:$10))<>1,ROW($1:$10))				
4		1			Row	CountIf	<>1	Result
5		7		Row 1	1	1	FALSE	FALSE
6		4		Row 2	2	0	TRUE	2
7		6		Row 3	3	1	FALSE	FALSE
8		3		Row 4	4	1	FALSE	FALSE
9		10		Row 5	5	0	TRUE	5
10				Row 6	6	1	FALSE	FALSE
11				Row 7	7	1	FALSE	FALSE
12				Row 8	8	0	TRUE	8
13				Row 9	9	0	TRUE	9
14				Row 10	10	0	TRUE	10

Figure 52. Range E4:H14 shows how half the formula calculates cell B9.

- Cells E5:E14 show the results of the ROW function, numbers 1 to 10.
- Cells F5:F14 count how many times the number in E already appears in the previous random numbers in B4:B8.
- Cells G5:G14 check to see if the result in F is equal to 1.
- The IF function in H says that if the value in G is TRUE, bring over the number from E; otherwise, Excel puts in a FALSE.

At this point, the array action of the formula is complete. PGC01 has succeeded in building an array of the available numbers. At this point, you simply have to ask for one of the numbers from that remaining array. Basically, the formula is then:

```
=SMALL(H5:H14,RANDBETWEEN(1,5))
```

Of course, figuring out that there are five numbers left is more difficult than in the above line. To make the formula compatible with Excel 2003, `PGC01` uses `RAND()` instead of `RANDBETWEEN`. The `RAND` function returns a random integer between 0 and 0.99999. `=INT(RAND()*5)` returns a random integer between 0 and 4. `1+INT(RAND()*5)` returns a random integer between 1 and 5.

Because the 5 portion of that formula has to be different in each row of the formula, you can use `(10-ROW()+ROW(B$4))` instead of hard-coding the 5.

Alternate Strategy: Let's say that you wanted to return a random check number between 1501 and 1850 in cells H11:H35.

Note that the first random number cannot be generated in row 1 because there always has to be a blank anchor cell above the first random number. In this case, the first random number is in H11, so the anchor cell becomes H10.

The start of the formula refers to the anchor cell twice, once with a dollar sign before the row and once without:

```
=SMALL(IF(COUNTIF(H$10:H10,
```

Next, you specify the first and last numbers in the range twice:

```
=SMALL(IF(COUNTIF(H$10:H10,ROW($1501:$1850))<>1,ROW($1501
:$1850)),
```

Note: You cannot use this method to generate numbers larger than 65,536 in Excel 2003 and earlier. In Excel 2007, you are limited to 1,048,576.

For the final portion of the formula, you need to figure out how many numbers are in the pool of numbers. In this case, 1850–1501+1 is 350 numbers. Plug in the 350 where shown and then plug in the address of the first cell in this fragment of the formula:

Note: While the first portion of the formula uses H10 as the anchor cell, this portion uses H11—the cell that contains the first random number.

```
1+INT(RAND()*(350-ROW()+ROW(H$11))))
```

The entire formula is:

```
=SMALL(IF(COUNTIF(H$10:H10,ROW($1501:$1850))<>1,ROW($1501
:$1850)),1+INT(RAND()*(350-ROW()+ROW(H$11))))
```

Type this formula in H11 and press Ctrl+Shift+Enter.

Copy cell H11 and paste it to H12:H35.

Tip: The sample file for this chapter includes a worksheet where you can type in three values, and the worksheet builds the formula for you.

	B	C	D	E	F	G
3	Fill in the yellow cells:					
4						
5	What is the first cell you will use?				Z2	
6	The anchor cell is one cell above that				Z1	
7	What is the first number in the range?				75	
8	What is the last number in the range?				95	
9	How many total numbers in the range?				21	
10	Anchor Row:				1	
11	Anchor Column:				26	
12	Anchor Cell Address, row absolute				Z$1	
13	Anchor Cell Address, relative				Z1	
14	First cell address, row absolute				Z$2	
15	Formula Part 1				=SMALL(IF(COUNTIF(	
16	Formula Part 2				:	
17	Formula Part 3				,ROW($	
18	Formula Part 4				:$	
19	Formula Part 5				))<>1,ROW($	
20	Formula Part 6				)),1+INT(RAND()*(	
21	Formula Part 7				-ROW()+ROW(	
22	Formula Part 8				))))	
23						
24	Copy B26 and paste as values in another cell. Then array-enter that formula in cell Z2					
25						
26	=SMALL(IF(COUNTIF(Z$1:Z1,ROW($75:$95))<>1,ROW($75:$95)),1+INT(RAND()*(21-ROW()+ROW(Z$2)))))					

Figure 53. Type in values in F5, F7, F8 and this worksheet will build the formula to use..

Summary: A fairly complex array formula can generate random numbers without any duplicates.

Source: http://www.mrexcel.com/forum/showthread.php?t=222922

This formula was nominated by Barry Houdini.

SORT WITH A FORMULA

Challenge: You have a range of numbers in cells D2:D11. You want a formula to rearrange the numbers into ascending or descending sequence.

Solution: You can use either the SMALL or LARGE function to solve this problem quickly. =SMALL(D2:D11,1) returns the smallest number in the range, =SMALL(D2:D11,2) returns the second-smallest number, and so on. Unlike the RANK function, the SMALL and LARGE functions deal well with ranges that contain ties.

Of course, you need to make the first argument absolute by adding dollar signs: $D$2:$D$11. In addition, you need to find a way to change the 1 in the second argument to 2, 3, 4, and so on as you copy down the range.

Instead of typing a 1 in the formula, you can use ROW(A1). This function returns a 1, and as you copy the formula down the page, it changes to ROW(A2), ROW(A3), etc.

In Figure 54, the SMALL formulas in column F sort the data in ascending sequence. The formula =LARGE($D$2:$D$11,ROW(A1)) in H3 and copied down sorts the numbers in descending sequence.

	F3			▼	ƒx =SMALL($D$2:$D$11,ROW(A1))		
	A BC	D	E	F	G	H	
1		Values					
2		10		Low to High		High to Low	
3		23		3		23	
4		3		10		22	
5		14		10		21	
6		17		11		17	
7		10		14		15	
8		21		15		14	
9		22		17		11	
10		15		21		10	
11		11		22		10	
12				23		3	

Figure 54. Formulas in F and H sort the data from D in ascending or descending sequence.

Note: Excel properly handles the duplicate values. Cells F4 and F5 show both of the 10s from the original data set. Excel returns 10 as the answer for the second- and third-smallest items in the range.

In Figure 55, notice how the ROW(A1) argument changes as you copy it down the range.

Low to High
=SMALL($D$2:$D$11,ROW(A1))
=SMALL($D$2:$D$11,ROW(A2))
=SMALL($D$2:$D$11,ROW(A3))
=SMALL($D$2:$D$11,ROW(A4))
=SMALL($D$2:$D$11,ROW(A5))
=SMALL($D$2:$D$11,ROW(A6))
=SMALL($D$2:$D$11,ROW(A7))
=SMALL($D$2:$D$11,ROW(A8))
=SMALL($D$2:$D$11,ROW(A9))
=SMALL($D$2:$D$11,ROW(A10))

Figure 55. Using ROW(A1) is an easy way to make the second argument change from 1 to 2, 3, 4, etc. as it copied down.

Summary: You can use the SMALL or LARGE function to sort with a formula.

DEAL WITH DATES BEFORE 1900

Challenge: Excel stores a date as the number of days that have elapsed since January 1, 1900. This means that all the cool date functions do not work for dates in the 1800s. This is a problem for historians and genealogists.

Solution: A formula proposed by Boller calculates elapsed days going back to January 1, 1000. I've adapted this formula a bit. Boller's original formula solved the problem by adding 1,000 years to the date. Thus, a valid date such as January 23, 2009, would become January 23, 3009. An invalid date such as February 17, 1865, would become February 17, 2865. Because Excel can deal with dates up through the year 9999, this method works sufficiently.

Part I

You need to enter a start date in A4 and an end date in B4. Use a format such as 2/17/1865 when entering dates. If your date is after 1900, Excel automatically converts the date to a date serial number. If the date is before 1900, Excel stores the date as text.

If the cell contains a real date, you want to add 1,000 years. An easy way to do this is to use the `EDATE` function and add 12,000 months to the date. `=EDATE(A4,12000)` returns a date that is 1,000 years after a valid date in A4. Note that this function requires the Analysis Toolpak in versions prior to Excel 2007. If you can ensure that the Analysis Toolpak is installed, you can use `=DATE(YEAR(A4)+1000,MONTH(A4),DAY(A4))`.

If the cell does not contain a real date, you need to break the date apart, add 1,000 years, put the date back together, and convert it to a real date:

- To get the left portion of the date, use `=LEFT(A4,LEN(A4)-4)`
- To get the year portion of the date, use `=RIGHT(A4,4)`
- To add 1,000 years to the date, use `=RIGHT(A4,4)+1000`
- To put the month, day, and year+1,000 back together, use `=LEFT(A4,LEN(A4)-4)&RIGHT(A4,4)+1000`
- To convert that result back to a true date, use `=DATEVALUE(LEFT(A4,LEN(A4)-4)&RIGHT(A4,4)+1000)`

You now need to selectively use either the `EDATE` or the `DATEVALUE` portion of the formula, depending on whether Excel sees the date in A4 as text. Enter this IF statement in cell C4:

```
=IF(ISTEXT(A4),DATEVALUE(LEFT(A4,LEN(A4)-4)&RIGHT(A4,4)+1
000),EDATE(A4,12000))
```

Copy it to cell D4 to get a modified date from column B.

You can now use these results with any available date functions.

In Figure 56, cell E4 calculates the number of elapsed days with `=D4-C4`. Cell F4 calculates the number of years with `=DATEDIF(C4,D4,"y")`. Note that you can combine the formulas from C4, D4, and E4 into a single mega-formula:

```
=IF(ISTEXT(B4),DATEVALUE(LEFT(B4,LEN(B4)-4)&RIGHT(B4,4)+1
000),EDATE(B4,12000))-IF(ISTEXT(A4),DATEVALUE(LEFT(A4,LEN
(A4)-4)&RIGHT(A4,4)+1000),EDATE(A4,12000)).
```

	A	B	C	D	E	F
3	Start	End	Start Modified	End Modified	Delta Days	Delta Years
4	2/17/1850	5/15/1960	2/17/2850	5/15/2960	40264	110
5	1/6/1888	3/5/1955	1/6/2888	3/5/2955	24529	67
6	8/12/1823	10/4/1858	8/12/2823	10/4/2858	12837	35
7	9/8/1782	8/27/1792	9/8/2782	8/27/2792	3641	9
8	11/12/1865	10/6/1893	11/12/2865	10/6/2893	10190	27
9	8/13/1739	3/19/1801	8/13/2739	3/19/2801	22499	61
10	9/22/1831	4/1/1883	9/22/2831	4/1/2883	18819	51
11	4/6/1878	2/1/1930	4/6/2878	2/1/2930	18928	51
12	2/2/1930	3/5/1950	2/2/2930	3/5/2950	7336	20
13	7/20/1815	1/23/1889	7/20/2815	1/23/2889	26851	73
14	3/5/1621	2/17/1965	3/5/2621	2/17/2965	125628	343

Figure 56. Excel seems to be able to handle dates from before 1900 when you use this formula.

Gotcha: Historians note that calendar reform in 1752 removed 12 days from the calendar. Be particularly careful when figuring dates before this period. The formula here does not deal with that anomaly. For details, see http://www.adsb.co.uk/date_and_time/calendar_reform_1752/.

Summary: Although Excel doesn't deal with pre-1900 dates, you can do date math with these dates by adding enough years to bring them into the post-1900 era.

Source: http://www.mrexcel.com/forum/showthread.php?p=1382146

This formula was nominated by Barry Houdini

USE VLOOKUP TO GET THE NTH MATCH

Challenge: Your lookup table contains multiple occurrences of each key field. You would like to return the second, third, or fourth occurrence of the key.

Solution: VLOOKUP cannot solve this problem. OFFSET with MATCH could do it, provided that the lookup table is sorted by key. But if your table is not sorted, you need to turn to this user-defined function from Zack Barresse and Peter Moran:

```
Function VLOOKUPNTH(lookup_value, table_array As Range, _
            col_index_num As Integer, nth_value)
' Allows for finding the nth item
' that matches the lookup value.
Dim nRow As Long
Dim nVal As Integer
Dim bFound As Boolean
    VLOOKUPNTH = "Not Found"
    With table_array
        For nRow = 1 To .Rows.Count
            If .Cells(nRow, 1).Value = lookup_value Then
                nVal = nVal + 1
                ' Check to see if this is the nth match
                If nVal = nth_value Then
                    VLOOKUPNTH = .Cells(nRow, col_index_num).Text
                    Exit Function
                End If
            End If
        Next nRow
    End With
End Function
```

You need to add this function to your workbook's VBA project. It works like VLOOKUP, but instead of specifying FALSE as the fourth argument, you specify which value match you want to return.

In Figure 57, a regular VLOOKUP appears in column F, and VLOOKUPNTH appears in columns G:H.

I2			*fx*	=VLOOKUPNTH($E2,$A$2:$C$209,3,10)				
	A	B	C	D	E	F	G	H	I
1	Rep	Invoice	Amount		Rep	First	2nd	3rd	10th
2	R104	1002	9985		R100	9916	9761	9572	6232
3	R102	1099	9980		R101	9970	9791	9747	8381
4	R101	1016	9970		R102	9980	9843	9744	7424
5	R100	1040	9916		R103	9781	9560	9258	7917
6	R102	1130	9843		R104	9985	9626	9553	7076

Figure 57. Formulas in G:H grab the nth match from the lookup table.

Breaking It Down: `table_array` is a range passed to the function. When the function uses table_array, the future references to `CELLS(nRow, 1).Value` always look through the first column of the lookup table. Later, `VLOOKUPNTH` is assigned to be `Cells(nRow, Col_index_number)`. If `Col_Index_Number` contains the number N, this refers to the nth column of the lookup table.

Additional Details: In my seminars, I frequently lament that `VLOOKUP` cannot grab a value that appears to the left of the key field. You could use a similar approach to Barresse and Moran's user-defined function to build a `VLOOKUP` that will work to the left of the key field:

```
Function VLOOKNEW(lookup_value, table_array As Range, _

        col_index_num As Integer, CloseMatch As Boolean)

` Allows for col_index_num to be negative

` that matches the lookup value.

Dim nRow As Long

Dim nVal As Integer

Dim bFound As Boolean

    VLOOKNEW = "Not Found"

    ` if positive, treat as a regular VLOOKUP

    If col_index_num > 0 Then

        VLOOKNEW = Application.WorksheetFunction.VLookup(lookup_value, _

            table_array, col_index_num, CloseMatch)

    Else

        ` Do a VLOOKUP Left

        nRow = Application.WorksheetFunction.Match(lookup_value, _

            table_array.Resize(, 1), CloseMatch)

        VLOOKNEW = table_array(nRow, 1).Offset(0, col_index_num)

    End If

End Function
```

`VLOOKNEW` is similar to `VLOOKUP`, except that you can use a negative value for the column index number (Figure 58).

C2		▼		*fx*	=VLOOKNEW(A2,$G$2:$G$6,-1,FALSE)				
	A	**B**	**C**	**D**	**E**	**F**	**G**	**H**	**I**
1	Rep	Name	Region			Region	Rep	Name	
2	R104	Edwards	East			East	R100	Adams	
3	R102	Clinton	East			East	R102	Clinton	
4	R101	Bush	West			East	R104	Edwards	
5	R100	Adams	East			West	R101	Bush	
6	R102	Clinton	East			West	R103	Delano	
7	R101	Bush	West						

Figure 58. VLOOKNEW returns a value that appears to the left of the key field

Summary: User-defined functions can provide improvements on the VLOOKUP function.

Source: http://www.mrexcel.com/forum/showthread.php?t=112275

The post was nominated by Matt Hohbein. Thanks to Zack Barresse and Peter Moran.

USE A SELF-REFERENCING FORMULA

Challenge: Shades was looking for a formula to reverse letters in a cell. This can easily be accomplished using a VBA function. However, Shades had challenged people to write a formula. A new member, Hady, came along with this solution.

Gotcha: The technique in this topic is not compatible with the Evaluate Formula feature. If you use Evaluate Formula on a self-referencing formula, you run the risk of crashing Excel and losing your work.

Solution: To solve this problem, you use a self-referencing formula. Follow these steps:

1. Select Tools, Options, Calculation. Choose Iteration and set the maximum iterations to 100.

2. Enter any sentence in A1.

3. In cell B1, enter this formula and press Enter: =IF(LEN(B1)<LEN(A1)+1,B1&MID(A1,LEN(A1)+1-LEN(B1),1),IF(MID(B1,1,1)<>"0",B1,RIGHT(B1,LEN(A1))&" ")), When you press Enter, you get a result of 0 and the last character from cell A1. This is normal.

4. Press F9 again, and you get 0, the last character, and the second-to-last character.

5. Press F9 again, and you get 0 and the last three characters in reverse.

6. Keep pressing F9. When you have 0 and all of the characters, press F9 one last time, and the 0 is removed.

7. To start over, go to B1, press F2 to put the formula in Edit mode, and press Ctrl+Shift+Enter.

Breaking It Down: Let's say you put AbCdWxYz in cell A1. When the formula starts, the value of B1 is 0. The LEN of A1 is 8, and the LEN of B1 is 0, so the formula takes whatever is in B1 and concatenates it with the MID of A1. The MID function says to start at the character that is the LEN of A1 minus the LEN of B1 + 1. In the first calculation, this appends the starting 0 with the final character, and you will have 0z in cell B1 (Figure 59).

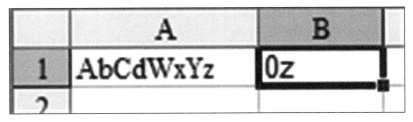

Figure 59. Initially, you get a 0 and the last character.

As the result in B1 gets longer, the formula keeps appending characters further from the end of A1. After you press F9 a few more times, you have 0zY in B1. The LEN of A1 is still 8. The LEN of B1 is 3. You are using 8+1–3, so you are now asking for the sixth character to be appended to B1, and you now get 0zYx in B1, as shown in Figure 60.

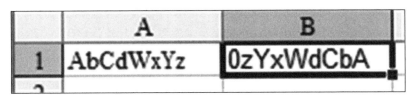

Figure 60. With each press of the F9 key, you get an additional character.

You eventually get to the point where you have a 0 and the complete text from A1, in reverse, as shown in Figure 61.

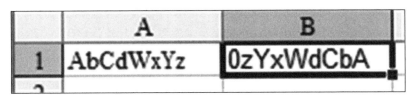

Figure 61. After gathering all the characters, you still have a starting 0.

The formula finally gets to use the last part of the formula, where it takes the RIGHT characters from B1, this time grabbing only the LEN of A1. This strips out the leading 0, as shown in Figure 62.

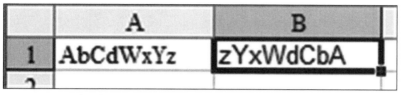

Figure 62. The final portion of the formula strips off the leading 0 when the LEN of B1 is greater than the LEN of A1.

Additional Details: Although this formula can do something VBA-like without using any VBA, it has limited use. You cannot copy the formula down to any other cells. And if you change A1, you need to start over and press F9 a bunch of times.

However, it is an interesting technique, and there have been a few instances at the MrExcel message board where Hady's approach was suggested:

http://www.mrexcel.com/forum/showthread.php?t=309945

http://www.mrexcel.com/forum/showthread.php?t=325172

http://www.mrexcel.com/forum/showthread.php?t=150637

Summary: You can use a self-referencing formula to replace a VBA user-defined function.

Source: http://www.mrexcel.com/forum/showthread.php?p=1107631

The post was nominated by Andrew Fergus.

USE TWO-WAY INTERPOLATION WITH A SINGLE FORMULA

Challenge: Many engineering design problems require designers to use tables to compute values of design parameters. Such tables contain values of the required parameter for a range of values of a control parameter, arranged in discrete intervals, and the designer is permitted to use linear interpolation for obtaining the parameter value for intermediate values of the control parameter.

A simple example is a two-column table comprising height above ground (the control parameter) and wind

Height	Velocity
20	10
30	40
40	130
50	180
60	240

velocity (a design parameter to be read from the table). In the table above, if you need to find the velocity corresponding to a height of 47 meters, it is a fairly simple matter to devise a formula that computes $130 + (180 - 130) * 7 / 10 = 165$ meters/sec.

How would you do this for a two-way table in which there are two control parameters? Is it possible to do so using a single formula? The table in Figure 63 illustrates values of wind pressure for the control parameters Height of structure and Span, and you need to compute the wind pressure for a height of 25 meters and a span of 300 meters.

	A	B	C	D	E	F	G
1		200	400	600	800	1000	Span
2	20	10	20	160	210	260	
3	30	40	60	190	240	290	
4	40	130	180	230	280	330	
5	50	180	230	280	330	380	
6	60	240	290	340	390	440	
7	70	310	360	410	460	510	
8	80	390	440	490	540	590	
9	90	750	800	850	900	950	
10	Height						

Figure 63. Interpolate values from column B and row 2.

Solution: The procedure you use to solve this problem is essentially an extension of the method used for the single control parameter table. Follow these steps:

1. Start with the worksheet shown in Figure 63. Add input cells for height and span in J1 and J2 respectively.
2. For ease of formula readability, define the following names:

```
ColHd      =Sheet1!$B$1:$F$1
RoHd       =Sheet1!$A$2:$A$9
Dat        =Sheet1!$B$2:$F$9
Ht         =Sheet1!$J$1
Sp         =Sheet1!$J$2
```

	I	J	K
1	Height	25	Input cell
2	Span	300	Input cell
3	Row1	1	=MATCH(J1,RoHd)
4	Row2	2	=J3+1
5	Col1	1	=MATCH(J2,ColHd)
6	Col2	2	=J5+1
7	Val(1,1)	10	=INDEX(Dat,J3,J5)
8	Val(2,1)	40	=INDEX(Dat,J4,J5)
9	Val(1,2)	20	=INDEX(Dat,J3,J6)
10	Val(2,2)	60	=INDEX(Dat,J4,J6)
11	HtDiff	5	=J1-INDEX(RoHd,J3)
12	SpanDiff	100	=J2-INDEX(ColHd,J5)
13	HtInterval	10	=INDEX(RoHd,J4)-INDEX(RoHd,J3)
14	SpanInterval	200	=INDEX(ColHd,J6)-INDEX(ColHd,J5)
15	Val(Ht,Span1)	25	=J7+(J8-J7)*J11/J13
16	Val(Ht,Span2)	40	=J9+(J10-J9)*J11/J13
17	Result	32.5	=J15+(J16-J15)*J12/J14
18			
19	Single formula	32.5	

Figure 64. The formulas in J3:J17 finds the result.

You can solve the problem using a series of formulas as shown in J3:J17 of Figure 64:

- The MATCH in J3 finds the row number in Figure 63 that is less than or equal to the height in cell J1.

- The MATCH in J5 finds the column number in Figure 63 that is less than or equal to the span in J2.

- Formulas in J4 and J6 add one to the previous cell.

- Formulas in J7:J10 use INDEX functions based on rows J3 & J4 and columns J5 & J6 to get the lower & higher height & spans.

- The HtDiff in J11 is the amount at which the sought height is in excess of the previous height.

- The SpanDiff in J12 is the amount at which the sought span is in excess of the previous span.

- The intervals in J13:J14 calculate the delta between the previous and next height or span.

- Cells J15:J17 then complete the interpolation

Part

I

Building the Mega-formula

You can now integrate the formulas in J3:J17 into a single formula to get the required wind pressure:

1. Copy the text of the formula in J17 to, say, J20—so the formula in J20 is:

```
=J15+(J16-J15)*J12/J14
```

2. Substitute the cell references for each precedent cell in this formula with the formula in the cell. To illustrate, the first cell reference is J15, which occurs at two places in the formula:

```
=J15+(J16-J15)*J12/J14
```

The formula in cell J15 is:

```
=J7+(J8-J7)*J11/J13
```

3. Copy the text of the formula (without the = sign) and replace the J15s in the formula in J20 so that the formula now becomes:

```
= J7+(J8-J7)*J11/J13 +(J16- J7+(J8-J7)*J11/J13)*J12/J14
```

4. Do the same with the remaining references J16, J12, and J14.

5. Successively repeat the procedure of back-substitution for the new set of references until all references in the formula are reduced to the defined names ColHd, RoHd, Dat, Ht, and Sp.

The resulting formula, after all substitutions, is:

```
=((INDEX(Dat,(MATCH(Ht,RoHd)),(MATCH(Sp,ColHd))))+((INDEX(Dat,
((MATCH(Ht,RoHd))+1),(MATCH(Sp,ColHd))))-(INDEX(Dat,(MATCH(Ht,
RoHd)),(MATCH(Sp,ColHd)))))*(Ht-INDEX(RoHd,(MATCH(Ht,RoHd))))/
(INDEX(RoHd,((MATCH(Ht,RoHd))+1))-INDEX(RoHd,(MATCH(Ht,RoHd)))))+((
(INDEX(Dat,(MATCH(Ht,RoHd)),((MATCH(Sp,ColHd))+1)))+((INDEX(Dat,((M
ATCH(Ht,RoHd))+1),((MATCH(Sp,ColHd))+1)))-(INDEX(Dat,(MATCH(Ht,Ro
Hd)),((MATCH(Sp,ColHd))+1))))*(Ht-INDEX(RoHd,(MATCH(Ht,RoHd))))/
(INDEX(RoHd,((MATCH(Ht,RoHd))+1))-INDEX(RoHd,(MATCH(Ht,RoHd))))
)-((INDEX(Dat,(MATCH(Ht,RoHd)),(MATCH(Sp,ColHd))))+((INDEX(Dat,
((MATCH(Ht,RoHd))+1),(MATCH(Sp,ColHd))))-(INDEX(Dat,(MATCH(Ht,
RoHd)),(MATCH(Sp,ColHd)))))*(Ht-INDEX(RoHd,(MATCH(Ht,RoHd))))/
(INDEX(RoHd,((MATCH(Ht,RoHd))+1))-INDEX(RoHd,(MATCH(Ht,RoHd))))))*(Sp-
INDEX(ColHd,(MATCH(Sp,ColHd))))/(INDEX(ColHd,((MATCH(Sp,ColHd))+1))-
INDEX(ColHd,(MATCH(Sp,ColHd)))))
```

This impressive-looking formula is 867 characters long and, of course, totally incomprehensible in its final form.

Summary: You can build a single formula from a multiple-step calculation, using successive back-substitution, starting with the last formula.

FIND THE SUM OF ALL DIGITS OCCURING IN A STRING

Part
I

Challenge: You want to build a formula to return the sum of all the digits in a string of text. For example, applying the formula on the text string "I am 24 years old and my Dad is 43" should yield 13 (2+4+4+3).

Setup: Assume that the text is in cell A1. Enter/copy the following formula in B1:

`=SUM((LEN(A1)-LEN(SUBSTITUTE(A1,{1,2,3,4,5,6,7,8,9},"")))*{1,2,3,4,5,6,7,8,9})`

Seemingly incomprehensible, eh? Read on…

Background: You could do this manually. You know that the digits that are significant for an addition operation are the digits 1 through 9. So an algorithm of the sum you are looking for would be:

1 × the number of 1s in the string +
2 × the number of 2s in the string +

…

…

9 × the number of 9s in the string = `RESULT`

You could consider substituting all occurrences of a digit (say, 4) with a null string, using the `SUBSTITUTE` function. `SUBSTITUTE(Txt,4,"")` returns the text without any 4s (i.e., 'I am 2 years old, and my Dad is 3').

Consider the formula fragment `SUBSTITUTE(A1,{1,2,3,4,5,6,7,8,9}, "")`. This successively substitutes the digits 1 through 9 with a null string, to yield an array of 9 modified string values, stripped of all occurrences of the corresponding digits.

Because the number of 4s in the string is 2, the length of the resultant string is 2 less than that of the original: `LEN(A1)`. Thus `LEN(A1)-LEN(SUBSTITUTE(A1,4,"")` gives you 2. Accordingly, one step further up the structure of the formula, `LEN(A1)-LEN(SUBSTITUTE(A1,{1,2,3,4,5,6,7,8,9},""))` gives you an array of 9 values, indicating the number of occurrences of each digit in the string. The array is {0,1,1,2,0,0,0,0,0}, reflecting one occurrence each of 2 and 3, two occurrences of 4, and no occurrences of the other digits.

At this point, the formula:

`=SUM((LEN(A1)-LEN(SUBSTITUTE(A1,{1,2,3,4,5,6,7,8,9},"")))*{1,2,3,4,5,6,7,8,9})`

translates to:

`=SUM({0,1,1,2,0,0,0,0,0} *{1,2,3,4,5,6,7,8,9})`

This is the summation of products of corresponding elements of two arrays:

0×1 + 1×2 + 1×3 + 2×4 + 0×5 + 0×6 + 0×7 + 0×8 + 0×9 = 13 (Required result)

Alternate Strategy: If you replace SUM in the original formula with SUMPRODUCT and replace the multiplication sign * with a comma, you could enter the formula as:

`=SUMPRODUCT((LEN(A1)-LEN(SUBSTITUTE(A1,{1,2,3,4,5,6,7,8,9},""))),{1,2,3,4,5,6,7,8,9})`

This form would probably look a bit more intuitive to some users.

Illustrative Examples:

Text	Comments	Result
76432		22
*****(8,121)		12
76*432		22
764 test 32		22
1 test 2		3
156.546		27
3127543.791		44
t=18317; p=239317		45
24 / 12		9
30°54'43"		19
SSN 421-89-7322		38
800/555-1212		29
3.142	PI() displayed to 14 decimal points	77
06:00 PM	Underlying value = 0.75	12

Summary: You can use SUM (or SUMPRODUCT) to build a formula that returns the sum of all the digits in a string of text.

Source: http://www.mrexcel.com/forum/showthread.php?p=242929

GET AN ARRAY OF UNIQUE VALUES FROM A LIST

Challenge: You want to extract all unique values from a column of text data that may contain several instances of a particular value. A procedure like this is useful when you need to populate a list box or combo box with unique values for user selection.

Solution: Assume that your spreadsheet contains a list of names in the range A2:A30 on Sheet1. Cell A1 contains the header Name.

You can manually solve this problem by selecting Data, Filter, Advanced Filter dialog.

In the Advanced Filter dialog, select Copy to Another Location, set List Range to `Sheet1!$A$1:$A$30`, leave Criteria Range blank, set Copy To to $H$1, select Unique Records Only, and click OK.

The list of unique names (with the header Name) is pasted at H1.

After it is pasted, you can sort the list in alphabetical order, if required.

Alternate Solution: This topic demonstrates two approaches for obtaining the unique values: one using the `Collection` object and the other using the `Dictionary` object. The two approaches are similar in mechanism in that they make use of the fact that a collection as well as a dictionary cannot contain duplicates.

Part I

The `Collection` Object Approach

The code for the `Collection` object approach is:

```
Sub GetUnique_Collection() 'Using the Collection object
  Dim SourceRng As Range
  Dim UniqColl As New Collection
  Set SourceRng = Range("A2:A30")
  On Error Resume Next
  For Each cell In SourceRng.Cells
    UniqColl.Add cell.Value, cell.Value
  Next
  On Error GoTo 0
  ReDim UniqArray(1 To UniqColl.Count)
  For i = 1 To UniqColl.Count
    UniqArray(i) = UniqColl(i)
  Next
  'Optional sort routine can be inserted here
      Range("H1").Resize(UniqColl.Count,    1).Value    =
WorksheetFunction.Transpose(UniqArray)
End Sub
```

This code creates a new collection, `UniqColl`, and cycles through all the values in the list of names, attempting to add each name to the collection. Notice that the statement:

```
UniqColl.Add cell.Value, cell.Value
```

contains two references to cell.Value. This is because the first two arguments for the `Add` method are `Value` and `Key`. A collection cannot contain duplicate

`Key` values. Error trapping during the execution of the `For...Next` loop is disabled, using `On Error Resume Next,` so whenever the code encounters a duplicate value (which, if already present in the collection, cannot be added to it), it simply skips to the next cell, without screeching to a halt with an error message.

When all the items are added to the collection, the code creates an array `UniqArray` of the same size as the collection `UniqColl.Count` and adds each item of the collection to this array. The array is needed to transfer the contents to the spreadsheet. Notice the use of the `Transpose` function when transferring the array to a column in the sheet; this is needed because `UniqArray` is a horizontal array.

Before transferring the unique list to the worksheet or control, it may be desirable to sort the data alphabetically. To do this, simply insert the following code after the comment 'Optional sort routine can be inserted here:

```
For i = 1 To UniqColl.Count - 1
   For j = i + 1 To UniqColl.Count
     If UniqColl(i) > UniqColl(j) Then
        Temp1 = UniqColl(i)
        Temp2 = UniqColl(j)
        UniqColl.Add Temp1, before:=j
        UniqColl.Add Temp2, before:=i
        UniqColl.Remove i + 1
        UniqColl.Remove j + 1
     End If
   Next j
 Next i
```

The `Dictionary` Object Approach

The code for the `Dictionary` object approach is:

```
Private Sub GetUnique_Dictionary()  'Using the Dictionary object
   Dim UniqueDic As Object
   Dim cell As Range
   Set UniqueDic = CreateObject("Scripting.Dictionary")
   For Each cell In Range("A2:A30")
     If Not UniqueDic.Exists(cell.Value) Then
        UniqueDic.Add cell.Value, cell.Value
     End If
```

```
Next
UniqArray = UniqueDic.Items
Range("H1").Resize(UniqueDic.Count, 1).Value = WorksheetFunction.
Transpose(UniqArray)
End Sub
```

This code works similarly to the previous routine. The points of difference are:

- Instead of disabling error trapping, the `Exists` property of the `Dictionary` object is used to decide whether a value has already been added to the dictionary and needs to be skipped.

- The dictionary contents are transferred to `UniqArray` in one go with:

```
UniqArray = UniqueDic.Items
```

Instead of transferring the unique items to the worksheet, you can fill a combo box with the values, using a statement like:

```
UserForm1.ComboBox1.List=UniqArray
```

Summary: You can extract a list of unique values from a large list that may contain multiple instances of a given value. The extracted values can be put into a worksheet range or used to fill values in a combo box or list box.

Sources: http://www.mrexcel.com/forum/showthread.php?t=8485, http://www.mrexcel.com/forum/showthread.php?t=217977, and http://www.mrexcel.com/forum/showthread.php?t=41643

AUTO-NUMBER RECORDS AND COLUMNS IN AN EXCEL DATABASE

Challenge: You want to build formulas to automatically serially number records and column headers in a database to which AutoFilter is applied and in which selected columns are hidden.

In the database shown in Figures 65 and 66, the records as well as columns are numbered normally. Figure 66 illustrates how the database appears when AutoFilter is applied to show records for total marks > 335 and the columns for Chemistry and Math are hidden. You want to auto-number the records (1 through 7 in this example) and column headers (1 through 5 in this example) by using formulas.

	A	B	C	D	E	F	G
1	No.	Name	Physics	Chemistry	Math	Eng. Lit.	TOTAL
2	1 ▾	2 ▾	3 ▾	4 ▾	5 ▾	6 ▾	7 ▾
3	1	Aladin	76	85	88	88	337
4	2	Anne	92	75	93	82	342
5	3	Bill	78	75	84	88	325
6	4	Don	82	86	82	87	337
7	5	Juan	79	85	81	78	323
8	6	Kent	84	75	93	87	339
9	7	Lora	80	79	92	78	329
10	8	Mary	94	82	87	89	352
11	9	Philip	78	88	86	80	332
12	10	Tony	75	82	96	88	341
13	11	Wayne	85	80	98	79	342

Figure 65. The complete database.

	A	B	C	F	G
1	No.	Name	Physics	Eng. Lit.	TOTAL
2	1 ▾	2 ▾	3 ▾	4 ▾	5 ▾
3	1	Aladin	76	88	337
4	2	Anne	92	82	342
6	3	Don	82	87	337
8	4	Kent	84	87	339
10	5	Mary	94	89	352
12	6	Tony	75	88	341
13	7	Wayne	85	79	342
15					

Figure 66. Your goal is to have row labels in A and column labels in row 2 get renumbered as shown here.

Solution: You start by defining the name `Database` for the range A2:G13. This excludes row 1 from the default selection when you apply AutoFilter. You need to put a space in the first cell immediately following the last record (A14 in this case). (This is a workaround to an annoying Excel bug that shows the last record, regardless of whether it meets the filter criteria.)

In cell A3, enter the formula:

```
=SUBTOTAL(3,B$3:B3)
```

and copy this formula to the range A4:A13.

Notice that the first row reference is absolute and the second one is relative. The formula in A13 is thus:

```
=SUBTOTAL(3,B$3:B13)
```

In cell A2, enter the formula:

```
=IF(CELL("width",A1)=0,0,1)
```

In cell B2, enter the formula:

```
=IF(CELL("width",B1)=0,0,MAX($A2:A2)+1)
```

and copy it to the range C2:G2.

Notice that the first column reference is absolute and the second one is relative. The formula in G2 is thus:

```
=IF(CELL("width",G1)=0,0,MAX($A2:F2)+1)
```

Now you are set. Breaking It Down: Let's start with the auto-numbering of the records. The SUBTOTAL function has the syntax SUBTOTAL(type,ref). In your formula, you specified type as 3, which is the equivalent of the COUNTA function. Column B contains names and thus qualifies for use of this subtotal type because the COUNTA function counts the number of text values in a range. The formula makes use of the fact that SUBTOTAL excludes hidden cells from its calculation.

Consider the formula in A10: =SUBTOTAL(3,B$3:B10). The total number of text values in this range is eight, but only five values are visible, so the formula returns 5, which is the serial number you want!

For auto-numbering of the columns, you use the CELL function. The syntax for this function is CELL(info_type, [reference]). When you specify "width" as info_type, the function returns the column width of the top left cell in reference.

The formula in cell A2, =IF(CELL("width",A1)=0,0,1), returns 0 if column A is hidden and 1 if it is not.

To understand how the formulas in B2:G2 work, first consider the formula in D2:

```
=IF(CELL("width",D1)=0,0,MAX($A2:C2)+1)
```

Because CELL("width",D1)=0 (column is hidden), the formula evaluates to 0.

The formula in the cell in the next visible column, F2, is:

```
=IF(CELL("width",F1)=0,0,MAX($A2:E2)+1)
```

Because `CELL("width",F1)>0`, this evaluates to `MAX($A2:E2)+1`, which is `Max(1,2,3,0,0)+1 = 4`.

Gotcha: Although the record numbering auto-updates with changes in AutoFilter settings, the column header numbering does not update as you hide/show columns. You need to force a recalculation by pressing F9 in order for these formulas to update.

Summary: You can build formulas to automatically number records and column headers in a database to which AutoFilter is applied and in which selected columns are hidden.

PART 2

TECHNIQUES

USE AUTOFILTER WITH A PIVOT TABLE

Challenge: You've created a pivot table to summarize sales by customer. You now want to filter those results to show only the customers with sales between $20,000 and $30,000. The AutoFilter command is grayed out for pivot tables.

Solution: You can fool Excel into turning on the AutoFilter dropdowns by starting your selection one cell to the right of the pivot table headings. In Figure 67, select cell E4. Hold down the Shift key and press the left arrow key four times to select E4:A4.

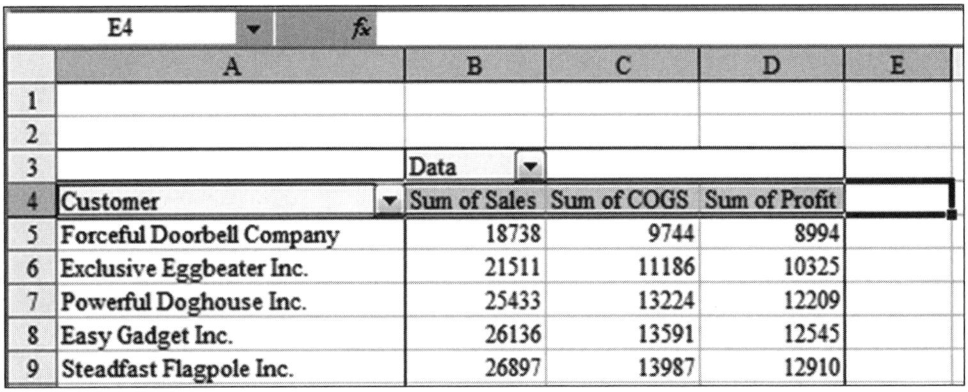

	A	B	C	D	E
	E4		f_x		
1					
2					
3		Data			
4	Customer	Sum of Sales	Sum of COGS	Sum of Profit	
5	Forceful Doorbell Company	18738	9744	8994	
6	Exclusive Eggbeater Inc.	21511	11186	10325	
7	Powerful Doghouse Inc.	25433	13224	12209	
8	Easy Gadget Inc.	26136	13591	12545	
9	Steadfast Flagpole Inc.	26897	13987	12910	

Figure 67. Start your selection just to the right of the pivot table headings.

In Excel 2003, you can select Data, Filter, AutoFilter to turn on the AutoFilter dropdowns. In Excel 2007, choose the Filter command from the Data tab.

Figure 68 shows how you apply a custom filter to limit the customers to those with sales between $20,000 and $30,000.

3		Data			
4	Customer	Sum of Sal	Sum of COG	Sum of Pro	
6	Exclusive Eggbeater Inc.	21511	11186	10325	
7	Powerful Doghouse Inc.	25433	13224	12209	
8	Easy Gadget Inc.	26136	13591	12545	
9	Steadfast Flagpole Inc.	26897	13987	12910	

Custom AutoFilter

Show rows where:
Sum of Sales

is greater than or equal to — 20000

● And ○ Or

is less than or equal to — 30000

Use ? to represent any single character
Use * to represent any series of characters

OK   Cancel

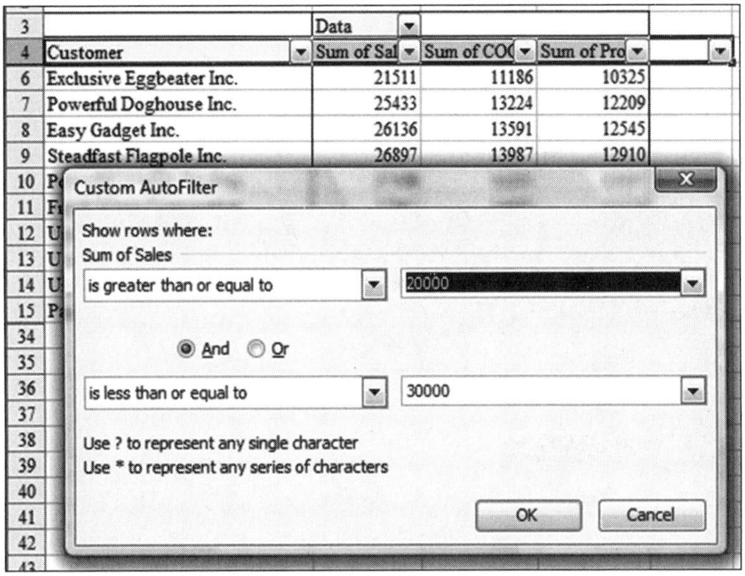

Figure 68. Use the filter dropdowns on the pivot table.

Summary: You can trick Excel into allowing filters in a pivot table by starting the selection outside the pivot table.

Source: Podcast episode 793 http://www.mrexcel.com/podcast/2008/07/episode-793-pivot-filter-hack.html

SORT SUBTOTALS

Part 2

Challenge: You want to chart the sales for the five largest customers in a data set.

Solution: You can sort the collapsed view of a subtotaled data set. Here's how:

1. Choose one cell in the customer column. Click the AZ button to sort in ascending order.

2. Choose Data, Subtotals. In the Subtotal dialog box, change the At Each Change In dropdown to Customer. Make sure the Use Function dropdown is Sum. Choose at least the Sales column from the Add Subtotal To section. Click OK. Excel adds subtotals for each customer.

3. Look at the left of column A. Excel has added three group and outline buttons, labeled 1, 2, and 3. Click the 2 button to see one line per customer.

4. Choose one cell in the Sales column. Click the ZA button to sort the largest customers to the top of the list.

5. Select cell A1 through the fifth customer total. In Excel 2003, press F11 to create a chart. In Excel 2007, press Alt+F1 to create a chart on the current page.

As shown in Figure 69, Excel creates a chart of the five largest customers.

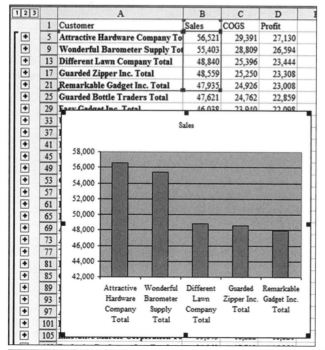

Figure 69. You can quickly create a chart of your five largest customers.

Breaking It Down: There are two amazing features here. First, you can successfully sort a subtotaled data set when it is in the collapsed state. Excel actually rearranges groups of rows while doing the sort. (Each group contains the hidden detail rows for one customer and the visible subtotal row.)

Second, in step 5, you take advantage of the fact that charts by default hide data that is hidden in the worksheet. Although your selection might include rows 1 through 21, the chart shows only the visible subtotals in rows 5, 9, 13, 17, and 21.

Summary: Excel properly sorts data when you've collapsed the view to show only the subtotals. After you sort the data to find the five largest customers, you can use Excel to create a chart based on the data.

COPY AN EXACT FORMULA BY USING DITTO MARKS

Challenge: You've entered total formulas in row 23 of Figure 70. Immediately below those formulas, you want to enter average formulas. However, if you copied cell B23 to B24, the range referenced in the formula would automatically change.

	B23	▼	f_x =SUM(B2:B22)			
	A		**B**	**C**	**D**	**E**
1	Customer		Q1	Q2	Q3	Q4
14	Ideal Luggage Inc.		Copy Here as Formats Only		,163	53,087
15	Superior Bottle Company		Link Here		,211	34,539
16	Functional Quilt Company		Create Hyperlink Here		,373	72,229
17	Leading Doorbell Supply				,965	65,362
18	First-Rate Tackle Supply		Shift Down and Copy		,619	67,536
19	Forceful Instrument Company		Shift Right and Copy		,118	65,224
20	Wonderful Shoe Partners		Shift Down and Move		,111	20,915
21	First-Rate Instrument Corporation		Shift Right and Move		,365	26,818
22	Supreme Clipboard Corporation		Cancel		,169	19,744
23	Total				,580	$916,573
24	Average					

Figure 70. You want to replicate the total formulas in row 23 as averages in row 24.

Solution: Do you remember back in school, when you used to use ditto marks to mean "repeat the same value as above"?

Title	Author
Learn Excel 2007 from MrExcel	Jelen, Bill
" " " "	" "

Well, the quotation mark key on your keyboard operates sort of like a ditto mark shortcut!

Follow these steps:

1. Select cells B24:E24.

2. Hold down the Ctrl key while pressing the apostrophe/quotation mark key. Excel copies the exact formula from cell B23 in cell B24. Excel leaves the formula in Enter mode, with the insertion point at the end of the formula.

3. Press F2 to change the mode from Enter to Edit.

4. Press Home to move to the beginning of the formula. Press the right arrow key. Type Average. Press the Delete key three times.

5. Press Ctrl+Enter to enter similar formulas in B24:E24.

Alternate Strategy: Another solution to this problem is to copy the result of the formula as a value. If you go to cell B24 and press Ctrl+Shift+", Excel copies the result from B23 as a value in cell B24. Unfortunately, you cannot use this method to fill an entire range, such as B24:E24. In that case, you could follow these steps:

1. Select cells B23:E23

2. Right-click the border of the selection. While holding down the right mouse button, drag down to row 24.

3. Release the mouse button and choose Copy Here as Values Only.

Summary: Use the Ctrl+quotation mark to make an exact copy of a formula.

RIGHT-DRAG BORDER TO ACCESS MORE COPYING OPTIONS

Challenge: You once stumbled upon a handy menu for accessing extra copying options. But how did you open it, and what can it do for you?

Solution: Excel has an incredibly useful but obscure shortcut menu, as shown in Figure 71. To open it, you select a cell or a range of cells. Then you right-click and drag the border of the range to a new location. When you release the right mouse button, Excel opens this menu, which has the following options, among others:

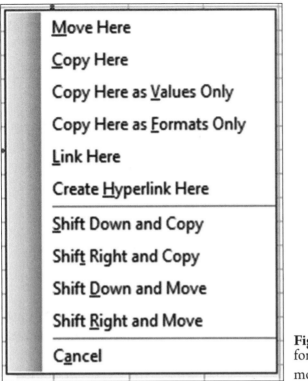

Move Here

Copy Here

Copy Here as **V**alues Only

Copy Here as **F**ormats Only

Link Here

Create **H**yperlink Here

Shift Down and Copy

Shif**t** Right and Copy

Shift **D**own and Move

Shift **R**ight and Move

C**a**ncel

Figure 71. This menu offers faster ways for Paste Values, Format Painter, and more. How do you find the menu?

- **Copy Here as Values Only:** Using Copy Here as Values Only is an incredibly fast way to convert a range of formulas to values. A good method is to select a range of formulas, right-click, drag right, drag back to the original location, let go of the right mouse button, and choose Copy Here as Values Only.

- **Copy Here As Formats Only:** You can copy numeric formatting, borders, and more by using Copy Here As Formats Only. For example, you can copy column widths by selecting a range of entire columns, such as A:C. Then you right-click and drag the border to E:G. When you let go of the mouse button, if you choose Copy Here As Formats Only, Excel changes the column widths of E:G to match those of A:C.

- **Link Here:** For a faster way to set up formulas to point to a range, you can select A1:A10, right-click and drag the border to C5, and select Link Here. Cell C5 now contains the formula `=A1`, and cell C14 contains the formula `=A10`.

- **Create Hyperlink Here:** This is a cool option but is rather difficult to use, and it does not work in an unsaved file. For details on how to use it, see "Quickly Create a Hyperlink Menu."

Gotcha: When you click on the border of a selection, do not click on the square dot in the lower-right corner of the cell. This dot is the fill handle, and clicking it invokes the AutoFill options instead of this menu.

Summary: By right-clicking and dragging the border of a selection, you can get quick access to several options.

QUICKLY CREATE A HYPERLINK MENU

Challenge: You are building a reporting package for people who are not familiar with Excel, and you want to add a menu worksheet to help them navigate through the workbook (see Figure 72). Usually, creating hyperlinks to another place in a document is kind of a pain, and you'd like to create a menu more quickly.

Part 2

019FasterHyperlink.xls:2					019FasterHyperlink.xls:1		
	A	B	C	D		A	B	C
1	XYZ Company				1	Abstract		
2	Reporting Worksheet				2			
3					3			Data
4					4			Data
5					5			Data
6					6			Data

Figure 72. You want to repeat the titles and headings at the top of each printed page.

Solution: Make sure your workbook is saved and is the only workbook open in Excel.

In Excel 2007, select View, New Window. In Excel 2003 and earlier, select Window, New Window. This will open two views of the same workbook.

In Excel 2007, select View, Arrange All. Then choose Vertical and click OK. In Excel 2003, select Window, New Window, Vertical, OK. This allows you to see one worksheet in the left window and another sheet of the same workbook in the right window.

In the left window, navigate so you can see the menu worksheet. In the right window, press Ctrl+Page Down to move to the first page of the report.

The goal is to take an identifying title from each worksheet of the workbook and build a hyperlink to that worksheet on the menu sheet. In Figure 73, select the A1 title from the right window. Right-click the border of A1, drag to cell B4 in the menu worksheet, and select Create Hyperlink Here.

019FasterHyperlink.xls:2						019Fast
	A	B	C	D		
1	XYZ Company					1 Abs
2	Reporting Worksheet					2
3						3
4						
5			Move Here			
6			Copy Here			
7			Copy Here as Values Only			
8						
9			Copy Here as Formats Only			
10			Link Here			
11			Create Hyperlink Here			
12						

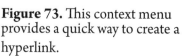

Figure 73. This context menu provides a quick way to create a hyperlink.

To repeat this with the next sheet, use Ctrl+Tab to switch to the right window and press Ctrl+Page Down to go to the next sheet. Right-click the border of A1, drag to B5 in the left window, and select Create Hyperlink Here. Repeat for each additional sheet.

Additional Details: If you want to also provide a "Return to Menu" hyperlink at the top of each worksheet in the reporting workbook, follow these steps:

1. In the right window, move to the first report worksheet.

2. In the left window, type Return to Menu in cell A3 of the menu.

3. Select cell A3. Right-click the border and drag to cell H1 of the right window. Choose Create Hyperlink Here.

4. In the right window, put the worksheets in Group mode. With the first worksheet selected, Shift+click the last worksheet.

5. In Group mode, go to cell H1. Press F2 and then press Enter to copy the words `Return to Menu` in cell H1 of all the worksheets. (Unfortunately, this by itself does not establish the hyperlink in each worksheet.)

6. Press Ctrl+C to copy the hyperlink from the first worksheet.

7. Press Ctrl+Page Down and Ctrl+V to paste the hyperlink on the next worksheet. Repeat this step for each additional worksheet.

8. Close the second window by clicking the X at the top of the right window.

Summary: Dragging titles as hyperlinks is a fast way to create a hyperlink menu.

QUICKLY CREATE MANY RANGE NAMES

Challenge: Quickly create many range names in a worksheet. If you decide that complicated formulas would benefit from referring to named ranges instead of cell addresses, you might have a daunting task of individually naming many ranges.

Setup: If your headings are suitable range names, you can use them to quickly create the range names. The commands are slightly different in Excel 2003 and earlier and in Excel 2007.

Solution: In any Excel version, select the data set, including the headings that will be used a range names.

In Excel 2003 and earlier, choose Insert, Name, Create. In the Create Names dialog, choose Top Row and click OK (Figure 74).

	A	B	C	D	E	F
1						
2		Sales	COGS	GP	Expenses	Income
3	Atlanta	114,945	52,530	62,415	22,299	40,116
4	Boston	183,681	88,351	95,330	23,674	71,657
5	Charlotte	153,487	70,144			60,274
6	Dallas	124,998	59,			42,624
7	Eden Prarie	187,889	91,			72,817
8	Fargo	114,700	55,			37,350
9	Galveston	141,324	67,			50,945
10	Homer	164,235	76,			64,581
11	Islip	149,636	69,			57,063
12	Jacksonville	166,847	78,			64,925
13	Kansas City	118,117	56,			38,822
14	Louisville	199,441	95,			79,521
15						

Create Names ✕

Create names in
☑ Top row
☐ Left column
☐ Bottom row
☐ Right column

OK   Cancel

Figure 74. Excel 2003 creates five named ranges in this selection.

In Excel 2007, with the data set selected, from the Formulas tab, choose Create from Selection. In the Create Names from Selection dialog, choose Top Row and click OK (Figure 75).

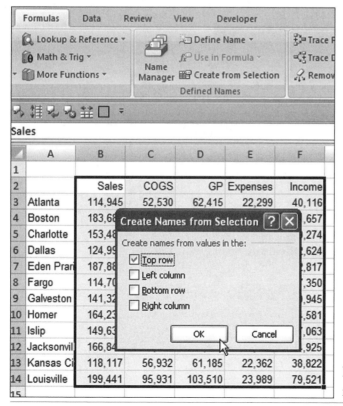

Figure 75. Excel 2007 creates five named ranges in this selection.

In this example, Excel creates five named ranges. The `Sales` range includes B3:B14. You can now use `=SUM(Sales)` as a valid formula (Figure 76).

Name Manager

New...	Edit...	Delete		
Name	**Value**	**Refers To**	**Scope**	
COGS	{"52,530";"88,351"...	=Sheet1!$C$3:$C$14	Workbook	
Expenses	{"22,299";"23,674"...	=Sheet1!$E$3:$E$14	Workbook	
GP	{"62,415";"95,330"...	=Sheet1!$D$3:$D$14	Workbook	
Income	{"40,116";"71,657"...	=Sheet1!$F$3:$F$14	Workbook	
Sales	{"114,945";"183,68...	=Sheet1!$B$3:$B$14	Workbook	

Figure 76. You can create five named ranges using a single command.

Gotcha: If your headings contain a space or other punctuation that is not valid in a named range, Excel substitutes an underscore for each invalid character. If your heading happens to contain a name that is also a valid cell address, Excel appends an underscore to the end of the name. Figure 77 shows several examples in which dashes, spaces, at symbols, and colons are all replaced with underscores when the names are created. Note that the heading I42 in cell G1 generates the range name I42_ to differentiate it from the cell address I42.

C	D	E	F	G	H	I
Atlanta	B-C	DEF	G@H	I42	J:K	
123	123	123	123	123	123	

Define Name

Names in workbook:

	OK
Atlanta	
B_C	Close
D_E_F	
G_H	Add
I42_	
J_K	Delete

Figure 77. Created range names differ from the headings if the headings contained invalid characters.

Additional Details: The following characters are valid in a range name:

- Letters A through Z and a through z
- Digits 0 through 9
- Period, question mark, backslash, underscore
- Euro symbol (character 128)

- Script f (character 131)
- Letters in other alphabets (such as characters 192–214, 216–246, and 248–255)

Additional Details: Formulas that existed before the named ranges were created do not automatically update to use the new named ranges. To retroactively apply a name to formulas, you can use Insert, Name Apply in Excel 2003. In Excel 2007, the Apply command is hidden behind a dropdown at the end of the Define Name command.

Summary: Rather than define range names individually, you can use existing headings to create many names at once.

ADD FORMULAS TO SMARTART

Challenge: For Excel fans, the biggest disappointment with Excel 2007 SmartArt diagrams is that their text is static. You cannot have the text for a SmartArt diagram dynamically calculated by Excel.

Solution: As a workaround, you can use the SmartArt tools to build a diagram and then convert the diagram to shapes. You can then apply formulas to the shapes.

In Figure 78, a database query feeds individual sales figures in columns A: C. SUMIF formulas in G4:G6 show the current sales for each rep. RANK formulas in E4:E6 figure out which rep is in the lead. VLOOKUP formulas in F8: H10 combine an associate's name and sales total. This report is functional, but it lacks visual interest.

	A	B	C	D	E	F	G	H	I	J
1	Sales Log					Summary by Associate				
2										
3	Associate	Ticket	Revenue							
4	Ted	1891	33.6			3 Ted	377.7			
5	Bob	1892	63.77			1 Mary	718.22			
6	Mary	1893	105.2			2 Bob	559.6			
7	Ted	1894	10.76							
8	Mary	1895	210.47			1 Mary	718.22	1. Mary is the daily star with $7		
9	Ted	1896	13.84			2 Bob	559.6	2. Bob has sales of $560		
10	Bob	1897	95.85			3 Ted	377.7	3. Ted has sales of $378		
11	Bob	1898	137.73							

Figure 78. Formulas create a functional but uninteresting report.

Follow these steps:

1. Build a SmartArt diagram that has three shapes. Use dummy text of about the right length. Use the SmartArt tools to format the diagram. In Figure 79, the Format ribbon was used to resize the individual shapes.

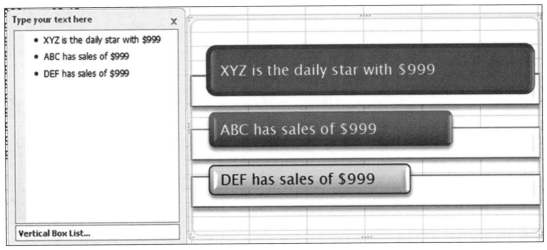

Figure 79. The text is still static text as this point. It is there to help with sizing the boxes.

2. Click inside the SmartArt but not on any shape. Press Ctrl+A to select all the shapes in the SmartArt diagram (Figure 80).

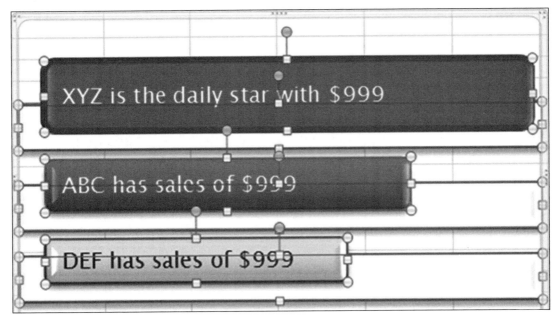

Figure 80. All the shapes are selected.

3. Press Ctrl+C to copy the shapes.
4. Click outside the SmartArt and press Ctrl+V to paste the shapes onto the worksheet.
5. Delete the original SmartArt diagram.
6. Click the first shape in the worksheet. Drag to select the text in the shape. Click in the formula bar, type =H8, and press Enter. The text in the selected shape changes to reflect the result of the formula in H8.

7. Repeat step 6 to assign =H9 to the second shape and =H10 to the third shape.

You now have something that looks like a SmartArt diagram, but the text for the shapes comes dynamically from the worksheet (Figure 81).

	A	B	C	D	E	F	G	H	I	J	K
1	Sales Log					Summary by Associate					
2											
3	Associate	Ticket	Revenue								
4	Ted	1891	33.6			3 Ted	377.7				
5	Bob	1892	63.77			1 Mary	718.22				
6	Mary	1893	105.2			2 Bob	559.6				
7	Ted	1894	10.76								
8	Mary	1895	210.47			1 Mary	718.22 1. Mary is the daily star with $718				
9	Ted	1896	13.84			2 Bob	559.6 2. Bob has sales of $560				
10	Bob	1897	95.85			3 Ted	377.7 3. Ted has sales of $378				
11	Bob	1898	137.73								
12	Bob	1899	117.82								
13	Bob	1900	82.42			1. Mary is the daily star with $718					
14	Bob	1901	23.33								
15	Ted	1902	102.45								
16	Ted	1903	29.85								
17	Mary	1904	70.05			2. Bob has sales of $560					
18	Mary	1905	242.74								
19	Bob	1906	20.06								
20	Mary	1907	89.76								
21	Bob	1908	18.62			3. Ted has sales of $378					
22	Ted	1909	43.22								
23	Ted	1910	143.98								

Figure 81. Now the text in the diagram is a live result from the data.

As the query in A:C updates with new sales, the formulas in E:H and thus the text in the diagram automatically update. While Mary was on a break, Ted made a $395 sale. The worksheet updates as shown in Figure 82.

11	Bob	1898	137.73	
12	Bob	1899	117.82	
13	Bob	1900	82.42	1. Ted is the daily star with $773
14	Bob	1901	23.33	
15	Ted	1902	102.45	
16	Ted	1903	29.85	
17	Mary	1904	70.05	2. Mary has sales of $718
18	Mary	1905	242.74	
19	Bob	1906	20.06	
20	Mary	1907	89.76	
21	Bob	1908	18.62	3. Bob has sales of $560
22	Ted	1909	43.22	
23	Ted	1910	143.98	

Figure 82. Excel dynamically calculates the text in this SmartArt.

Summary: Although SmartArt in Excel 2007 cannot dynamically update, you can use SmartArt to create a diagram and then convert it to shapes and dynamic formulas.

CREATE A PIVOT TABLE FROM DATA IN MULTIPLE WORKSHEETS

Challenge: You have more data than will fit on a single worksheet. You would like to create a pivot table from the data spread across multiple worksheets. The Multiple Consolidation feature only works when your data has a single column of text labels on the left with additional numeric columns to the right. You'd like to be able to grab similar data from multiple worksheets and summarize it in a pivot table.

Background: Fazza from Perth, Australia, posted a remarkable bit of code in 2008 that allows you to build a pivot cache from multiple worksheets or even multiple workbooks. Amazingly, the pivot cache is stored with the workbook, so you can effectively build a report from more than 65,536 rows in Excel 2003.

Solution: The solution here involves building a SQL statement to grab data from each worksheet into an array. You then merge the worksheets into a single recordset. You open a new workbook and create a pivot table to an external dataset—in this case, the recordset you just created. The result is a blank workbook with a blank pivot table and the cache stored in memory behind the scenes.

Breaking it Down: You create code that sets up an array of SQL statements. The complete code is as follows:

```
Sub BuildPivotCache()

    Dim i As Long
    Dim arSQL() As String
    Dim objPivotCache As PivotCache
    Dim objRS As Object
    Dim wbkNew As Workbook
    Dim wks As Worksheet

    With ActiveWorkbook
      ReDim arSQL(1 To .Worksheets.Count)
      For Each wks In .Worksheets
        i = i + 1
        arSQL(i) = "SELECT * FROM [" & wks.Name & "$]"
      Next wks
      Set wks = Nothing
      Set objRS = CreateObject("ADODB.Recordset")

      objRS.Open Join$(arSQL, " UNION ALL "), _
          Join$(Array("Provider=Microsoft.Jet.OLEDB.4.0; Data Source=", _
          .FullName, ";Extended Properties=""Excel 8.0;"""), vbNullString)
```

```
   End With

   Set wbkNew = Workbooks.Add(Template:=xlWBATWorksheet)

   With wbkNew
     Set objPivotCache = .PivotCaches.Add(xlExternal)
     Set objPivotCache.Recordset = objRS
     Set objRS = Nothing

     With .Worksheets(1)
               objPivotCache.CreatePivotTable   TableDestination:=.
   Range("A3")
         Set objPivotCache = Nothing
         Range("A3").Select
     End With
   End With
   Set wbkNew = Nothing
End Sub
```

If the active workbook contains five worksheets, the array might look as shown in Figure 83.

```
        objRS.Open Join$(arSQL, " UNION ALL "), Join$(.
            .FullName, ";Extended Properties=""Excel 8
    End With

    Set wbkNew = Workbooks.Add(Template:=xlWBATWorks
```

Expression	Value	Type
arSQL		String(1 to 5)
arSQL(1)	"SELECT * FROM [Jan$]"	String
arSQL(2)	"SELECT * FROM [Feb$]"	String
arSQL(3)	"SELECT * FROM [Mar$]"	String
arSQL(4)	"SELECT * FROM [Apr$]"	String
arSQL(5)	"SELECT * FROM [May$]"	String

Figure 83. You build multiple SQL statements to grab all the data from each worksheet.

Part
2

The code then builds a new recordset that unions all the queries from Figure 83. This recordset will contain all records from all worksheets.

Where is the recordset saved? It is simply resident in memory as the object variable objRS.

Later, the code adds a new workbook and uses the recordset as the source for an external pivot cache:

```
Set objPivotCache = .PivotCaches.Add(xlExternal)
Set objPivotCache.Recordset = objRS
```

You end up with a new workbook that appears to be blank. An empty pivot table is in cell A3. As shown in Figure 84, the pivot table field list contains a list of all fields from your worksheets.

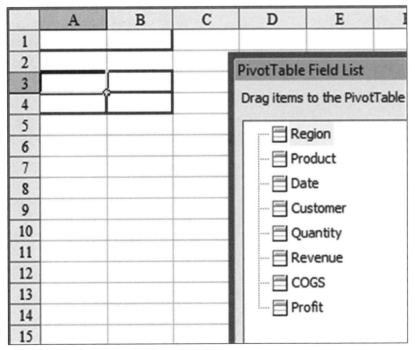

Figure 84. Although the workbook contains no visible data, the fields are in the pivot cache.

From this point, you can drag fields into the pivot table.

If the pivot cache contains fewer records than there are rows in your worksheet, you can try double-clicking the Grand Total cell. You then see the data that is stored in the pivot cache.

Note: It is interesting that the workbook containing the data stored in the pivot table cache is much smaller than the original workbook. Excel doesn't have to store fonts, styles, formulas, etc.

Gotcha: Unlike pivot tables built from data in a worksheet, this pivot table does not calculate until you drag one field to the data area. Don't worry if you drag a region to the row area and nothing happens. As soon as you add Revenue to the data area, the pivot table calculates, and the regions fill in.

Summary: You can create code that grabs similar data from multiple worksheets and summarizes it in a pivot table.

Source: http://www.mrexcel.com/forum/showthread.php?t=315768

This topic was nominated by Denis Wright (aka SydneyGeek), who builds custom Excel and Access solutions in Sydney, Australia, and loves to solve problems. Among other things, he maintains a website with Excel and Access tutorials; see http://www.datawright.com.au.

Part 2

DETERMINE THE HEIGHT AND WIDTH OF THE DATALABEL OBJECT

Challenge: The `DataLabel` object does not have either a height or width property, and Excel does not permit the user to resize a data label. In some situations, you may need to determine these properties. A case in point is a series with long, wrapping label text or labels of points that are very close to each other, where it is intended to programmatically adjust label position to get rid of any overlaps (Figure 85).

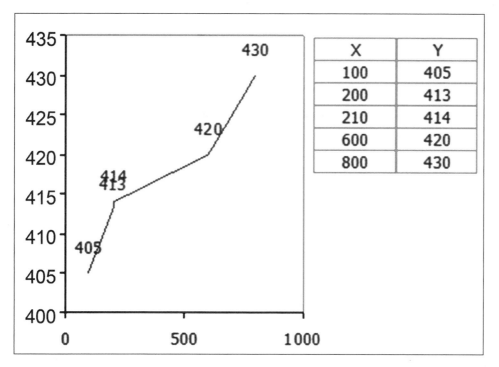

X	Y
100	405
200	413
210	414
600	420
800	430

Figure 85. You want to find the height and width of the DataLabel object for point 210, 414.

Background: The solution to this problem makes use of the fact that it is not possible to move a data label (or, for that matter, any movable chart element, such as a legend, a chart title, an axis title etc.) even partially off the chart area. To verify this, select a single data label with two single clicks and try dragging it off the chart through the bottom-right corner. You cannot drag it beyond the point where the bottom-right corners of the data label and the chart coincide.

Figure 86 illustrates the situation that prevails when the label is moved to the bottom-right corner of the chart area. The origin (0,0) for the chart coordinates is the top-left corner of the chart area.

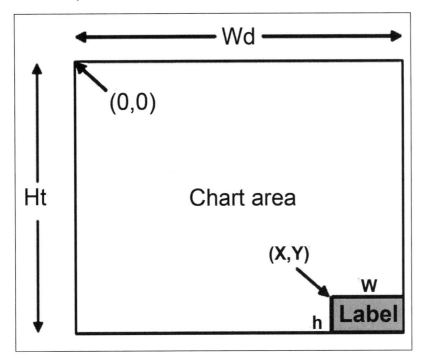

Figure 86. The label has been moved to the bottom-right corner.

Using VBA, Wd =ChartArea.Width,   Ht = ChartArea.Height

The values of x and y are obtained from the Top and Left properties of the DataLabel object.

.

The height and width of the label can be calculated as:

h = Ht − y

w = Wd − x

 Solution: Ensure that the chart in question is the active chart and use the following code:

```
Sub FindLblSize()

    Dim Lbl As DataLabel
    Set Cht = ActiveChart
    Set Lbl = Cht.SeriesCollection(1).Points(3).DataLabel

    'Get height and width of the chart area
    ChartWd = Cht.ChartArea.Width
    ChartHt = Cht.ChartArea.Height

    'Store old position of data label
    OldTop = Lbl.Top
    OldLeft = Lbl.Left

    'Attempt to move data label so that top left corner
    'coincides with bottom right corner of chart area
    Lbl.Top = ChartHt
    Lbl.Left = ChartWd

    'Above move makes bottom right corner of data label
    'to coincide with bottom right corner of chart area
    'as it cannot be moved any further

    'Calculate and display the label dimensions
    LblWd = ChartWd - Lbl.Left
    LblHt = ChartHt - Lbl.Top
    MsgBox "Label dimensions:   Width = " & LblWd & "    Height
= " & LblHt

     'Restore label to a slightly staggered position to remove
overlap
    Lbl.Left = OldLeft
    Lbl.Top = Cht.SeriesCollection(1).Points(2).DataLabel.Top -
LblHt
End Sub
```

Part
2

With the background discussed earlier, the comments in the code are self-explanatory. Figure 87 shows the chart after the label's position has been adjusted

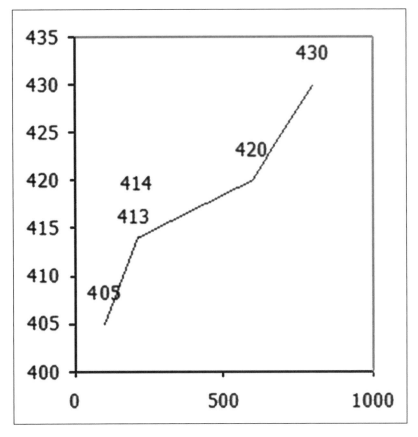

Figure 87. The label position has been adjusted.

Summary: Excel restricts movement of objects on a chart to within the chart boundaries in order to programmatically determine the height and width of a data label. By itself, the code in this solution is not of much use, but the technique illustrated could form the basis of a larger routine for programmatically examining a series for overlapping data labels and staggering them, if required.

ADJUST XY CHART SCALING FOR CORRECT ASPECT RATIO

Challenge: You want to adjust an XY (scatter) chart so that both axes have the same scale per unit axis value. That is, you need to adjust the chart in Figure 88 so the square and a circle appear as shown in Figure 89. You want to adjust an XY (scatter) chart so that both axes have the same scale per unit axis value. That is, you need to adjust the chart in Figure 88 so the square and a circle appear as shown in Figure 89.

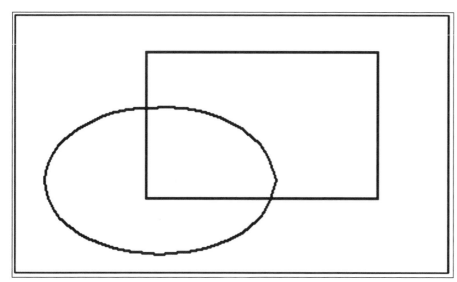

Figure 88. You start with an oval and a rectangle.

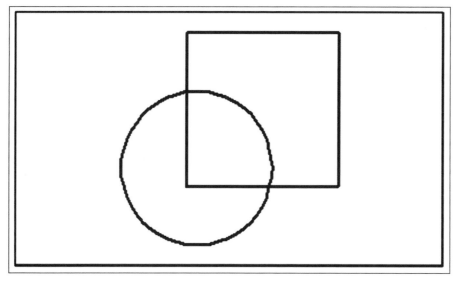

Figure 89. You want a circle and a square, as shown here.

Solution: The following code works on both embedded charts and chart sheets. Ensure that the chart is selected or that the chart sheet is activated and then run the following code:

```
Sub ScalePlot()
    Dim Cht As Chart, Ser As Series, AxX As Axis, AxY As Axis
    Set Cht = ActiveChart

    With Cht
        'Determine MinX, MinY, MaxX, MaxY across all series
        For i = 1 To Cht.SeriesCollection.Count
```

```
    Set Ser = Cht.SeriesCollection(i)
    XVals = Ser.XValues
    YVals = Ser.Values
    If i = 1 Then
      MinX = WorksheetFunction.Min(XVals)
      MaxX = WorksheetFunction.Max(XVals)
      MinY = WorksheetFunction.Min(YVals)
      MaxY = WorksheetFunction.Max(YVals)
    Else
      MinX = WorksheetFunction.Min(MinX, XVals)
      MaxX = WorksheetFunction.Max(MaxX, XVals)
      MinY = WorksheetFunction.Min(MinY, YVals)
      MaxY = WorksheetFunction.Max(MaxY, YVals)
    End If
Next

'Maximize the plot area and get its dimensions
With .PlotArea
    .Top = 0
    .Left = 0
    .Width = Cht.ChartArea.Width
    .Height = Cht.ChartArea.Height
    PWd = .Width
    PHt = .Height
    PWd1 = .InsideWidth
    PHt1 = .InsideHeight
End With

Set AxX = .Axes(xlCategory)
Set AxY = .Axes(xlValue)

'Range of X and Y Values from series data
XDiff = MaxX - MinX
YDiff = MaxY - MinY

'Set a buffer space of 10% of XDiff and YDiff so there is
'a margin between series boundary and plot area
Buffer = 0.1

'Adjust values of Max/Min X/Y for buffer
```

```
            MaxX = MaxX + Buffer * XDiff
            MinX = MinX - Buffer * XDiff
            MaxY = MaxY + Buffer * YDiff
            MinY = MinY - Buffer * YDiff


            'Revised range of X and Y Values with buffer
            XDiff = MaxX - MinX
            YDiff = MaxY - MinY


            'Rescale Axes for max possible magnification
            With AxX
               .MaximumScale = MaxX
               .MinimumScale = MinX
            End With
            With AxY
               .MaximumScale = MaxY
               .MinimumScale = MinY
            End With


            'Calculate scaling of plot area per unit X and Y
            WdScale = PWd1 / XDiff
            HtScale = PHt1 / YDiff


            If WdScale > HtScale Then
               'X axis needs to be adjusted
               'keeping Y axis scale unchanged
               XDiff1 = (XDiff * WdScale / HtScale - XDiff) / 2
               AxX.MinimumScale = MinX - XDiff1
               AxX.MaximumScale = MaxX + XDiff1
            Else
               'Y axis needs to be adjusted
                'keeping X axis scale unchanged
               YDiff1 = (YDiff * HtScale / WdScale - YDiff) / 2
               AxY.MinimumScale = MinY - YDiff1
               AxY.MaximumScale = MaxY + YDiff1
            End If
       End With
   End Sub
```

The sample chart in Figure 89 is a plot of a circle of radius 4 units, with a center at (5,5), and a square of side 8 units, with the top-left corner at (4.5,12).

Breaking It Down: This problem crops up in situations where the x and y data are of similar orders of magnitude—for example, when you are plotting a shape rather than an algebraic function. In the general case, when such a chart is created, the scaling of the x and y axes are not the same. The height and width of the plot area also contribute to the degree of distortion of the plotted series. The idea is to determine which of the two axes needs to be set to a larger range of `Min/Max` scale values so the series appears with the correct aspect ratio, so the required `Min/Max` scale values are calculated, and so the axis scale is set accordingly.

The following section of code calculates the `Min/Max` x and y across all series in the chart:

```
For i = 1 To Cht.SeriesCollection.Count
  Set Ser = Cht.SeriesCollection(i)
  XVals = Ser.XValues
  YVals = Ser.Values
  If i = 1 Then
    MinX = WorksheetFunction.Min(XVals)
    MaxX = WorksheetFunction.Max(XVals)
    MinY = WorksheetFunction.Min(YVals)
    MaxY = WorksheetFunction.Max(YVals)
  Else
    MinX = WorksheetFunction.Min(MinX, XVals)
    MaxX = WorksheetFunction.Max(MaxX, XVals)
    MinY = WorksheetFunction.Min(MinY, YVals)
    MaxY = WorksheetFunction.Max(MaxY, YVals)
  End If
Next
```

The following section maximizes the plot area to the chart boundaries and gets the inside dimensions of the plot area (these dimensions are required for the scaling exercise):

```
With .PlotArea
     .Top = 0
     .Left = 0
     .Width = Cht.ChartArea.Width
     .Height = Cht.ChartArea.Height
     PWd = .Width
```

```
      PHt = .Height
      PWdl = .InsideWidth
      PHtl = .InsideHeight
End With
```

The next section calculates the range of extreme x and y values,:

```
XDiff = MaxX - MinX
YDiff = MaxY - MinY


'Set a buffer space of 10% of XDiff and YDiff so there is
'a margin between series boundary and plot area
Buffer = 0.1


'Adjust values of Max/Min X/Y for buffer
MaxX = MaxX + Buffer * XDiff
MinX = MinX - Buffer * XDiff
MaxY = MaxY + Buffer * YDiff
MinY = MinY - Buffer * YDiff


'Revised range of X and Y Values with buffer
XDiff = MaxX - MinX
YDiff = MaxY - MinY


'Rescale Axes for max possible magnification
With AxX
   .MaximumScale = MaxX
   .MinimumScale = MinX
End With
With AxY
   .MaximumScale = MaxY
   .MinimumScale = MinY
End With
```

Part 2

A buffer of 10% of x and y ranges is set to accommodate the series comfortably within the plot area, the ranges are recalculated (including the buffer zone), and the Min/Max scales of the axes are set to the newly calculated Min/Max values.

The final section of code calculates the new scaling of the internal dimensions of the plot area for the modified x and y ranges:

```
WdScale = PWd1 / XDiff
HtScale = PHt1 / YDiff

If WdScale > HtScale Then
    'X axis needs to be adjusted keeping Y axis scale unchanged
    XDiff1 = (XDiff * WdScale / HtScale - XDiff) / 2
    AxX.MinimumScale = MinX - XDiff1
    AxX.MaximumScale = MaxX + XDiff1
Else
    'Y axis needs to be adjusted keeping X axis scale unchanged
    YDiff1 = (YDiff * HtScale / WdScale - YDiff) / 2
    AxY.MinimumScale = MinY - YDiff1
    AxY.MaximumScale = MaxY + YDiff1
End If
```

If the horizontal scaling is greater than the vertical scaling, the x axis needs to be set to a larger scale range (XDiff1), which is calculated from the horizontal scaling of the inside width of the plot area. XDiff1 is applied symmetrically to the x axis scaling (i.e., the minimum scale for the x axis is reduced by XDiff1/2), and the maximum scale is incremented by the same amount. The same is done with the y axis if the vertical scaling is greater than the horizontal scaling.

Summary: The code in this solution programmatically adjusts a scatter chart containing series of similar orders of magnitude to display correctly proportioned series.

PART 3

MACROS

MAKE A PERSONAL MACRO WORKBOOK

Challenge: Macros stored in the Personal Macro Workbook are always at your disposal. You can run the macros on any workbook that you open on the computer. Also, you do not have to jump through security hoops to run macros stored in the Personal Macro Workbook.

If you have never used the Personal Macro Workbook, it does not exist on your computer. You need to create one.

Solution:

For Excel 2003 and Earlier

In Excel 2003 or an earlier version of Excel, open any workbook. Choose Tools, Macro, Record New Macro.

In the Macro Name field, type `HelloWorld` (without a space). Open the Store Macro In dropdown and choose Personal Macro Workbook. Leave the Shortcut Key field blank. There is no need to change the Description field for this tiny macro. The dialog should appear as in Figure 97. Click OK.

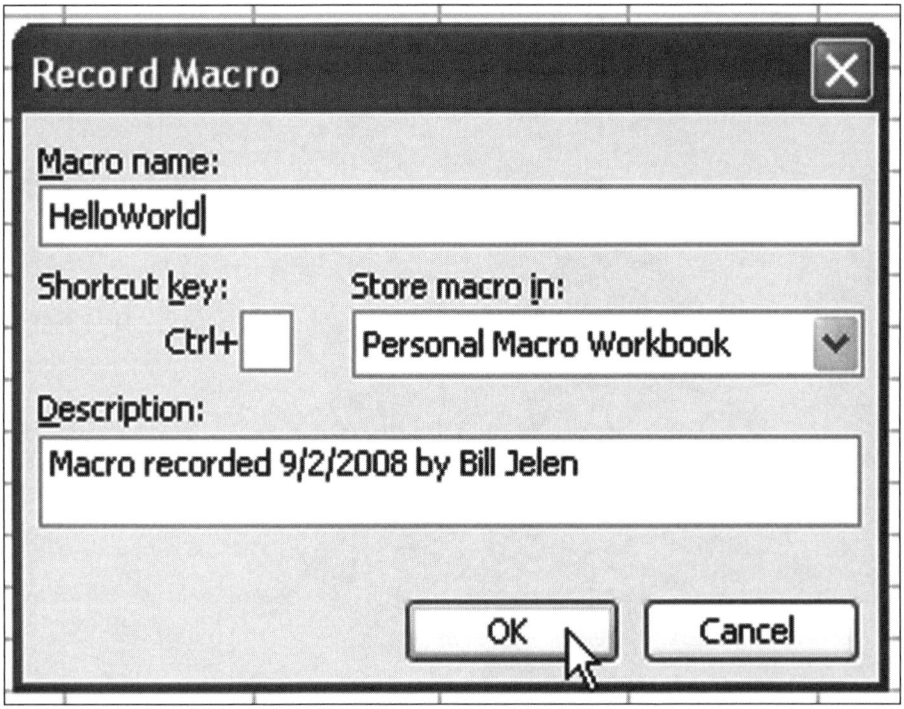

Figure 97. To force Excel to create a Personal Macro Workbook, record a tiny macro to go there.

When you click OK, the macro recorder runs. You have to do at least one action in Excel that is recordable. Perhaps you can press Ctrl+B to bold the current cell or type Hello in the current cell. After you have performed this action, you can stop recording. The reliable way to stop recording is to choose Tools, Macro, Stop Recording. You might also see the Stop Recording button on the tiny Stop Recording toolbar (Figure 98).

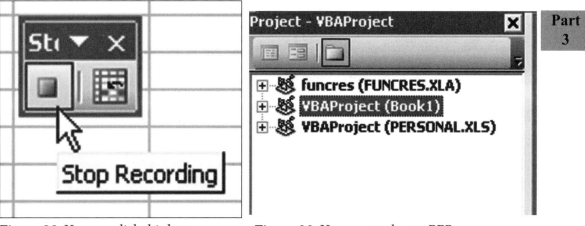

Part 3

Figure 98. You can click this button to stop recording.

Figure 99. You want to locate PERSONAL.XLS in the Project Explorer.

When you've recorded a macro, Excel creates the Personal Macro Workbook. On my Windows XP computer, the file is stored in C:\Documents and Settings\ Bill \Application Data\Microsoft\Excel\XLSTART\Personal.xls.

The Personal Macro Workbook is a hidden workbook. There is nothing special about the workbook. If you are curious, you can unhide it by selecting Window, Unhide and then selecting PERSONAL.XLS and clicking OK. It should contain one worksheet and will be completely blank. All the good stuff in the Personal Macro Workbook is visible from the VBA editor.

To see the code pane in the Personal Macro Workbook, follow these steps:

1. Press Alt+F11 or select Tools, Macro, Visual Basic Editor. If you have never used macros before, you see a menu bar, a toolbar, and a lot of gray.

2. Press Ctrl+R or select View, Project Explorer to show the Project Explorer pane. As shown in Figure 99, the Project Explorer lists each open workbook, plus one workbook for each standard add-in installed on your computer. Figure 99 shows the workbooks in collapsed mode. You might find that some of your workbooks have been expanded to show worksheets and modules.

3. Use the + sign next to PERSONAL.XLS to expand the tree view. Click the + sign next to Modules to see a list of modules. If you just recorded your first macro, you see only Module1. If you record more macros, Excel adds new modules such as Module2, Module3, and so on (Figure 100).

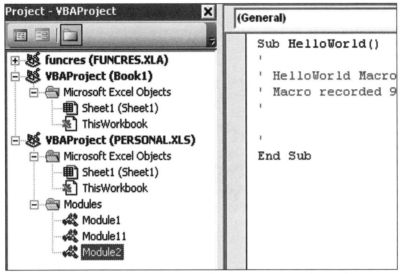

Figure 100. You double-click a module name to see the code in that module.

4. To see the code in any module, double-click the module in Project Explorer. Alternatively, right-click the module and choose View Code.

If you want to run a macro from this book, you can type or paste it in any existing module in PERSONAL.XLS. Note that after you change code in PERSONAL.XLS and then you close Excel, you are prompted about whether you want to save your changes to PERSONAL.XLS. Don't forget to save at this point!

For Excel 2007

In Excel 2007, follow these steps:

1. Open any workbook in Excel 2007.
2. Look near the lower-left corner of the Excel window. To the right of the word Ready in the status bar is the Record Macro icon. Click it (Figure 101). Excel displays the Record Macro dialog.

Figure 101. The Record Macro icon is one of the few icons outside the ribbon.

3. In the Record Macro dialog, enter a macro name, such as `HelloWorld` (no spaces). Leave the Shortcut Key field blank. Change the Store Macro In dropdown to Personal Macro Workbook. Leave the Description field blank. Click OK (Figure 102).

Record Macro [?][X]

Macro name:
HelloWorld

Shortcut key:
Ctrl+[ ]

Store macro in:
Personal Macro Workbook [v]

Description:
|

[OK]   [Cancel]

Figure 102. Choose to create this macro in the Personal Macro Workbook.

4. Perform one action that the macro recorder can record. Perhaps you can press Ctrl+B to bold the current cell or type `Hello` in the current cell.

5. Stop the macro recorder by pressing the square icon in the lower-left corner of the window, near the word Ready in the status bar (Figure 103). This icon and the Record Macro icon share the same location; the Stop Recording icon replaces the Record Macro icon while you are recording.

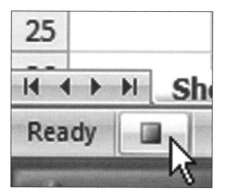

Figure 103. Look for the Stop Recording button in the same place you found the Record Macro icon.

Note: You can also record a macro by selecting View, Macros, Record Macro or Developer, Record New Macro. The Stop Recording button is found in these same locations while you are recording a macro.

The Personal Macro Workbook is a hidden workbook. There is nothing special about the workbook. If you are curious, you can unhide it with the Unhide command on the View tab. It should contain one worksheet and will be completely blank. All the good stuff in the Personal Macro Workbook is visible from the VBA editor.

To see the code pane in the Personal Macro Workbook, follow these steps:

1. Press Alt+F11 or select Developer, Visual Basic. If you have never used macros before, you see a menu bar, a toolbar, and a lot of gray.

2. Press Ctrl+R or select View, Project Explorer to show the Project Explorer pane. As shown in Figure 99, the Project Explorer lists each open workbook, plus one workbook for each standard add-in installed on your computer. Figure 99 shows the workbooks in collapsed mode. You might find that some of your workbooks have been expanded to show worksheets and modules.

3. Use the + sign next to PERSONAL.XLS to expand the tree view. Click the + sign next to Modules to see a list of modules. If you just recorded your first macro, you only see Module1. If you record more macros, Excel adds new modules, such as Module2, Module3, and so on (Figure 100).

4. To see the code in any module, double-click the module in the Project Explorer. Alternatively, right-click the module and choose View Code.

If you want to run a macro from this book, you can type or paste it in any existing module in PERSONAL.XLS. Note that after you change code in PERSONAL. XLS and then you close Excel, you are prompted about whether you want to save your changes to PERSONAL.XLS. Don't forget to save at this point!

Summary: Several code samples in this book are appropriate for the Personal Macro Workbook. By following the steps in this selection, you can create the Personal Macro Workbook.

RUN A MACRO FROM A SHORTCUT KEY

Challenge: You recorded a macro but forgot to assign it to a shortcut key. Now you need to change the shortcut key used for the macro. Excel documents the shortcut key used when recording a macro in the comments at the top of the macro. However, changing the comment in the macro does not have any effect on the actual shortcut key used.

Solution: To change the shortcut key, press the F8 key to see a list of macros. Click the macro in question and click the Options button in the Macro Options dialog. You can edit the shortcut key here (Figure 104).

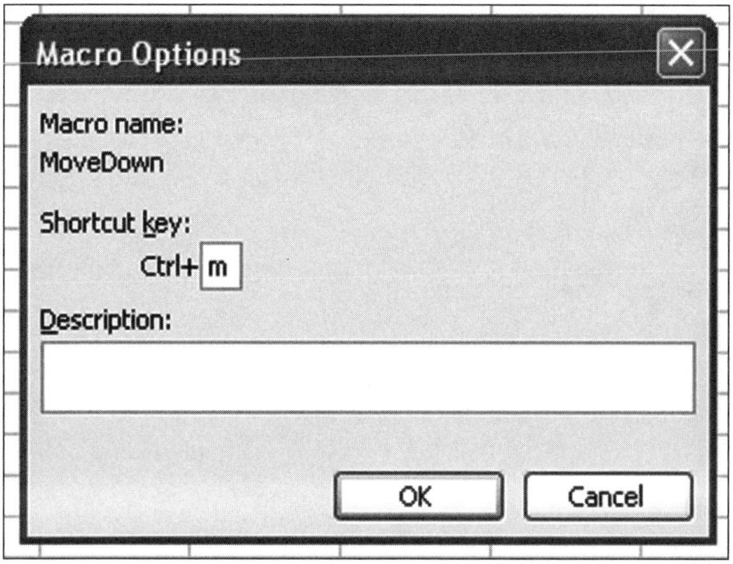

Figure 104. You can change the shortcut key using this dialog.

Additional Details: You can temporarily assign a macro to a shortcut key by using a macro. Perhaps you want to turn on a shortcut key during one section of a process and turn it off later in the process. The following line of code temporarily assigns the MoveDown procedure to Ctrl+m:

```
Application.OnKey Key:="^m", Procedure:="MoveDown"
```

To cancel this assignment and return Ctrl+m to its normal function, use:

```
Application.OnKey Key:="^m"
```

To permanently change the shortcut key via code, use:

```
Application.MacroOptions Macro:="MoveDown", ShortcutKey:="m"
```

Additional Details: Excel stores the shortcut key in the code module, but it is not visible in the Visual Basic editor. You have to export the module from VBA. Follow these steps:

1. Right-click the module in the Project Explorer and choose Export File.

2. Save the file in a place where you can find it later. Excel proposes a name such as Module1.bas. You can use this name.

3. Open the .bas file in Notepad.

4. You see an attribute near each module. The shortcut key is listed, followed by /n14. So, in Figure 105, the g\n14 attribute means the macro is assigned to Ctrl+g. The G\n14 attribute means the macro is assigned to Ctrl+Shift+G.

Part
3

```
Module1.bas - Notepad
File  Edit  Format  View  Help
Sub AssignKey()
Attribute AssignKey.VB_ProcData.VB_Invoke_Func = "s\n14"
    Application.OnKey Key:="^m", Procedure:="MoveDown"
End Sub

Sub ShortcutKeyLowerCaseG()
Attribute ShortcutKeyLowerCaseG.VB_ProcData.VB_Invoke_Func = "g\n14"
    MsgBox "This macro is assigned to Ctrl+g"
End Sub

Sub ShortcutKeyUpperCaseG()
Attribute ShortcutKeyUpperCaseG.VB_ProcData.VB_Invoke_Func = "G\n14"
    MsgBox "This macro is assigned to Ctrl+Shift+G"
End Sub
```

Figure 105. You can export the module to see all the shortcut keys used.

Summary: There are several ways to assign the shortcut key associated with a macro.

Source: http://www.mrexcel.com/archive2/39200/45444.htm

RUN A MACRO FROM A BUTTON

Challenge: You want an easy way to run a macro. Can you run it from a button on the worksheet?

Solution: There are many ways to run a macro. Figure 106 shows seven different methods in Excel 2003. All of them except the custom toolbar translate to Excel 2007.

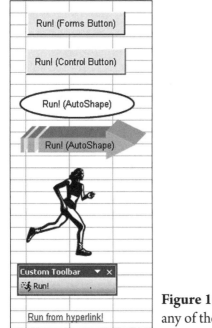

Figure 106. You can run a macro from any of these elements.

Method 1: Forms Button

To run a macro from a forms button, in Excel 2003, select View, Toolbars, Forms. Click the Button icon (Figure 107) and then drag in the worksheet to draw a button.

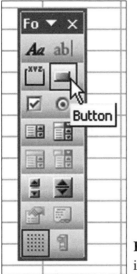

Figure 107. This is how you create the forms button in Excel 2003 and earlier.

Part
3

In Excel 2007, go to the Developer tab. Open the Insert dropdown and choose the icon shown in Figure 108. Drag a rectangle on the worksheet to draw your button.

Figure 108. If you can't find the Developer tab in Excel 2007, use Office Icon, Excel Options, Popular, Show Developer Tab in the Ribbon. The Insert dropdown then offers the forms button.

The Assign Macro dialog appears. Click your macro and then click OK.

The button initially appears with the generic name Button 1. To change the name: Ctrl+click the button to select the button without running the macro. The button is surrounded by dots. Drag across the words on the button to select them for editing. The button is now surrounded by diagonal lines. Type new words.

You can change the font, font size, alignment, and color of the button. If you are in Text Edit mode, click the diagonal lines surrounding the button to return to the dots border. Otherwise, Ctrl+click the button to select the button. Press Ctrl+1 to edit the font, alignment, size, and more. Right-click the button and choose Assign Macro to change the macro assigned to the button.

Method 2: ActiveX Button

An ActiveX button looks like a forms button, but it is more flexible, as you will soon learn. Follow these steps to build one in Excel 2003:

1. Select View, Toolbars, Control Toolbox.

2. Click the Button icon and drag in the worksheet. Notice in Figure 109 that the Design Mode icon is turned on when you draw a new control. Design Mode is the icon in the top left, with the ruler, triangle, and pencil. Design mode has to be on when you are working with this control. When you exit Design mode, the button you create acts as a button when you click on it.

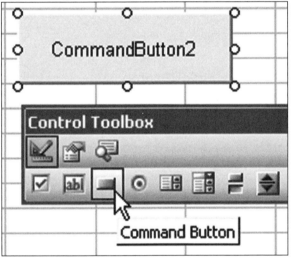

Figure 109. Design mode must be on to work with the button.

3. Click the second button, the Properties button, to display the properties for the button. Find the line for Caption. Click in the second column of the Properties dialog, next to the word Caption, and type the words that should appear on the button (Figure 110). Note that you can change the appearance of the button by using properties such as BackColor, ForeColor, and Font. While the Caption property is a simple text box where you can type a new caption, many choices lead to fly-out menus or even to new dialog boxes. You can add a picture to the button, change the color, etc. These features make the ActiveX controls far more flexible than the forms controls. Note that you still have not assigned a macro to the button.

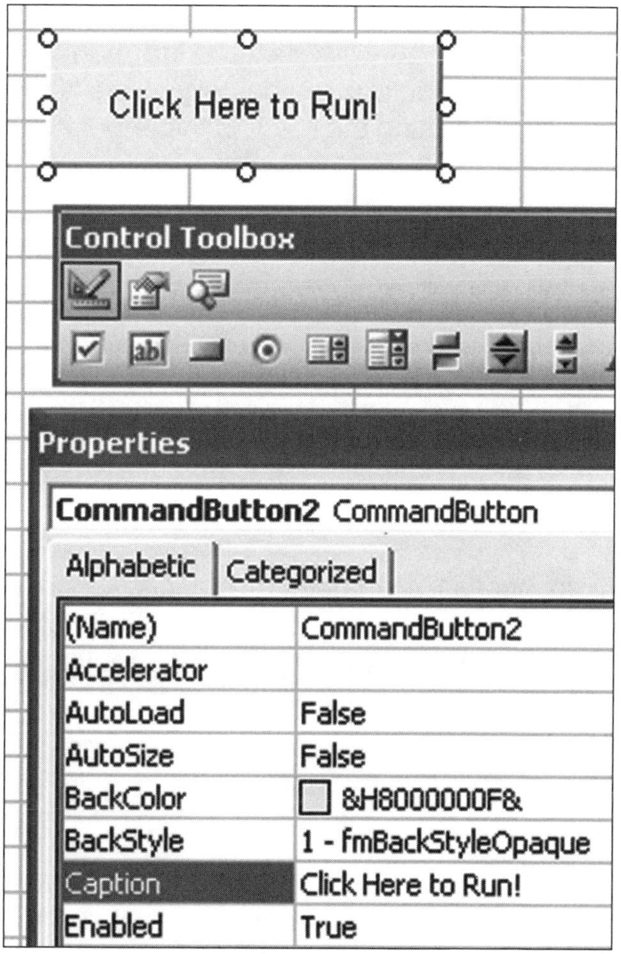

Figure 110. You can change properties in the
Properties dialog to change the appearance of the
button.

4. With the button still in Design mode, click the View Code icon. This is the third icon in the Control Toolbox—a magnifying glass looking at a sheet. When you click View Code, you are taken to a brand new macro in the VBA editor. The new macro lives on the code sheet for the workbook.

5. You can write the macro steps in this new macro. Or, if you want to call an existing macro, simply type the name of the macro as the only code in the macro, as shown in Figure 111.

```
Private Sub CommandButton1_Click()
    TestMacro
End Sub
```

Figure 111. When you click View Code, you are taken to a
new macro on the code pane for the worksheet.

Part
3

Back in the Excel worksheet, you need to close the Properties dialog by clicking the red X in the upper-right corner. You also need to exit Design mode by clicking the Design Mode icon in the Control Toolbox toolbar. If you are done adding buttons, hide the Control Toolbox by clicking the red X in the upper-right corner.

In Excel 2007, the process is similar. You use the Button icon at the bottom of the Insert dropdown. The Design Mode, Properties, and View Code icons are in the same group on the Developer tab. Microsoft nicely added words so you can easily identify each icon.

Method 3: From Any Shape, Picture, SmartArt, or Clip Art

To set up a macro to run from any shape, picture, SmartArt, or clip art, add an AutoShape or clip art to your worksheet. Right-click the object and choose Assign Macro. You can assign a macro to the shape just as in Method 1 for the forms button.

In Excel 2003, use Insert, Picture to access a number of objects. Choose ClipArt, Picture, or AutoShape. If you are going to use AutoShapes, it is best to display the Drawing toolbar. You can use the icons on the Drawing toolbar to change the color, shadow, text, number of dimensions, and so on.

In Excel 2007, use the Insert tab of the ribbon. AutoShapes have been renamed Shapes. You can also add SmartArt. Right-click the diagram when you are done and choose Assign Macro.

Method 4: From a Hyperlink

Setting up a macro to run from a hyperlink is tricky but possible. To begin, add some text to a cell—perhaps `Run the Macro!`. Then choose Insert, Hyperlink and make the hyperlink jump to the cell that contains the text. This basically prevents the hyperlink from going anywhere.

Next, switch to VBA. In the Project Explorer, look for the entry for the worksheet where the hyperlinks are. Right-click that sheet name and choose View Code, as shown in Figure 112.

Figure 112. The code to intercept the hyperlink has to be on the code pane for the worksheet.

There are two dropdowns above the code pane. From the left dropdown, choose Worksheet. From the right dropdown, choose FollowHyperlink.

You now have the makings of a `Worksheet_FollowHyperlink` macro. Every time someone clicks a hyperlink on this worksheet, this bit of code will run. The Target variable tells you about the hyperlink that was clicked.

If there is only one hyperlink on the worksheet, then you can simply run the macro:

```
Private   Sub   Worksheet_FollowHyperlink(ByVal   Target   As
Hyperlink)


      TestMacro
End Sub
```

Part 3

However, if you have multiple hyperlinks on the worksheet, you can use the Target.TextToDisplay property to distinguish between hyperlinks:

```
Private   Sub   Worksheet_FollowHyperlink(ByVal   Target   As
Hyperlink)
    Select Case Target.TextToDisplay
        Case "Run Report 2"
            TestMacro
        Case "Run Report 2"
            TestMacro2
        Case "Run Report 3"
            TestMacro3
    End Select
End Sub
```

Using a hyperlink to run a macro is a favorite trick when you want to toggle between different states. Perhaps you want to toggle between sorting ascending and sorting descending in a column. This macro will perform an action and change the text in the hyperlink so that a different action can be performed the next time:

```
Private   Sub   Worksheet_FollowHyperlink(ByVal   Target   As
Hyperlink)
    Select Case Target.TextToDisplay
        Case "A-Z"
            SortMacroAscending
            Target.TextToDisplay = "Z-A"
        Case "Z-A"
            SortMacroDescending
```

```
            Target.TextToDisplay = "A-Z"
       End Select
End Sub
```

Method 5: Custom Toolbar (Excel 2003 Only)

In Excel 2003, you can create your own floating toolbar. Choose Tools, Customize. In the Customize dialog, choose the Toolbars tab and then click New. Type a name for the toolbar and click OK.

Keep the Customize dialog open. Go to the Commands tab. In the left dropdown, choose Macros. In the right dropdown, drag either Custom Menu Item or the Custom Button to the new toolbar. Keep the Customize dialog open. Right-click the new icon in the toolbar. You can choose a new icon, choose a ToolTip, and assign a macro to the button (Figure 113).

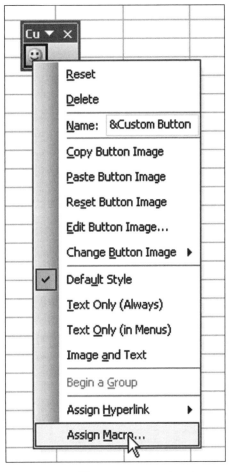

Figure 113. You can customize the button on the new toolbar.

Summary: There are several ways to start a macro by using controls that appear on a worksheet.

RUN A MACRO FROM AN ICON

Challenge: You want an easy way to run a macro, and you don't especially like the options presented in "Run a Macro from a Button." Can you run a macro from an icon on a toolbar?

Solution: The process of setting up a macro to run from a toolbar icon changed dramatically between Excel 2003 and Excel 2007. You have far more options in Excel 2003.

Part 3

For Excel 2007

In Excel 2007, the only non-programmatic method for adding a macro button to a toolbar is to add a button to the Quick Access toolbar. Follow these steps:

1. Right-click anywhere in the ribbon and choose Customize Quick Access Toolbar. Excel opens the Customize section of the Excel Options dialog.

2. Open the Choose Commands From dropdown and select the fourth item, Macros.

3. Choose a macro from the left list box.

4. Press the Add>> button in the center of the dialog.

5. Use the up or down arrow button on the right side of the dialog to rearrange the icon within the ribbon, if desired (Figure 114).

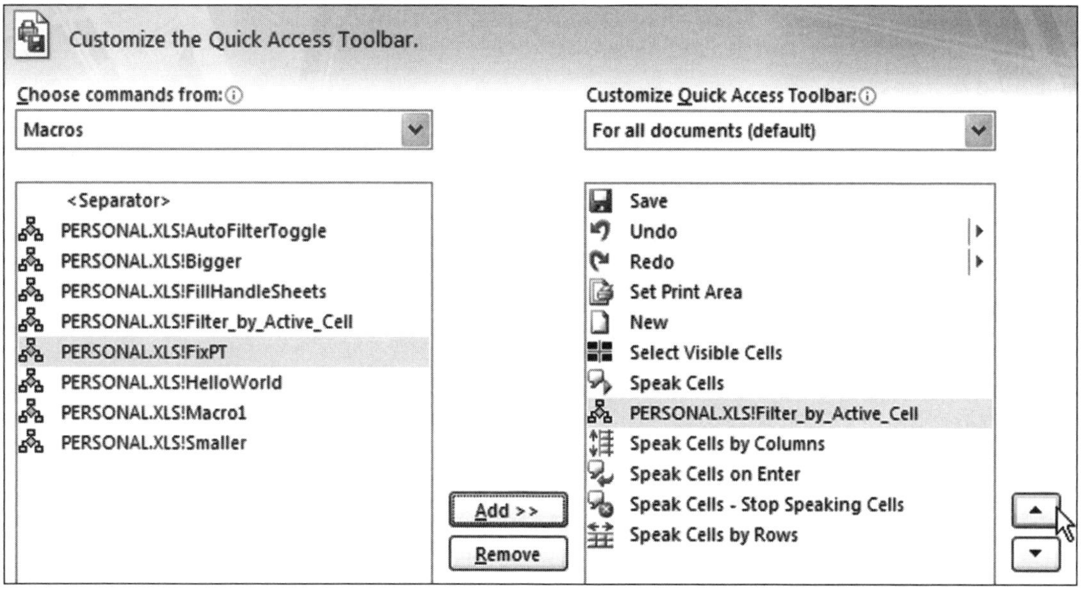

Figure 114. You can add an icon to the Quick Access toolbar and adjust its location.

6. By default, every macro starts out with an identical flowchart icon. To change the icon, click the Modify button, which appears below the right list box. There are 181 icons available (Figure 115). Choose one that will remind you of the action in the macro. Change the display name to something friendlier. This name will be displayed when you hover over the icon in the Quick Access toolbar.

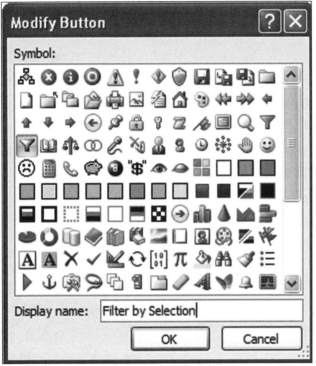

Figure 115. You customize the icon from this selection of icons.

7. Click OK to close the Excel Options dialog. The new icon appears in the Quick Access toolbar, as shown in Figure 116.

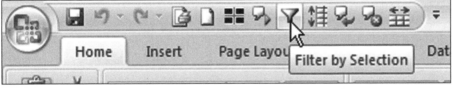

Figure 116. The new icon appears in the Quick Access toolbar.

Tip: There is one bit of new functionality in Excel 2007: You can add to the Quick Access toolbar an icon that appears only when a particular workbook is open. To add an icon for one workbook, use the top-right dropdown in the Customize dialog. Change the setting from For All Documents (Default) to For <workbook name>.

For Excel 2003

Excel 2003 and prior versions offer more options for adding icons to your toolbars. The icon can be added to any toolbar or even to a new toolbar. (See "Run a Macro from a Button" on page 102). You can use a selection of default icons, draw your own icon, or even copy an icon from another application. Here's how:

1. Right-click any toolbar and choose Customize or select Tools, Customize.

2. Select the Commands tab in the Customize dialog.

3. Scroll down in the left list box to almost the end. Choose Macros, the third item from the end of the left list box. The right list box offers two icons: a smiley face and an icon with nothing. Even if you hate the smiley face, use it for now.

4. Drag the smiley face icon from the right list box and drop it in the desired location on any toolbar or menu. Figure 117 shows the new icon being added to the Filter fly-out on the Data menu.

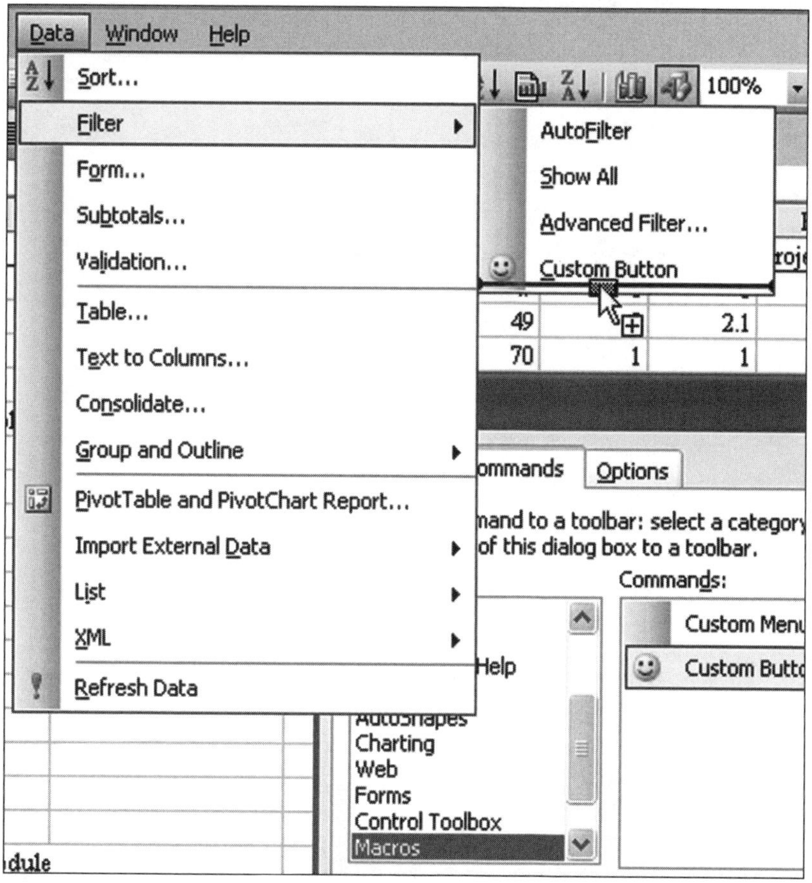

Part 3

Figure 117. You can drag the smiley face to any existing toolbar or menu.

5. Keep the Customize dialog box open. Find your new icon on the menu or toolbar. Right-click the icon or click it and choose Modify Selection in the Customize dialog. From the menu that appears, adjust the settings in step 6 and optionally follow any of steps 7 through 11.

6. From the bottom of the menu, choose Assign Macro. Choose the appropriate macro and click OK.

7. Choose Change Button Image and select one of the 48 default images instead of the smiley face (Figure 118).

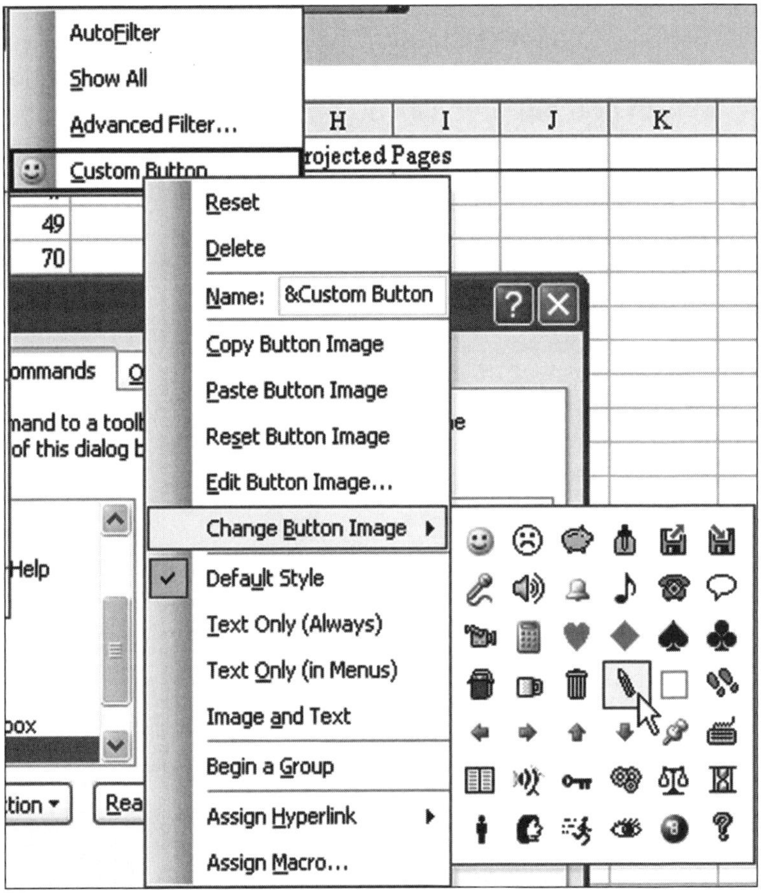

Figure 118. You are not stuck with the smiley face.

8. Type a new name for the button. This name will appear in menus and will appear as the ToolTip when the icon is in a toolbar.

Tip: If your icon is in a menu, add a shortcut key by preceding one letter in the name with an ampersand. For the menu shown in Figure 119, for example, the name is Filter &to Selection. This causes the t in to to be underlined, and it makes the command sequence to access the new button Alt+D+F+T (D opens to Data menu, Filter opens the Filter menu, and T selects Filter to Selection).

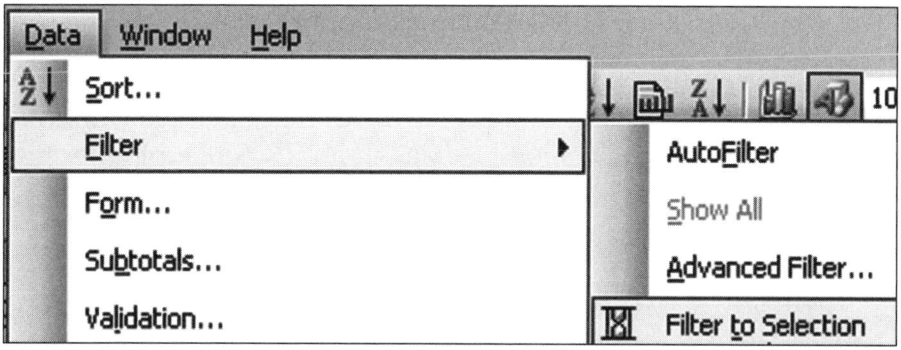

Figure 119. In menus, you can specify one letter to have an accelerator key.

9. If desired, use the Begin a Group menu item to tell Excel to insert a separator before the menu item.

10. If you have way too much time on your hands, choose Edit Button Image and create any icon that fits in a 16-by-16 grid (Figure 120). Before you try this, see if another Office application offers the icon you need and follow the instructions below for copying an icon from another Office application.

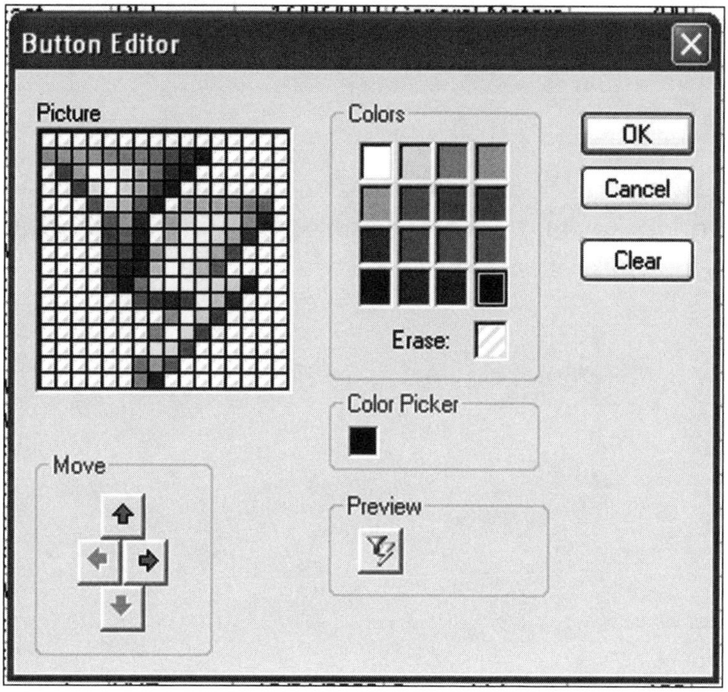

Figure 120. In Excel 2003 and earlier, you can edit to create
your own custom icons.

11.   By default, a custom menu item appears with an image and text. A custom toolbar item appears with only an image. You can override this style by using the Text Only or Image and Text settings in the menu.

Copying Icons from Other Office Applications

Rather than create your own icon using the Button editor, as shown in Figure 120, see if another application already has the icon. For example, the idea for Filter to Selection came from Access. It is likely that Access already has an icon called Filter to Selection. If so, you can copy the icon from one Office application to Excel. Follow these steps:

1. Keep Excel open and open Access (or Word or PowerPoint).

2. In Access (or Word or PowerPoint), find the Filter to Selection icon, which appears only when you are viewing a table. Finding the icon might require a few steps. If you don't have an Access table, use File, Import to import an Excel worksheet into a table. Then double-click the table to view it in Data Sheet mode. The desired icon now appears on the Table Datasheet toolbar.

3. Right-click the toolbar and choose Customize.

4. While the Customize dialog is displayed, right-click the desired icon and choose Copy Button Image.

5. Switch back to Excel.

6. Choose Tools, Customize.

7. Right-click the desired icon and choose Paste Button Image. A new menu item is added, with a shortcut key and a professional-looking icon. As shown in Figure 121, this item looks like it is part of the core Excel product.

Figure 121. A custom button with an image copied from Access runs the macro in the Personal Macro Workbook.

Summary: Excel 2003 is better than Excel 2007 for adding custom menu items.

CREATE A REGULAR MACRO

Challenge: You've found a cool VBA macro on the MrExcel message board. Your workbook doesn't currently have any macros. How can you get the macro into your workbook?

Solution: You can type regular macros in a module in the VBA editor. Follow these steps to insert a new module:

1. Open the workbook in which you want to save the macro.
2. Switch to the VBA editor by pressing Alt+F11. Alternatively, you could select Tools, Macro, Visual Basic Editor in Excel 2003 or Developer, Visual Basic in Excel 2007.
3. From the VBA editor menu, choose Insert, Module. A new blank code pane appears on the right side of the screen.
4. Copy the code from the webpage. Click in the blank code module and choose Paste.

Part 3

If it is not already visible, display the Project Explorer by pressing Ctrl+R. In the Project Explorer, you should be able to see the Module1 entry listed below your workbook. If you plan to have several macros, you can organize them into multiple modules. To rename a module from a generic name, follow these steps:

1. Display the Properties window by pressing F4.
2. Click Module1 in the Project Explorer.
3. The Properties window shows only one property: (Name).
4. Click in the text box for (Name) and type a new name, such ad ModuleReports.

As you add modules, you can name them to make it easier to locate particular macros later (Figure 122).

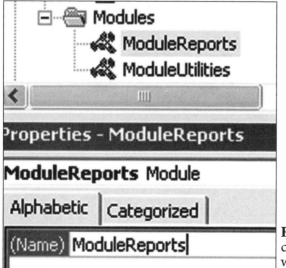

Figure 122. Organize your modules by changing their name in the Properties window.

Tip: You may get to the point where you have many macros spread across many modules. You can quickly find a macro in the regular Excel interface by pressing Alt+F8 to bring up an alphabetical list of all the macros. Find the desired macro and click the Edit button. Excel switches to VBA, opens the correct module, and scrolls so this module is in view. Unfortunately, this trick does not work for macros in hidden workbooks, such as the Personal Macro Workbook.

Summary: You type regular VBA macros into standard modules in the VBA editor.

CREATE AN EVENT HANDLER MACRO

Challenge: While typical macros are entered in modules, a few special macros, called event handler macros, are run automatically in response to an event that happens in Excel.

Background: Some common event handler macros are:

- `Workbook_Open`: This macro runs when a workbook is opened.
- `Workbook_BeforeClose`: This macro runs after someone tries to close a workbook but before the person is asked whether to save changes.
- `Workbook_BeforePrint`: This macro runs when someone issues a print command but before the job is sent to the printer. This macro allows you to adjust something in the workbook, such as adding the current file location and the user name in the footer of the worksheet.
- `Worksheet_Change`: This amazing macro runs every time someone enters a value in any cell in the worksheet.
- `Worksheet_Activate`: This is sort of a a `Workbook_Open` macro but for an individual worksheet. Maybe you want certain menu items to appear only when someone is on a particular worksheet.
- `Worksheet_SelectionChange`: This macro runs every time someone moves to a new cell in the worksheet.

Event handler macros are powerful, but they do not work correctly unless they are entered properly in the VBA editor. The VBA code is not entered in a traditional module but is entered in the code pane attached to the worksheet or to the `ThisWorkbook` object.

Solution: Say that you have found some code for the `BeforePrint` event. This is a workbook-level event, so it needs to go on the code pane for the workbook. Follow these steps:

1. Open the workbook in Excel.
2. Switch to the VBA editor by pressing Alt+F11.
3. Open the Project Explorer by pressing Ctrl+R.
4. Find your workbook in the Project Explorer list. If necessary, click the + sign to the left of the workbook name to expand the tree view for the workbook.

5. If necessary, click the + sign to the left of Microsoft Excel Objects to expand the view of worksheets and the workbook. You now see an entry for each worksheet in the workbook and an entry for `ThisWorkbook`.

6. Double-click `ThisWorkbook`. Alternatively, right-click `ThisWorkbook` and choose View Code (Figure 123).

Part
3

Figure 123. You need to access the code pane for the `ThisWorkbook` object.

7. If you are copying a macro from the web, paste it to the code window now. If you are typing the macro yourself, follow steps 8 and 9.

8. From the left dropdown at the top of the code window, choose `Workbook`. By default, Excel types the start of a `Workbook_Open` macro in the code window. You can delete it later, if needed.

9. Open the right dropdown at the top of the code window. These are all the workbook-level events that can have a macro associated with them. Choose `BeforePrint` from the dropdown. Excel types the start of the `Workbook_BeforePrint` macro in the code window.

The process is similar if you want to create a worksheet-level event handler. In that case, you follow the steps above, but in step 6, you double-click the worksheet name in the Project Explorer, and in step 8, you choose Worksheet from the left dropdown. Excel automatically creates the start of the `Worksheet_SelectionChange` macro.

Summary: You need to type event handler macros in special code panes attached to the worksheet or workbook.

EXTRACT AN E-MAIL ADDRESS FROM A CELL CONTAINING OTHER TEXT

Challenge: You have cells that contain e-mail addresses as well as other text. You need to extract just the e-mail address from a cell.

Solution: There are three solutions to this problem: Use a macro, use a user-defined function, or use a very large formula.

Macro Solution

The macro solution makes use of the SPLIT function in VBA. Let's say that a cell contains the text Write to `lora@mrexcel.com to book a seminar.` If you pass this text to the SPLIT function and indicate that the text should be split at every space character, VBA will return an array, with each word at a new position of the array. Figure 124 shows the value of x after you use SPLIT.

```
Sub getEmailMacro()
    Dim x As Variant
    Dim i As Integer
    Dim note As String

    For Each cell In Selection
        x = Split(cell.Value, " ")

        For i = 0 To UBound(x)
            If x(i) Like "*@*.*" Then
                cell.Offset(0, 1) = x(i)
                Exit For
            End If
        Next i

    Next cell
```

Watches		
Expression	**Value**	**Type**
x		Variant/String(0 to 6)
x(0)	"Write"	String
x(1)	"to"	String
x(2)	"lora@mrexcel.com"	String
x(3)	"to"	String
x(4)	"book"	String
x(5)	"a"	String
x(6)	"seminar"	String

Figure 124. The SPLIT function returns a 0-based array, with each word broken out.

The macro then simply loops through each position in the x array, looking for a word that matches the pattern *@*.*. (Rather than test for equality, the LIKE operator looks for a word that matches a pattern.)

When a match is found, the macro writes the e-mail address to the right of the original cell.

With the following macro, you select all the cells that contain text e-mail addresses somewhere within the cell:

```
Sub getEmailMacro()
    Dim x As Variant
    Dim i As Integer
       For Each cell In Selection
        x = Split(cell.Value, " ")

        For i = 0 To UBound(x)
            If x(i) Like "*@*.*" Then
                cell.Offset(0, 1) = x(i)
                Exit For
            End If
        Next i


    Next cell
End Sub
```

Part 3

When you run the macro, the e-mail address portion of the cell is written to the right of the original values.

User-Defined Function Solution

You can adapt the macro above into a user-defined function that accepts one cell value as an argument and returns the e-mail portion of the text:

```
Public Function getEmail(note As String) As String
Dim x As Variant
Dim i As Integer
x = Split(note, " ")
For i = 0 To UBound(x)
    If x(i) Like "*@*.*" Then
        getEmail = x(i)
        Exit Function
    End If
Next i
End Function
```

Formula Solution

While the following formula would take some time to build, it is clever and remarkably simple in its operation:

```
=TRIM(MID(SUBSTITUTE(" "&A1," ",REPT(" ",20)),FIND("@",SUBST
ITUTE(" "&A1," ",REPT(" ",20)))-20,40))
```

The formula initially uses the `SUBSTITUTE` function to replace every occurrence of a space with 20 spaces. This serves to separate every word in the text by many spaces:

Original Text: `Tell bill@mrexcel.com hello`

New Text: `Tell`   `bill@mrexcel.com`
`hello`

The `FIND` function locates the @ sign in the new text. The `MID` function starts 20 characters before the @ and grabs text for 40 characters. I used 40 characters because that should be long enough to handle any possible e-mail address. In fact, it would fail if you had `john.jacob.jingleheimer.schmidt@gmail.com` in your database. However, for a normal-sized e-mail address, you end up with something like:

        `bill@mrexcel.com`

Finally, the `TRIM` function removes all leading and trailing spaces, so you end up with:

`bill@mrexcel.com`

Figure 125 shows the result of the formula.

=TRIM(MID(SUBSTITUTE(" "&A3," ",REPT(" ",20)),FIND("@",SUBSTITUTE(" "&A3," ",REPT(" ",20)))-20,40))			
A	B	C	D
1 now is the time for bill@mrexcel.com to buy a book	bill@mrexcel.com		
2 Write to lora@mrexcel.com to book a seminar	lora@mrexcel.com		
3 Get a consulting quote from tracy@mrexcel.com	tracy@mrexcel.com		

Figure 125. The formula isolates the e-mail portion of the text.

Summary: You can use three different methods to extract the e-mail address from a cell that contains an e-mail address as well as other text

Source: http://www.mrexcel.com/forum/showthread.php?t=226840

FIND THE CLOSEST MATCH

Challenge: People enter data in various ways. If you ask 50 sales reps to record a forecast for General Motors, you will find that there are a dozen ways to spell and/or abbreviate the name of that customer. Combine all the forecasts from all the sales reps, and you will have the same customer spelled a multitude of ways. Column A in Figure 126 shows some of the different ways to enter the names of customers whose official names are listed in column D.

	A	B	C	D
1	Abbott			**Official List**
2	Abbott Laboratories			Abbott Laboratories
3	Abbott Labs			Associated Grocers
4	A/G Kansas			General Motors
5	A/G Nebraska			IBM
6	Associated Grocers / Kansas			Wal*Mart
7	Associated Grocers / Nebraska			
8	General Motors			
9	GM			
10	GM Lordstown			
11	I B M			
12	IBM			
13	International Business Machines			
14	Wal*Mart			
15	WalMart			
16	Wal-Mart			

Figure 126. When asked to type customer names, various employees will spell or abbreviate them in various ways.

Setup: This is a classic problem known as the fuzzy match problem. The problem was first discussed at the MrExcel message board back in fall 2001, with the fuzzy match challenge of the month. At that time, Juan Pablo Gonzalez wrote in with a routine to determine the percentage match between two strings. Damon Ostrander and others later followed up.

The question arose again at the message board in late 2003. Al_B_Cnu adapted the code from the challenge to write complete `FuzzyVLOOKUP`, `FuzzyHLOOKUP`, and `FuzzyPercent` functions. I won't reprint the 373 lines of code here, but you can examine them in the sample file for this topic (download from www.MrExcel.com/gurufiles.html).

Solution: The `FuzzyPercent` function compares text from two cells and determines what percentage of the characters in the first cell are in the same sequence in the second cell. In Figure 127, cells A2 and B2 share 11 characters in common. Because cell A2 contains 11 characters total, 73% of the characters match cell B2, and the `FuzzyPercent` is 73%. Note that if you reverse A2 and B2, the result may be different, as shown in row 3. Here, A3 and B3 share the same 11 characters, but 11 characters is only 50% of the 22 characters found in A3.

	C2	▼	f_x =fuzzyPercent(A2,B2,1)	
	A		B	C
1	String 1		String 2	FuzzyPercent
2	Ask MrExcel.com		MrExcel.com Consulting	73%
3	MrExcel.com Consulting		Ask MrExcel.com	50%
4	I B M		IBM Corporation	40%
5	IBM Corporation		I B M	20%
6	A. Schulman		A Schulman	91%
7	A Schulman		A. Schulman	100%
8	Elvis		lives	60%

Figure 127. The `FuzzyPercent` user-defined function in this workbook calculates the percentage of the characters that are in the same sequence.

Note that the algorithm is not perfect. `Elvis` and `lives` contains exactly the same characters, but in a completely different order. But is it completely different? Both cells have the characters l-v-s in the same sequence, so it appears to be a 3-out-of-5, or 60%, match.

The problem becomes more complex when you have to find the best matches from two lists. In Figure 128, a two-dimensional table shows how well each item from the forecast list in column A matches up with the official customer list in row 1.

Note that GM Lordstown shares just as many characters in common with General Motors as it does with Abbott Laboratories. To combat this, AI_B_Cnu offered alternative algorithms for the `FuzzyPercent` test. You can try out =`FuzzyPercent2()` in the sample workbook to see if is matches up your data better.

	B2	▼	f_x =fuzzyPercent($A2,B$1)	
	A		B	C
1	Abbott		Abbott Laboratories	Associated Grocers
2	Abbott Laboratories		89%	37%
3	Abbott Labs		82%	45%
4	A/G Kansas		40%	40%
5	A/G Nebraska		33%	42%
6	Associated Grocers / Kansas		19%	63%
7	Associated Grocers / Nebraska		17%	59%

Figure 128. This table highlights the best match in each row using `FuzzyPercent`.

To make Juan Pablo Gonzalez's function easier, Al_B_Cnu wrote `Fuzzy-VLOOKUP` and `FuzzyHLookup`. Like `VLOOKUP`, the `FuzzyVLOOKUP` function can return a specific column from a table. It can also return the best match, second-best match, and so on. In Figure 129, `FuzzyVLOOKUP` returns the three best matches for each forecasted customer. Someone is going to have to go through the choices to figure out which entries are correct matches.

	B2	▼		fx	=fuzzyPercent($A2,B$1)				
	A		B	C	D	E	F	
1	Abbott		Abbott Laboratories	Associated Grocers	General Motors	IBM	Wal*Mart	Part
2	Abbott Laboratories		89%	37%	32%	5%	21%	3
3	Abbott Labs		82%	45%	36%	9%	18%	
4	A/G Kansas		40%	40%	30%	0%	10%	
5	A/G Nebraska		33%	42%	42%	8%	17%	
6	Associated Grocers / Kansas		19%	63%	19%	4%	7%	
7	Associated Grocers / Nebraska		17%	59%	17%	7%	7%	
8	General Motors		50%	36%	100%	7%	29%	
9	GM		0%	50%	100%	50%	50%	
10	GM Lordstown		42%	33%	42%	8%	25%	
11	I B M		40%	40%	40%	60%	20%	
12	IBM		33%	33%	33%	100%	33%	
13	International Business Machines		16%	19%	19%	10%	13%	
14	Wal*Mart		63%	25%	50%	25%	88%	
15	WalMart		71%	29%	57%	14%	100%	
16	Wal-Mart		63%	25%	50%	13%	88%	

Figure 129. `FuzzyVLOOKUP` compares every item in the list to find the best, second-best, and third-best matches.

Summary: Custom functions in VBA help solve the fuzzy match problem.

Source: http://www.mrexcel.com/forum/showthread.php?t=69491

USE TIMER TO MICRO-TIME EVENTS

Challenge: Two Excel gurus walk into a bar. One of them says it is faster to use =MAX(0,MIN(A2,B2)), and the other thinks it is better to use =MEDIAN(0,A2,B2). Which one is correct?

Solution: You can find the answer by firing up a VBA macro to calculate each formula 50,000 times. Before the macro starts, you save the value of `Timer` to a variable. When the 50,000 calculations end, you can compare the original and final values of `Timer`.

On a Windows PC, `Timer` shows the number of seconds and fractional seconds elapsed since midnight. On a Mac, the function returns only whole seconds but no fractions. You need to make the process repeat enough times to actually show a difference in the number of seconds. Also, you need to make sure that the process does not extend past midnight!

The following code compares MIN(MAX to MEDIAN on 60,000 cells:

```
Sub TestMinMaxVsMedian()
    Application.ScreenUpdating = False
    Range("A1:B65000").Formula = "=Randbetween(-1000,1000)"
    Range("A1:B65000").Value = Range("A1:B50000").Value

    StartTime = Timer
    Range("C1:C65000").FormulaR1C1 = "=MAX(0,MIN(RC1,RC2))"
    Application.Calculate
    Range("C1:C65000").Value = Range("C1:C65000").Value
    ElapsedTime1 = Timer - StartTime

    StartTime = Timer
    Range("C1:C65000").FormulaR1C1 = "=MEDIAN(0,RC1,RC2)"
    Application.Calculate
    Range("C1:C65000").Value = Range("C1:C65000").Value
    ElapsedTime2 = Timer - StartTime

    Application.ScreenUpdating = True
    MsgBox "MAX(MIN takes: " & ElapsedTime1 & vbCr & "MEDIAN
takes: " & ElapsedTime2

End Sub
```

By comparing the Timer values before and after critical sections of code, you can compare the times required for various approaches. As shown in Figure 130, using the functions MIN and MAX is faster than using the MEDIAN function.

Figure 130. MEDIAN is just a bit slower than MAX and MIN.

Additional Details: Different computers might run at different speeds, so it is important to test the two processes on the same computer, preferably with similar items running in both cases.

Also, note that the difference in Figure 130 is just over two-hundredths of a second for 60,000 cells. The actual time difference for one cell is 3.9E-7 seconds—a time that will not matter to most end users. However, you, as the reader of this book, know that even such a small difference makes a difference between winning and losing a bar bet.

Summary: You can use the `Timer` function to calculate how long a process takes.

Source: http://www.mrexcel.com/forum/showthread.php?t=258950 and http://www.mrexcel.com/pc17.shtml

Part
3

DISCOVER THE TEMP FOLDER PATH

Challenge: I want to find the path to my computer's temp folder in VBA.

Solution: To discover the path to your computer's temp folder, use this code:

```
TempPath = Environ("Temp")
```

The `Environ` function provides a remarkable amount of information about a system. However, you should be careful because the variables available on one computer may not be available on another computer.

To discover which variables are available on your system, use this code:

```
Sub ListEnvironVariables()
    For i = 1 To 99
        Cells(i, 1).Value = Environ(i)
    Next i
End Sub
```

When you run this code, you get a listing similar to the one shown in Figure 131.

	A	B	C	D	E	F	G
1	ALLUSERSPROFILE=C:\ProgramData						
2	APPDATA=C:\Users\Bill\AppData\Roaming						
3	CLASSPATH=.;C:\Program Files\Java\jre1.5.0_07\lib\ext\QTJava.zip						
4	CommonProgramFiles=C:\Program Files\Common Files						
5	COMPUTERNAME=SUPERJOE						
6	ComSpec=C:\Windows\system32\cmd.exe						
7	FP_NO_HOST_CHECK=NO						
8	HOMEDRIVE=C:						
9	HOMEPATH=\Users\Bill						
10	LOCALAPPDATA=C:\Users\Bill\AppData\Local						

Figure 131. A list of environment variables and their values for one particular system.

Each entry in the list contains the environment variable name, an equals sign, and the value on that computer. When you know what variable names are available, you can pass the variable name in quotes:

```
Msgbox "You are signed in as " & Environ("USERNAME") & " to
domain " & _
    Environ("USERDOMAIN")
```

Some common environment variables that appear on most systems include:

```
ALLUSERSPROFILE
APPDATA
CommonProgramFiles
COMPUTERNAME
ComSpec
FP_NO_HOST_CHECK
HOMEDRIVE
HOMEPATH
LOGONSERVER
NUMBER_OF_PROCESSORS
OS
Path
PATHEXT
PROCESSOR_ARCHITECTURE
PROCESSOR_IDENTIFIER
PROCESSOR_LEVEL
PROCESSOR_REVISION
ProgramFiles
SESSIONNAME
SystemDrive
SystemRoot
TEMP
TMP
USERDOMAIN
USERNAME
```

Additional Details: The `Environ` function does not work in the Excel grid. You can build a user-defined function to make it available to the Excel interface. To do so, use this code:

```
Function MyEnviron(ByVal Key)
    MyEnviron = Environ(Key)
End Function
```

You can then use `=myenviron("COMPUTERNAME")` in a cell in Excel.

Summary: On a Windows PC, the VBA `Environ` function provides information about the path to the temp folder, the path to the application data folder, and more.

Source: http://www.mrexcel.com/forum/showthread.php?t=240975

USE EVALUATE IN VBA INSTEAD OF LOOPING THROUGH CELLS

Part 3

Challenge: You need to change all the cells in a range based on a calculation. You are planning on looping through all the cells with this code:

```
For Each cell In Selection
    cell.Value = -1 * cell.Value
Next cell
```

Solution: The Evaluate function can perform this function faster than a loop. Replace the above code with this single line of VBA:

```
Selection.Value = Evaluate(Selection.Address & "*-1")
```

I used the Timer code to compare the two methods. The loop method required 8.3 seconds for 100,000 cells. The evaluate method ran in 0.09 seconds—a 99% improvement in processing time!

Breaking It Down: You might thinking that this is a cool function that could be used to quickly transform any range of data. Unfortunately, most of Excel's functions will fail when used inside `Evaluate`. For example:

```
Range("C2:C99").Value = Evaluate("lower(C2:C99)")
```

will fill the range with the lowercase version of just cell C2. The general rule is that if the Excel function does not normally accept an array, the `Evaluate` function will not return an array.

However, PGC01 at the MrExcel message board wrote an excellent tutorial, demonstrating how to coax `Evaluate` to work on a range by introducing an extra dummy range outside the function. PGC01 would use the following expression to solve the above problem:

```
Range("C2:C99").Value = Evaluate("if(ROW(2:99),LOWER(C2:C99))")
```

In this case, `ROW(2:99)` returns the numbers from 2 to 99. When a logical test returns any numeric value other than 0, the result will be considered `TRUE`. Thus, the text inside the function is saying, "Here are 98 vertical true values. For each one, calculate the lowercase version of the corresponding cell from C2:C99."

Additional Details: You can also use Evaluate to change a horizontal vector:

```
Range ("A1:J1") = Evaluate ("if(row(1:10),upper(A1:J1))")
```

Using Evaluate on a rectangular range is a bit trickier. You need to introduce both a vertical array such as `ROW(1:10)` and a horizontal array such as either `COLUMN(A:J)` or `TRANSPOSE(ROW(1:10))`. The following code uses two IF functions, the first of which introduces a vertical array and the second of which introduces a horizontal array:

```
Range ("A1:L23") = Evaluate ("IF(ROW(1:23),IF(TRANSPOSE(ROW(1:
12)),LOWER(A1:L23)))")
```

You can generalize this code to work on any range. The following code performs the `UPPER` function on all cells in the selection:

```
Sub RectangularProper()
    ' Convert all cells in the selection to proper case
    Dim rngRectangle As Range, rngRows As Range, rngColumns
As Range
    Set rngRectangle = Selection
    ' Define a vertical vector array
    Set rngRows = rngRectangle.Resize(, 1)
    ' define a horizontal vector array
    Set rngColumns = rngRectangle.Resize(1)
    rngRectangle = Evaluate("IF(ROW(" & rngRows.Address & "),
    —
        IF(COLUMN(" & rngColumns.Address & _
        "),PROPER(" & rngRectangle.Address & ")))")
End Sub
```

While the examples here deal with changing the case of text using `UPPER`, `LOWER`, and `PROPER`, you can use them to perform calculations with most of Excel's functions.

Gotcha: Although this method improves the speed of your code substantially, it also makes your code far more difficult for someone else to understand.

Summary: You can use Evaluate to perform simple transformations on vector ranges.

Source: http://www.mrexcel.com/forum/showthread.php?t=246143

RENAME EACH WORKSHEET BASED ON ITS A1 VALUE

Challenge: You have a workbook that has numerous worksheets. The title of each worksheet is in cell A1. You want to name each worksheet based on its cell A1 value.

Solution: You can quickly and automatically solve this problem by using a tiny bit of VBA code. Here's how:

Part 3

1. Press Alt+F11.
2. Press Ctrl+G to open the immediate pane.
3. Type the following code and then press Enter:

```
For Each ws In Worksheets : ws.Name = Left(ws.Cells(1, 1).Value, 31) : Next
```

This is actually a three-line macro, with the lines separated with colons.

Additional Details: If any value in cell A1 contains more than 31 characters, the name is shortened to 31 characters.

If any worksheet has an illegal character in cell A1, the macro stops with an error. For worksheet names, the illegal characters are ', *, /, :, ?, [, \, and]. To simply skip the worksheets that contain illegal characters, you can use this macro:

```
Sub NoErrorNameThem()
    On Error Resume Next
    For Each ws In ThisWorkbook.Worksheets
        ws.Name = Left(ws.Cells(1, 1).Value, 31)
    Next
    On Error GoTo 0
End Sub
```

To use alternate characters instead of the illegal characters, use this macro:

```
Sub ReplaceIllegalCharactersNameThem()
    For Each ws In ThisWorkbook.Worksheets
        NewName = ""
        For i = 1 To Len(ws.Name)
            ThisChar = Mid(ws.Name, i, 1)
            Select Case ThisChar
                Case "'", "*", "/", ":", "?", "[", "\", "]"
                    NewName = NewName & " "
                Case Else
```

```
                NewName = NewName & ThisChar
        End Select
     Next i
     ws.Name = Left(NewName, 31)
   Next
End Sub
```

Summary: You can use a short macro to rename worksheets.

USE A CUSTOM PULL FUNCTION INSTEAD OF INDIRECT WITH A CLOSED WORKBOOK

Challenge: As you know from several other topics, the `INDIRECT` function is fairly cool. Say that you want to use `INDIRECT` to go out to a variable workbook and grab a value. You store each day's records in a workbook with a name similar to `C:\aaa\Sales20090801.xls`. `INDIRECT` does not work in this situation because it cannot point to a closed workbook. It can point to an open workbook, but you would not want to open 365 workbooks every time you had to calculate the worksheet.

Solution: As documented by Frank Kabel, at http://www.dailydoseofexcel. com/archives/2004/12/01/indirect-and-closed-workbooks/, there are three workarounds for this problem. The one I use is Harlan Grove's custom function `PULL`. The function can even return a range of cells from the closed workbook, so it can be used as the table range in a `VLOOKUP`.

Follow these steps to install PULL in your workbook:

1. Browse to http://members.aol.com/hrlngrv/pull.zip to get the latest version of PULL.
2. Unzip pull.bas from the zip file.
3. Open the workbook where you want to use `PULL`.
4. Switch to the VBA editor by pressing Alt+F11.
5. From the VBA editor menu, choose File, Import.
6. Browse to and select pull.bas.

Figure 132 illustrates the use of `PULL`. Column A contains a date. Based on this date, you want to look up sales from a different daily workbook. All the workbooks are stored in `C:\aaa\`, with names such as SALESyymmdd.xls.

Cell C3 formats the date in YYYYMMDD format using the formula `=TEXT(A3,"yyyymmdd")`.

Cell D3 builds the file path and name with `="C:\aaa\[Sales"&C3&".xls]"`.

Cell E3 contains the worksheet name in the external workbook.

Cell F3 contains the range name in the external workbook.

Cell G3 builds an external VLOOKUP using =VLOOKUP(B3,PULL("'"&D3&E3& "'!"&F3),2).

In real life, you may opt to forgo columns C:G and use this single formula:

```
=VLOOKUP(B3,PULL("'C:\aaa\[Sales"&TEXT(A3,"yyyymmdd")&".xls]
Sheet1'!$A$4:$B$12"),2,FALSE)
```

		f_x =VLOOKUP(B3,PULL(""&D3&E3&"!"&F3),2)				
	A	B	C	D	E	F	G
1							
2	Date	Product		File Name	WS Name	Range	Result
3	8/1/08	A	20080801	C:\aaa\[Sales20080801.xls]	Sheet1	$A$4:$B$12	1203

Figure 132. Harlan Grove's custom PULL function can replicate INDIRECT for external workbooks.

Gotcha: Be careful with PULL. The function actually opens a new instance of Excel, opens the external workbook, and then builds an array using a cell from the external workbook. This works fine for a few cells, but it would take a very long time to calculate 10,000 formulas, each containing a PULL function.

Summary: You can use the custom PULL function to extend the INDIRECT concept to closed external workbooks.

IN VBA, DETERMINE THE NUMBER OF THE ACTIVE WORKSHEET

Challenge: You want to refer to the worksheet two sheets to the right of the active worksheet in VBA. How can you figure out the index number of the current worksheet?

Solution: You can figure out the index number of the current worksheet by using ActiveSheet.Index.

	A	B	C	D	E	F	
1							
2							
3							
4							
5							

◄ ◄ ► ►│ \ E.R. \ **Patient Accounting** / Adoptive Center / Laboratory /

Figure 133. How can a macro tell that you are on worksheet 2?

In Figure 133, the active worksheet could be referred to as either `Worksheets(2)` or `Worksheets("Patient Accounting")`. In my VBA books and seminars, I tell people that it is better to use `Worksheets("Patient Accounting")`. However, in some situations, you might really need to refer to a worksheet with an index number. Perhaps if you needed to refer to a sheet two sheets to the right of the active sheet, you could refer to `Worksheets(x+2)`. Is there an easy way to figure out the index number of the active sheet?

You might figure it out using a brute-force loop:

```
Ctr = 1
For each WS in Activeworkbook.Worksheets
    If WS.Name = ActiveSheet.Name then Exit For
    Ctr = Ctr + 1
Next WS
```

However, this is the long way around. The `Index` property of a worksheet identifies the location of the worksheet within the workbook. You could use `Worksheets("Patient Accounting")`.Index to return the number 2, or you could simply use `ActiveSheet.Index` to return the number 2.

Summary: The `Index` property returns the position of a worksheet in the workbook.

CREATE WORKSHEET NAMES BY USING THE FILL HANDLE

Challenge: You type `Jan` into a cell, grab the fill handle, and drag down five cells. Excel types `Marcia`, `Cindy`, `Bobby`, `Greg`, and `Peter`. No, sorry. Excel types `Feb`, `Mar`, `Apr`, `May`, `Jun`. The fill handle can do all sorts of amazing fills, handling months, quarters, weekdays, dates, and so on. If you set up a custom list, Excel can even extend your list of departments, products, or Brady Bunch kids. The fill handle is so useful, wouldn't it be cool if you could use it to copy the current worksheet into new worksheets that have appropriate names? For example, if you have a worksheet named Tuesday and used the fill handle, you could have Excel add new worksheets `Wednesday`, `Thursday`, and `Friday` to the right of `Tuesday`.

Solution: Add the following code to your Personal Macro Workbook:

```
Sub FillHandleSheets()
'
' Make copies of the current worksheet
' The new worksheets will have names as if using the Fill Handle
'
```

```
Dim ws As Worksheet ' original worksheet, the one to copy
Dim wst As Worksheet ' worksheet to hold fill handle series
Dim wb As Workbook ' temporary workbook to hold fill handle
series
Dim wbt As Workbook ' activeworkbook
Dim wsn As Worksheet ' most recently created sheet

Set ws = ActiveSheet
Set wbt = ActiveWorkbook
Application.ScreenUpdating = False

' Which index number is the current sheet?
' Note that Ctr will be 1 less than the current sheet, so that
in the loop, you can use Ctr+i
Ctr = ws.Index - 1

x = InputBox( _
    Prompt:="How many new worksheets to create?", _
    Title:="Fill Handle for Worksheets", Default:=11)

' Add a temporary workbook with a single worksheet
Set wb = Workbooks.Add(xlWBATWorksheet)
Set wst = wb.Worksheets(1)

' Enter current worksheet name in cell A1 of temp worksheet
wst.Cells(1, 1).Formula = "'" & ws.Name
' Using xlFillSeries instead of xlFillDefault will allow
' a number such as "1" to extend to "1", "2", "3".
wst.Cells(1, 1).AutoFill Destination:=wst.Cells(1, 1).Resize(x
+ 1, 1), Type:=xlFillSeries

For i = 2 To x + 1
    ws.Copy after:=wbt.Worksheets(Ctr + i - 1)
    Set wsn = ActiveSheet
    ' if duplicate name, don't bother renaming
    On Error Resume Next
    wsn.Name = wst.Cells(i, 1).Value
    On Error GoTo 0
Next i

' Close the temporary workbook
```

Part 3

```
wb.Close SaveChanges:=False

` Go back to the original worksheet
wbt.Activate
ws.Select
Application.ScreenUpdating = True


End Sub
```

This macro creates a temporary workbook. It types the sheet name into cell A1 of the temporary workbook and then fills the series. A loop then starts copying the original worksheet and uses names from the filled series.

Press Alt+F8, choose the macro, choose Options, and assign the shortcut key Ctrl+Shift+F to the macro.

When you run the macro, Excel asks how many sheets you want to insert (Figure 134). Because my most common situation is copying Jan to the remaining 11 months, I used 11 as the default in the input box. Feel free to adjust it to your most common situation.

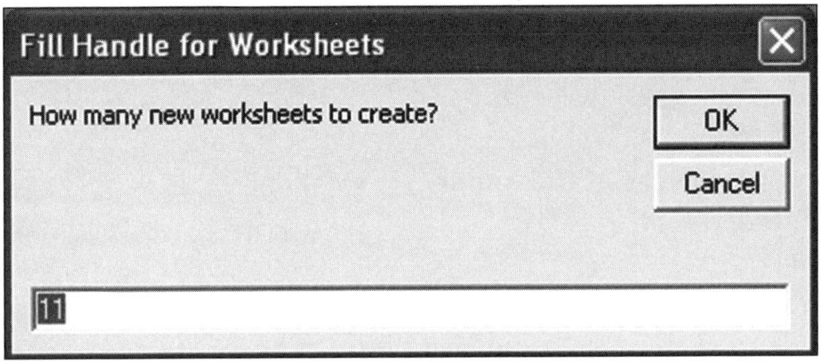

Figure 134. Excel asks how many sheets to copy.

The macro works well for months, day names, and quarters. It even works for numbers, a slight improvement on the fill handle because you need to hold down the Ctrl key to coax 1 to fill 1, 2, 3. However, the macro has problems with dates.

The standard U.S. date format is 9/15/2009 for September 15, 2009. This is an illegal sheet name because you cannot include slashes in a worksheet name. So, although no one would have a worksheet name like 9/15/2009 to begin with, you might have worksheet names that spell out dates in another format. For example, 9-15, Sep 15, and 9-15-2009 are all valid worksheet names. Here is the problem: When the macro types those names into cell A1 of a temporary worksheet, Excel instantly converts the value to 9/15/2009. The filled series contains slashes, which are invalid worksheet names.

Even more frustrating, the logic to figure out the custom number format to replicate the original date is difficult. You can't learn the correct format from

`Cells(1, 1).NumberFormat` because in most cases, typing the value causes Excel to change the number format.

As a compromise, the macro types the worksheet name preceded by an apostrophe. This allows `9-15` and `Sep 15` entries to work through the end of the month. Note that these text entries work just like `Room 101` works in the fill handle. `Sep 15` accurately jumps to `Sep 16`, but `Jan 31` inaccurately jumps to `Jan 32`! Figure 135 shows several examples of workbooks where the first worksheet was copied using the macro in this chapter.

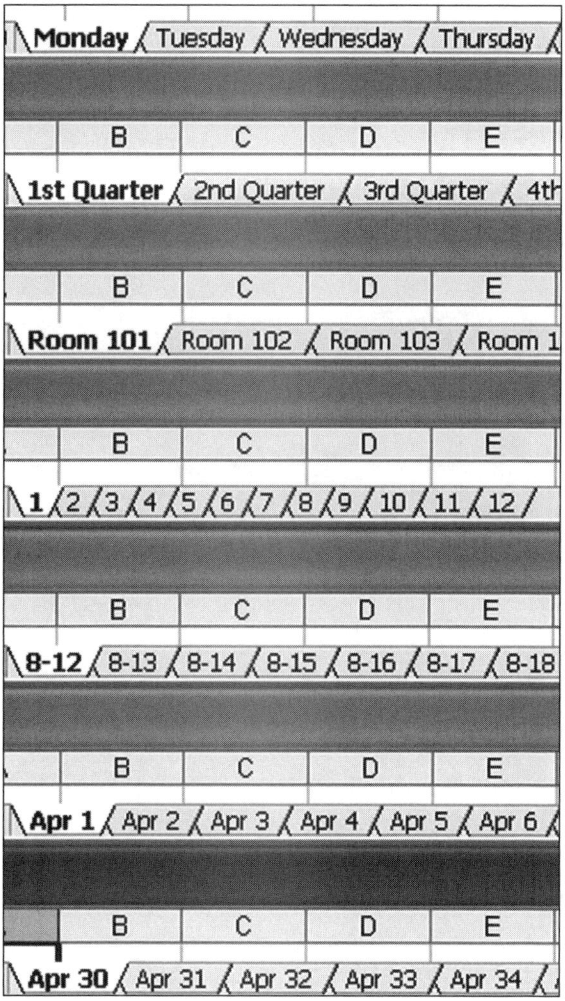

Figure 135. The macro correctly handles many items but fails when extending Apr 30.

Tip: If you define a custom list, you can have this macro use the names in the custom list.

Summary: Perhaps Microsoft will add this functionality to a future version of Excel. Until it does, use this macro to copy worksheets and change their names to a known series.

COPY THE PERSONAL MACRO WORKBOOK TO ANOTHER COMPUTER

Challenge: You have a bunch of cool macros in your Personal Macro Workbook. You would like to get them in a co-worker's Personal Macro Workbook.

Setup: This process is not as daunting as it may seem. Basically, you need to save your Personal.xls file with a new name, send that file to the co-worker, and drag modules from your workbook to your co-worker's workbook in the VBA editor.

Solution: Follow these steps to save your Personal.xls file:

1. Open the VBA editor by pressing Alt+F11.

2. Find Personal.xls in the Project Explorer. Click on this entry once.

3. Click the Save icon in the toolbar to ensure that your latest changes are saved (Figure 136).

4. Press Ctrl+G to display the immediate window.

5. In the immediate window, type `ThisWorkbook.SaveAs "C:\MyPersonal.xls"`. You can use any folder you like, but make sure to save it with a name other than Personal.xls.

6. Close Excel.

7. Navigate to the folder from step 5. E-mail `MyPersonal.xls` to your co-worker.

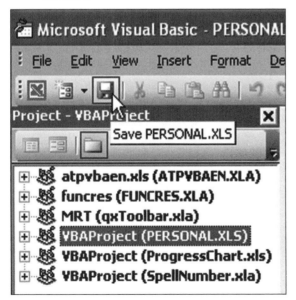

Figure 136. You choose Personal.xls in the Project Explorer.

On your co-worker's computer, follow these steps:

1. Open Excel.
2. Open to VBA editor by pressing Alt+F11. If this computer does not already have a Personal.xls file in the Project Explorer, create one by choosing to record a new macro and specifying that it should be saved in Personal. xls. When the macro recorder starts, move to a new cell and then stop recording. This will create the Personal.xls in the proper folder.
3. Open MyPersonal.xls on this computer.
4. In the VBA Project Explorer, expand Personal.xls so you can see the modules entry. Expand MyPersonal.xls so you can see each individual module.
5. Drag the modules from MyPersonal.xls into the Modules folder in Personal. xls (Figure 137).
6. Close Excel. Reopen Excel. All the macros will have been copied into `Personal.xls` on the new computer.

Part 3

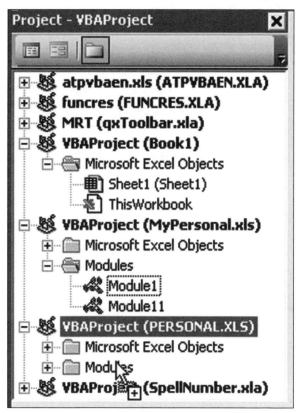

Figure 137. You drag modules from `MyPersonal.xls` to `Personal.xls` on the new computer.

Summary: You can copy macros from your `Personal.xls` file to other computers.

ADD FILTER TO SELECTION FUNCTIONALITY

Challenge: Access offers a cool feature called Filter to Selection. If you are looking at a data sheet in Access, click the value `XYZ` in `Field22` and click Filter to Selection, Access shows you only the records where `Field22` is equal to `XYZ`. Excel does not offer this feature. Instead, you have to turn on the Filter (known as AutoFilter in Excel 2003 and before) and choose the desired value from the Filter dropdown.

Solution: It takes only a few lines of code to replicate this feature in VBA. Add the following macros to your Personal Macro Workbook. (To get a Personal Macro Workbook, see "Make a Personal Macro Workbook.")

```
Sub FilterToSelection()
    ColNum = ActiveCell.Column - _
        (ActiveCell.CurrentRegion.Column - 1)
    Selection.AutoFilter _
        Field:=ColNum, Criteria1:=ActiveCell
End Sub


Sub AutoFilterToggle()
    Selection.AutoFilter
End Sub
```

Assign the macros to shortcut keys or to custom buttons on your toolbar or Quick Access toolbar in Excel 2007.

Using the First Macro

To use the first macro, in any data set that has a row of headings at the top, select one cell in any column. Click the Filter to Selection icon, as shown in Figure 138.

	A	B	C	D	E	F	G
1			Region	Product	Date	Customer	Quantity
2			East	XYZ	1/1/2008	Ford	1000
3			Central	DEF	1/2/2008	Verizon	100
4			East	DEF	1/4/2008	Merck	800
5			East	XYZ	1/4/2008	Texaco	400
6			East	DEF	1/7/2008	State Farm	1000
7			East	ABC	1/7/2008	General Motors	400
8			Central	ABC	1/9/2008	General Motors	800
9			Central	XYZ	1/10/2008	Wal Mart	900

Figure 138. To see all the General Motors records, select one cell that contains General Motors and click Filter to Selection.

Excel hides all the rows that do not contain `General Motors` in column F (Figure 139).

	C	D	E	F	G
1	Region ▼	Produc ▼	Date ▼	Customer ▼	Quant ▼
7	East	ABC	1/7/2008	General Motors	400
8	Central	ABC	1/9/2008	General Motors	800
17	West	ABC	1/23/2008	General Motors	800
21	East	DEF	1/29/2008	General Motors	700
24	East	ABC	1/31/2008	General Motors	800
30	Central	ABC	2/9/2008	General Motors	300

Figure 139. You can filter the data set to show only General Motors records.

Note that the macro is additive: After filtering by customer, you can filter to just ABC records in column D by selecting D8 and clicking Filter to Selection again. You end up with just the sales of ABC to General Motors. Choose the word `Central` in C8 and click Filter to Selection. You now have just the Central region sales of ABC to General Motors.

To return to all records, you can run the `AutoFilterToggle` macro or simply turn off the Filter feature. In Excel 2007, you click the large Filter icon on the Data tab. In Excel 2003, you select Data, Filter, Show All or Data, Filter, AutoFilter.

How the Code Works

The heart of the code is the line with the `AutoFilter` method. In this case, the `AutoFilter` method is applied to the Selection. You are taking advantage of the fact that applying `AutoFilter` to a single cell automatically applies the filter to the current region. Two named parameters control `AutoFilter` in this macro. The first parameter is the Field parameter. This is an integer that identifies the column number. In Figure 138, notice that columns A and B are blank. Thus, the current region is C2:H564. The `AutoFilter` method numbers columns starting with 1 as the leftmost column in the data set. Because column C is the first column in the data set, you specify `Field:=1` to filter based on column C.

To make the macro more general, you filter to the field number of the active cell. This is stored in a variable called `ColNum`. You'll see how `ColNum` is assigned below.

The second parameter for the `AutoFilter` method is the Criteria1 parameter. To filter the data set to only Exxon customer records, you might use:

Selection.AutoFilter Field:=4, Criteria1:="Exxon"

The macro specifies a `Criteria1` of `ActiveCell`. The `ActiveCell` property returns a range object that contains the one cell that is the active cell. Note that someone might select a rectangular range such as C8:H13. Only one of these cells is the active cell. It is the cell listed in the name box. Technically, you should be asking for `ActiveCell`.Value, but it turns out that the .Value property is the default property returned from a range, so simply filtering to `ActiveCell` causes Excel to filter to General Motors in Figure 139.

Handling the Unexpected

Most data sets I encounter start in column A. Why would anyone leave columns A and B blank? If you could guarantee that your data sets would always start in column A, then it would be easy to identify the Field parameter as:

`Field:=ActiveCell.Column`

If you are in column C, then `ActiveCell.Column` is 3. Simple enough.

But the macro goes an extra step and envisions someone daring to start a data set in a column other than column A. The logic works sort of like this:

- What column is the active cell in? It's in column F, which is column 6.
- Okay. What column is the leftmost column in the data set? It's in column C, which is 3.
- Hmmm. Okay. Then how many blank columns are to the left of the first column? Well, that is the column number of column C minus 1 (i.e., 3 – 1, or 2). In most cases, the calculation for the number of blank columns evaluates to 0. Column A is column number 1, and 1 – 1 is 0.

To translate this logic to VBA, Figure 140 asks many of these questions in the VBA immediate window.

```
Immediate
 print activecell.Address
 $F$7
 Print activecell.column
  6
 print activecell.CurrentRegion.Address
 $C$1:$H$564
 print activecell.CurrentRegion.Columns.Count
  6
 print activecell.CurrentRegion.Columns(1).column
  3
 print activecell.CurrentRegion.Column
  3
 print activecell.CurrentRegion.Column - 1
  2
```

Figure 140. There are some logical steps in calculating the field parameter.

The active cell is F7.

Cell F7 is column number 6.

The current region around F7 is C1:H564. To find the current region, Excel proceeds from the active cell in all directions and stops when it encounters the edge of the spreadsheet or an edge of the data set. An edge of the data set requires the cells in the row below the data set to be completely blank.

When you ask for `CurrentRegion.Columns`, you are referring to six columns. You might feel compelled to ask for `CurrentRegion.Columns(1).Column` to find out that the data set starts in column 3. However, a shortcut is to ask for the Column property of `CurrentRegion.Columns`. The Column property happens to return the column number of the first column in the range. So, when you ask for `CurrentRegion.Column`, you get a 3, which indicates that the first column of the current region is in column C.

Part 3

The first line of the macro goes through all this logic to figure out that Customer is the fourth column in the current data set. `ActiveCell.Column` is 6. The number of blank columns to the left of the data set is 2. This is `ActiveCell.CurrentRegion.Column (3)` minus 1. So, the `ColNum` variable is 6 - 2, or 4.

In order to handle the unexpected, the macro grows to two lines of code. The first line calculates the column number within the current data set:

```
ColNum = ActiveCell.Column - _
    (ActiveCell.CurrentRegion.Column - 1)
```

The second line of code turns on `AutoFilter` and filters the specific column to the value in the current cell:

```
Selection.AutoFilter _
    Field:=ColNum, Criteria1:=ActiveCell
```

Using the Second Macro

The second macro needs to turn off `AutoFilter`. If you use the `AutoFilter` method with no parameters, it simply toggles the `AutoFilter` dropdown on or off. If a data set is filtered and you use `Selection.AutoFilter`, Excel turns off `AutoFilter` and shows all records again. So the second macro is one line of code:

```
Selection.AutoFilter
```

Tip: After this book was written, I learned that this functionality is already in Excel! See the Learn Excel podcast episode 851.

Summary: You can use macros to add the Filter to Selection functionality to Excel.

USE A MACRO TO HIGHLIGHT THE ACTIVE CELL

Challenge: Microsoft changed the selection highlighting in Excel 2007. If you select 20 cells, Excel highlights those cells in super-ultra-light blue. Imagine if you had 5 gallons of white paint and dropped in one drop of blue paint. That paint would have more color than the new selection color in Excel 2007. You want to highlight the active cell so it's easier to spot.

Solution: There is a cool event macro that can add a splash of color to the selection and draw crosshairs to help you locate the row and column where the active cell is located. In Figure 141, bright yellow highlight indicates the active cell in D16. Lighter yellow is used to mark column D and Row 16. As you move the cell pointer, the highlights change. Figure 142 shows the crosshairs pattern for B20.

D16			f_x 34277	
	A	B	C	D
11	Account 10	40460	21385	14956
12	Account 11	36457	30328	12320
13	Account 12	38841	18278	20592
14	Account 13	49218	45579	26504
15	Account 14	29406	15151	38375
16	Account 15	46226	41515	34277
17	Account 16	40699	40292	31350

Figure 141. The macro draws yellow highlights to help you locate the active cell.

B20			f_x 12168
	A	B	C
11	Account 10	40460	21385
12	Account 11	36457	30328
13	Account 12	38841	18278
14	Account 13	49218	45579
15	Account 14	29406	15151
16	Account 15	46226	41515
17	Account 16	40699	40292
18	Account 17	35101	37310
19	Account 18	44115	41904
20	Account 19	12168	20260
21	Account 20	36339	39528

Figure 142. As you move to a different cell, the yellow highlights move to track the active cell.

This macro runs every time you move to a new cell in the worksheet. The macro works for one worksheet.

Note: If you want it to work on all worksheets, put this code in the SheetSelectionChange macro in the ThisWorkbook code pane.

Follow the instructions in "Create an Event Handler Macro" to open the worksheet code module. Then paste in the following code:

```
Private Sub Worksheet_SelectionChange(ByVal Target As Range)
    Dim wi As Window
    Set wi = ActiveWindow
    Cells.Interior.ColorIndex = xlNone
    Target.Interior.ColorIndex = 6
    For i = wi.VisibleRange.Rows(1).Row To Target.Row - 1
        Cells(i, Target.Column).Interior.ColorIndex = 36
    Next i

    For i = wi.VisibleRange.Columns(1).Column To Target.Column - 1
        Cells(Target.Row, i).Interior.ColorIndex = 36
    Next i
End Sub
```

Here is how the code works:

The first line indicates that you will have access to a range variable called `Target`:

```
Private Sub Worksheet_SelectionChange(ByVal Target As Range)
```

This is an object variable, so it not only tells you the value of the active cell (`Target.Value` or simply `Target`), it can tell you information about the active cell, such as `Target.Row` or `Target.Column`

The `Dim` and `Set` lines define an objet variable to refer to the current window in Excel:

```
Dim wi As Window
Set wi = ActiveWindow
```

While many macros refer to the current worksheet, you need to refer to the active window here so you can capture the top row in the visible portion of the worksheet.

This line resets the color of all cells to have no fill:

```
Cells.Interior.ColorIndex = xlNone
```

This erases all the yellow highlighting drawn in by the last running of the macro. Because you don't specify which cells, this resets all cells in the entire worksheet.

This line changes the color of the selection to bright yellow:

```
Target.Interior.ColorIndex = 6
```

It uses the old Excel 2003 concept of ColorIndex so that it will work in either Excel 2003 or Excel 2007. Excel 2007 supports more than 56 colors, so you can use the RGB function to return any of 16 million colors.

```
Target.Interior.Color = RGB(200,200,228)
```

Next, you draw in the crosshairs in a lighter yellow. This involves looping from the top row in the visible section of the worksheet down to the row above the selection. To find the top row of the visible section of the worksheet, use `wi.VisibleRange.Rows(1).Row`. To find the row immediately above the selection, use `Target.Row - 1`. The following loop goes through each of the cells from the selection up to the top of the visible worksheet:

```
For i = wi.VisibleRange.Rows(1).Row To Target.Row - 1
    Cells(i, Target.Column). Interior.ColorIndex = 36
Next i
```

The line of code inside the loop colors the cell at the intersection of i and the same column as the `Target`. `36` is the color code for light yellow.

Only a minor adjustment is needed to build a second loop to color in all the cells in the current row from the left edge of the worksheet up to one column to the left of the selection:

```
For i = wi.VisibleRange.Columns(1).Column To Target.Column - 1
    Cells(Target.Row, i).Interior.ColorIndex = 36
Next i
```

You might be wondering what would happen if `Target` is the top row of the visible window. Say that you select cell A11 in Figure 142. The macro clears all the yellow formatting from all cells in the worksheet, resetting all cells back to their original color. The macro then colors the `Target` cell bright yellow. This colors A11.

The first line of the loop uses row 11 as the first row of the visible window. It uses row 10 as the row above the target cell. When the loop says `For i = 11 to 10`, Excel simply skips the loop. Nothing gets colored light yellow in the first loop. Similarly, the second loop is skipped as Excel tries to loop from 1 to 0.

Excel does a very quick and smooth job of running event handler macros run. As you move from cell to cell in the worksheet, Excel constantly redraws the yellow highlights to help you find the active cell.

Summary: An event handler macro can help you keep track of the active cell.

REMOVE THE CAPTION BAR
FROM A USER FORM

Challenge: You want to show a user form in Excel and prevent users from closing the form by clicking the red X close button in the corner.

Solution: You can hide the caption bar—and therefore also the red X close button—in a user form. Doing so requires a bit of Windows API.

One problem is that no one can move the form if the caption is missing. The last bit of code in the macro below therefore uses the `MouseDown` method to allow the form to be moved.

In VBA, you select Insert Userform. Draw one button on the form (or users won't have any way to close the form!). Right-click the form and choose View Code. Paste the following code into the code pane for the form:

```
Private Declare Function FindWindow Lib "user32" _
    Alias "FindWindowA" (ByVal lpClassName As String, _
    ByVal lpWindowName As String) As Long
Private Declare Function GetWindowLong Lib "user32" _
    Alias "GetWindowLongA" (ByVal hwnd As Long, _
    ByVal nIndex As Long) As Long
Private Declare Function SetWindowLong Lib "user32" _
    Alias "SetWindowLongA" (ByVal hwnd As Long, _
    ByVal nIndex As Long, ByVal dwNewLong As Long) As Long
Private Declare Function DrawMenuBar Lib "user32" _
    (ByVal hwnd As Long) As Long
Private Declare Function SendMessage Lib "user32" _
    Alias "SendMessageA" (ByVal hwnd As Long, _
    ByVal wMsg As Long, ByVal wParam As Long, _
    lParam As Any) As Long
Private Declare Function ReleaseCapture Lib "user32" () As Long
Private Const GWL_STYLE As Long = (-16)
Private wHandle As Long

Private Sub CommandButton1_Click()
    Unload Me
End Sub

Private Sub UserForm_Initialize()
    Dim frm As Long, frmstyle As Long
    If Val(Application.Version) >= 9 Then
        wHandle = FindWindow("ThunderDFrame", Me.Caption)
    Else
        wHandle = FindWindow("ThunderXFrame", Me.Caption)
```

```
    End If
    If wHandle = 0 Then Exit Sub
    frm = GetWindowLong(wHandle, GWL_STYLE)
    frm = frm Or &HC00000
    SetWindowLong wHandle, -16, frmstyle
    DrawMenuBar wHandle
End Sub


Private Sub UserForm_MouseDown(ByVal Button As Integer, _
    ByVal Shift As Integer, ByVal X As Single, ByVal Y As Single)
    'Code to drag the form

    If wHandle = 0 Then Exit Sub
    If Button = 1 Then
        ReleaseCapture
        SendMessage wHandle, &HA1, 2, 0
    End If
End Sub
```

In a regular module, use this line of code to launch the form:

```
Sub ShowForm()
    UserForm1.Show
End Sub
```

When you run the macro, you have a user form that must be dismissed using the button on the form instead of using the red X close button (Figure 143).

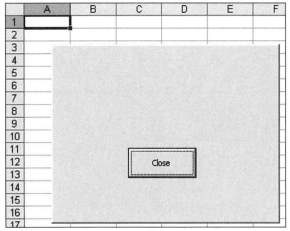

Figure 143. You can create a user form that doesn't have a red X close button.

Summary: You can prevent the red X close button from appearing in a user form.

Source: www.mrexcel.com/forum/showthread.php?t=45533

KEEP A BUTTON IN VIEW

Challenge: You have a worksheet that contains 10,000 rows of data. As people scroll through the workbook, you want the macro button to always be in view.

Solution: One option is to use Freeze Panes to keep a few rows visible at the top of the screen and place the button in that area. If you are in Excel 2003, you could use a custom floating toolbar for this. In any recent version of Excel, you could use a modeless user form to hold the button. Another method, as described in this topic, is to use the worksheet `SelectionChange` macro to reposition the button at the top of the screen.

Part 3

Add a forms button to your worksheet. If you use the Forms dialog, the button will have a name such as `Button 1`. If you use an ActiveX control, it will have a name such as `CommandButton1`. This concept works with any other control (such as a combo box). Simply replace the name of the control in the `ActiveSheet.Shapes("Button 1")` line of code.

Access the code pane for your worksheet by right-clicking the tab name in Excel and choosing View Code. Paste the following code into the code pane:

```
Private Sub Worksheet_SelectionChange(ByVal Target As Range)
    Dim ScrollRw As Long
    Dim ScrollCol As Integer
    ScrollRw = ActiveWindow.ScrollRow
    ScrollCol = ActiveWindow.ScrollColumn
    With ActiveSheet.Shapes("Button 1")
        .Top = Cells(ScrollRw, ScrollCol).Top
        .Left = Cells(ScrollRw, ScrollCol).Left
    End With
End Sub
```

As long as the user uses the keyboard to navigate the worksheet, the button will reliably stay in the top left of the window. Using Page Down, Page Up, Alt+Page Down, and Alt+Page Up to scroll works best. If a user scrolls by using the arrow keys, the button annoyingly dance around. If a user scrolls using the wheel mouse or the scrollbars, the button disappears until the user clicks inside the worksheet.

Additional Details: The button has a `Top` property and `Left` property. These indicate the distance from A1 in pixels or points. The macro finds the top row in the visible window by using `ActiveWindow.ScrollRow`. The macro finds the left column in the visible window by using `ActiveWindow.ScrollColumn`. These two lines might tell you that the top-left cell in the window is G501. Interestingly, you can learn the distance from the top-left corner of A1 to cell G501 by using `Range("G1").Top` and `Range("G1").Left`.

The lines inside the With block assign the `Top` property for the button to be the same as the `Top` property for the cell at the top-left corner of the visible window.

As you scroll through the worksheet, the button stays at the top of the window (Figures 144 and 145).

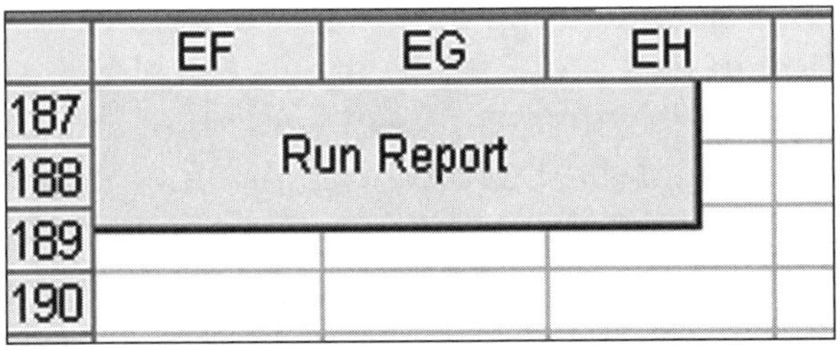

Figure 144. If you scroll down, the button moves.

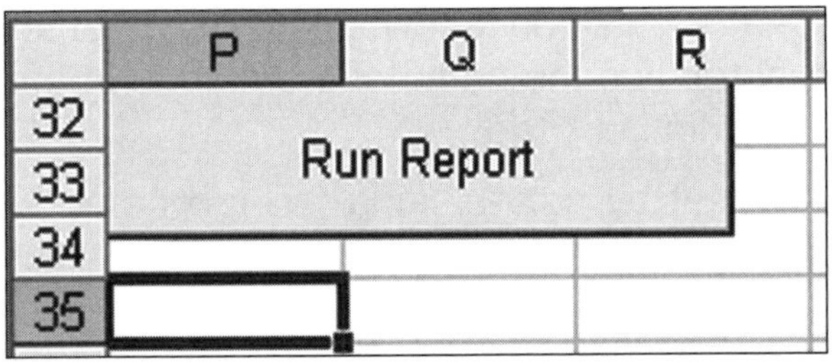

Figure 145. The button moves as you scroll through the worksheet.

Summary: You can use a macro to keep a button visible in a worksheet.

Source: http://www.mrexcel.com/forum/showthread.php?t=86319

ADD A RIGHT-CLICK MENU TO A USER FORM

Challenge: You've designed a custom user form. You want to add a right-click menu (also called a context menu) to it.

Solution: Many people are used to right-clicking in Excel. If you've designed a custom user form, people might want to right-click the form to get additional options. A solution Haluk posted at the MrExcel message board takes advantage of the user form's `MouseDown` event. This event is run when someone clicks on the user form. A variable called `Button` indicates whether the left or right mouse button is clicked. Another variable, `Shift`, indicates which combinations of the Shift, Ctrl, and Alt keys are held down.

For the `Button` variable, 1 indicates a left-click, and 2 indicates a right-click.

For the Shift variable, 0 indicates that no keys are used in combination with the mouse click, 1 indicates the Shift key, 2 indicates the Ctrl key, and 4 indicates the Alt key. If someone holds down multiple keys, Excel adds the values (for example, 5 indicates Alt+Shift). Here is the complete table of possible values for the `Shift` variable:

Shift Value	Meaning
0	No keys
1	Shift
2	Ctrl
3	Shift+Ctrl
4	Alt
5	Shift+Alt
6	Ctrl+Alt
7	Shift+Ctrl+Alt

The event handler macro first makes sure that `Button` is 2 and `Shift` is 0.

The macro uses API calls to build a menu. You can customize the menu by adding additional options to the menu, using:

```
AppendMenu hMenu, MF_STRING, 1, "Menu Text Here"
```

In this case, the 1 indicates the value returned to the macro if that menu item is selected.

The `TrackPopupMenu` function displays the menu and determines which item is selected by the person using the form. The selection is returned to the variable `ret`. After this line of code, the `ret` variable indicates the numeric menu value selected.

Later in the macro, a `Case Select` handles the possible menu choices and calls an appropriate procedure for each.

Place all this code in the code pane for the user form:

```
Private Type POINTAPI
    X As Long
    Y As Long
End Type
'

Private Declare Function CreatePopupMenu Lib "user32" () As Long
Private Declare Function TrackPopupMenuEx Lib "user32" _
        (ByVal hMenu As Long, ByVal wFlags As Long, ByVal X As Long,
ByVal Y As Long, _
ByVal hWnd As Long, ByVal lptpm As Any) As Long
```

Part
3

```
Private Declare Function AppendMenu Lib "user32" Alias "AppendMenuA"
_
        (ByVal hMenu As Long, ByVal wFlags As Long, ByVal wIDNewItem
As Long, _
        ByVal lpNewItem As Any) As Long
Private Declare Function DestroyMenu Lib "user32" (ByVal hMenu As
Long) As Long
Private Declare Function GetCursorPos Lib "user32" (lpPoint As
POINTAPI) As Long
Private Declare Function FindWindow Lib "user32" Alias "FindWindowA"
_
        (ByVal lpClassName As String, ByVal lpWindowName As String)
As Long
'
Const MF_CHECKED = &H8&
Const MF_APPEND = &H100&
Const TPM_LEFTALIGN = &H0&
Const MF_SEPARATOR = &H800&
Const MF_STRING = &H0&
Const TPM_RETURNCMD = &H100&
Const TPM_RIGHTBUTTON = &H2&
'
Dim hMenu As Long
Dim hWnd As Long
'
Private Sub UserForm_Initialize()
    hWnd = FindWindow(vbNullString, Me.Caption)
End Sub
'
Private Sub UserForm_MouseDown(ByVal Button As Integer, ByVal Shift
As Integer, ByVal X As Single, ByVal Y As Single)
 Dim Pt As POINTAPI
    Dim ret As Long
    If Button = 2 Then
        hMenu = CreatePopupMenu()
        AppendMenu hMenu, MF_STRING, 1, "Menu Item 1"
```

```
        AppendMenu hMenu, MF_STRING, 2, "Menu Item 2"
        AppendMenu hMenu, MF_SEPARATOR, 3, ByVal 0&
        AppendMenu hMenu, MF_STRING, 4, "Menu Item 3"
        GetCursorPos Pt
        ret = TrackPopupMenuEx(hMenu, TPM_LEFTALIGN Or TPM_RETURNCMD
Or _
                               TPM_RIGHTBUTTON, Pt.X, Pt.Y, hWnd,
ByVal 0&)
        DestroyMenu hMenu

            Select Case ret
                Case 1
                Call MenuProc1
                Case 2
                Call MenuProc2
                Case 4
                Call MenuProc3
            End Select
    End If
End Sub
'

Private Sub MenuProc1()
    MsgBox "PopUp menu-1 is activated !"
End Sub
'

Private Sub MenuProc2()
    MsgBox "PopUp menu-2 is activated !"
End Sub
'

Private Sub MenuProc3()
    MsgBox "PopUp menu-3 is activated !"
End Sub

Private Sub CommandButton1_Click()
    Unload Me
End Sub
```

Part 3

When someone right-clicks the form, the menu is displayed (Figure 146).

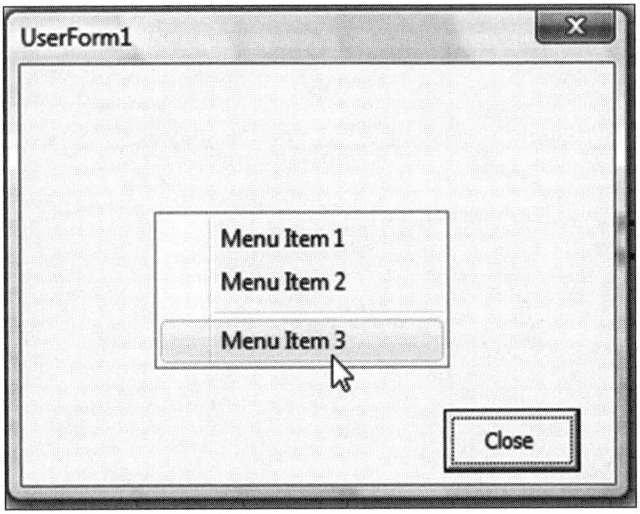

Figure 146. The custom right-click menu is displayed.

Summary: You can add right-click menu functionality to a user form.

Source: http://www.mrexcel.com/forum/showthread.php?t=97871

This topic was nominated by Microsoft MVP Greg Truby.

FORMAT A USER FORM TEXT BOX AS CURRENCY OR A PERCENTAGE

Challenge: You are building a custom user form to calculate a monthly payment, based on loan amount, number of payments, and interest rate. You would like one text box on the form to be formatted as currency and another to be formatted as a percentage. There do not appear to be a properties to format the text boxes.

Solution: You can use the `BeforeUpdate` code to grab what the person types into a text box and format it properly. If someone types `20`, you can have it automatically change to 20% when the user tabs out of the field.

In the VBA editor, right-click your text box and choose View Code. Excel takes you to the code pane and inserts a new procedure called `TextBoxName.Change`. This is a good guess on Excel's part, but you are going to use a different event. From the right dropdown at the top of the dialog, choose `BeforeUpdate`. Excel enters the start of the macro, and you need to fill in the remaining lines.

To format a value as currency with two decimal places, use:

```
Private   Sub   tbPrin_BeforeUpdate(ByVal   Cancel   As   MSForms.
ReturnBoolean)
    If Int(Me.tbPrin.Value) = tb.Prin.Value Then
        Me.tbPrin.Value = Format(Me.tbPrin.Value, "$#,##0")
    Else
        Me.tbPrin.Value = Format(Me.tbPrin.Value, "$#,##0.00")
    End If
End Sub
```

Part

3

To format a value as a percentage, you must handle the situation where the user already typed in a percentage. You also have to deal with the possibility that someone would enter 20% as 0.2 and someone else might enter 20. Use this code:

```
Private   Sub   tbInt_BeforeUpdate(ByVal   Cancel   As   MSForms.
ReturnBoolean)
    ' Handle if they entered a % sign already
    If Not Right(Me.tbInt.Value, 1) = "%" Then
        If Me.tbInt.Value >= 1 Then
            Me.tbInt.Value = Format(Me.tbInt.Value / 100, "0.00%")
        Else
            Me.tbInt.Value = Format(Me.tbInt.Value, "0.00%")
        End If
    End If
End Sub
```

The text box derived from this method will look great. The downside is that when you use those values, the percentage value is stored as text. Excel ignores the currency character, but it does not ignore the percent symbol. You need to use the following code to strip out the percent sign and divide the number by 100 before it can be used in a loan calculation:

```
Private Sub CommandButton1_Click()
    MyPct = tbInt.Value
    MyPct = Left(MyPct, Len(MyPct) - 1) / 100
    PmtAns = Application.WorksheetFunction.Pmt _
(MyPct / 12, Me.tbMonths, -Me.tbPrin.Value)
    Me.LabAns  =  "The  monthly  payment  is  "  &  Format(PmtAns,
"$#,##0.00")
End Sub
```

The resulting user form is shown in Figure 147.

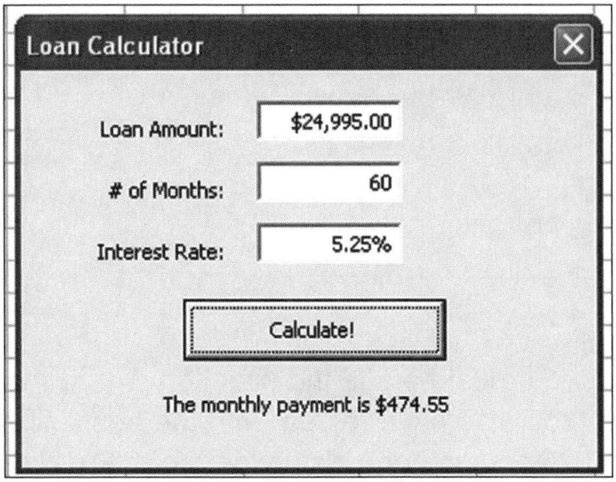

Figure 147. The BeforeUpdate procedure formats the entries in the text boxes.

Summary: Although text boxes on user forms do not offer a numeric format property, you can use code to format the values entered in the text box.

Source: http://www.mrexcel.com/forum/showthread.php?p=66754

Nate Oliver, Microsoft Excel MVP, provided this solution. He humbly serves as MrExcel.com's administrator, using the handle NateO. He resides in Minneapolis and entertains rather sophisticated finance and IT projects.

DELETE RECORDS IN VBA

Challenge: You need to delete records that match a certain criterion, and you'd like to do it by using a VBA macro.

Solution: The typical solution involves running a For...Next loop backward, from the last row up to row 1, checking each record and deciding whether that record should be deleted. The code to delete all the records with S29 in column D would be something like this:

```
Sub LoopWay()
    FinalRow = Cells(Rows.Count, 1).End(xlUp).Row
    For i = FinalRow To 2 Step -1
        If Cells(i, 4) = "S29" Then
            Cells(i, 1).EntireRow.Delete
        End If
    Next i
End Sub
```

Richard Schollar offered code that achieves this task quickly and efficiently by using the Excel AutoFilter command to isolate the desired records and then the SpecialCells property to delete only the visible cells.

For a 25,000-row data set, Excel can delete the matching records by running three commands instead of running through a loop and executing an IF statement 25,000 times. The code for this macro is:

```
Sub FasterWay()
    Dim rng As Range
    FinalRow = Cells(Rows.Count, 1).End(xlUp).Row

    ' While the headings are in row 1, this range start in row 2
    Set rng = Cells(2, 1).Resize(FinalRow - 1, 1)

    ' Apply a filter to the dataset
    Cells(1, 1).AutoFilter field:=4, Criteria1:="S29"

    ' Delete the visible cells starting in row 2
    rng.SpecialCells(xlCellTypeVisible).EntireRow.Delete

    ' Turn of the filter
    Cells(1, 1).AutoFilter
End Sub
```

The macro first finds how many rows are in the data set. It then defines an object variable that ignores the headings in row 1, starts in A2, and extends down through the data.

After you run the AutoFilter command, only the S29 records are visible, as shown in Figure 148.

	A	B	C	D
1	Regio ▼	Produ ▼	Date ▼	Rep ▼
9	Internal	XYZ	1/10/2008	S29
116	Internal	ABC	5/28/2008	S29
134	Internal	DEF	6/25/2008	S29
146	Internal	DEF	7/13/2008	S29
168	Internal	XYZ	8/6/2008	S29
221	Internal	ABC	10/15/2008	S29
234	Internal	ABC	10/30/2008	S29
254	Internal	DEF	11/27/2008	S29
255	Internal	XYZ	11/28/2008	S29
286	Internal	XYZ	1/3/2009	S29
318	Internal	DEF	2/19/2009	S29

Figure 148. One line of code turns on the AutoFilter dropdowns and chooses S29 from the sales rep dropdown.

In the next line of code, the rng variable points to A2:A999. Using `SpecialC ells(xlCellTypeVisible)` is equivalent to clicking the Special button on the GoTo dialog and choosing Visible Cells Only. This selects A9, A116, A134, and so on. In the same line of code, the EntireRow.Delete method removes all the rows that match the criterion.

The last bit of cleanup is to get rid of the `AutoFilter dropdowns`. You can issue the `AutoFilter` command without any arguments, as shown in the last line of code, to turn them off.

Summary: Using `AutoFilter` is a fast way to delete records that match a criterion.

Source: http://www.mrexcel.com/forum/showthread.php?t=185408

The code was proposed by Richard Schollar and nominated by Jon von der Heyden.

SELF-SIGN YOUR MACROS FOR CO-WORKERS

Challenge: You've created some macros for co-workers to use. Having them click Enable Macros each time is tiresome, but you don't want them to drop their macro security settings too low.

Solution: You can provide a self-signed certificate for your macros. Getting an "official" certificate can be pricey, but you can create one yourself.

To create the certificate, select Start, All Programs, Microsoft Office, Microsoft Office Tools, Digital Certificate for VBA Projects. Type a name for your certificate, as shown in Figure 149.

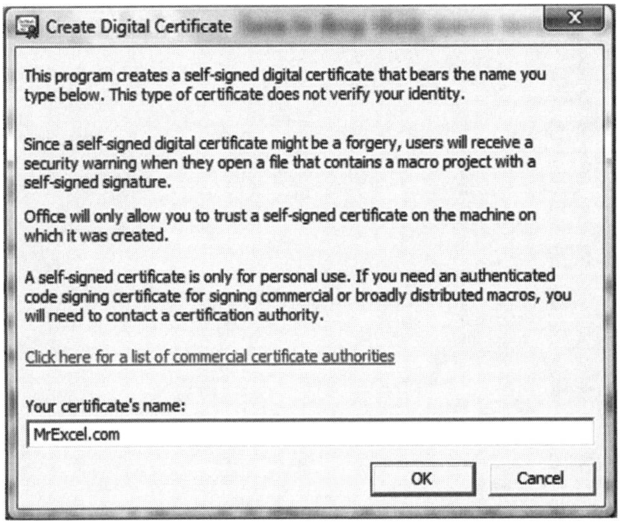

Figure 149. You can create your own certificate.

Excel confirms that a new signature has been created.

To sign a macro, follow these steps:

1. Go to the Visual Basic editor.
2. From the Visual Basic editor menu, choose Tools, Digital Signature.
3. Click the Choose button in the Digital Signature dialog.
4. Choose the signature you just created and click OK.

Excel now lists the project as signed, as shown in Figure 150:

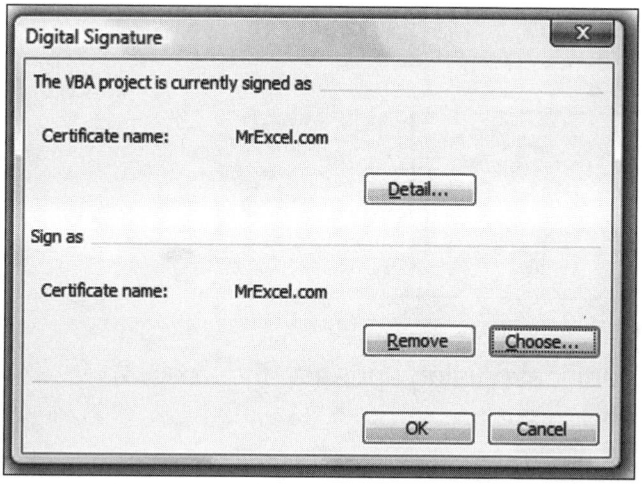

Figure 150. You attach the certificate to the project.

To enable the certificate on another computer, follow these steps for Excel 2003:

1. Open Excel.
2. Select Tools, Macro, Security. In the Security dialog, select Medium.
3. Open the workbook that is signed. Excel displays the Security Warning dialog shown in Figure 151.

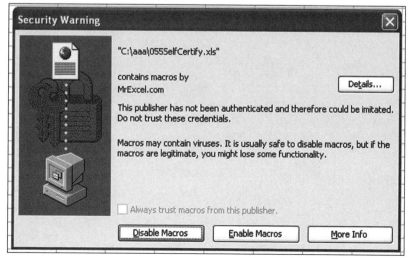

Figure 151. Excel indicates that the macro is signed by you.

4. Click the Details button in the Security Warning dialog. The Digital Signature Details dialog appears (Figure 152).

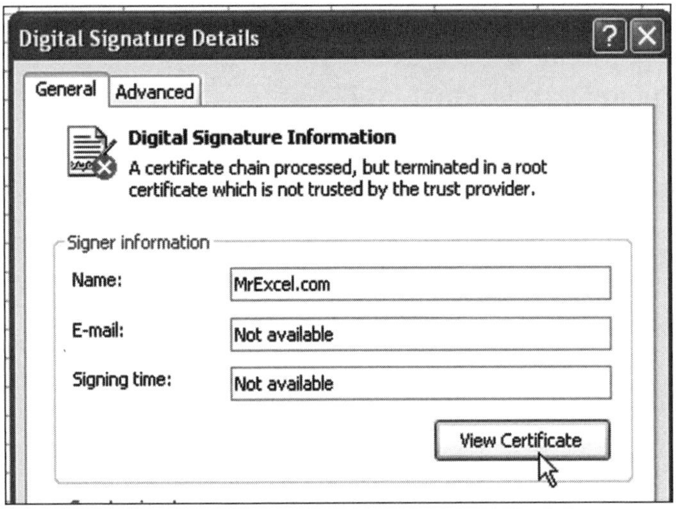

Figure 152. You can view the certificate.

5. Click View Certificate . The Certificate dialog appears (Figure 153).

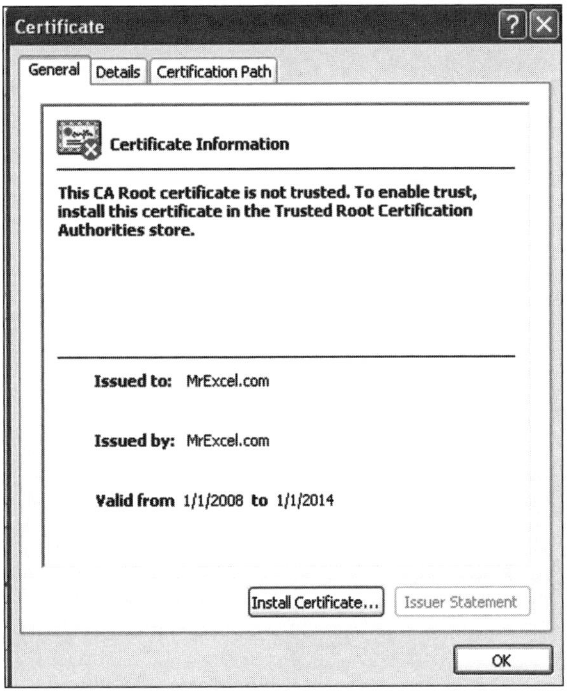

Figure 153. You use this dialog to install the certificate on this machine.

6. Click Install Certificate.

7. Click Next three times. Click Yes. Click OK three times to return to the Security Warning dialog.

8. Back in the Security Warning dialog, choose Enable Macros.

9. Close the workbook.

10. Reopen the workbook. You get the same security warning shown in Figure 152, but the checkbox for Always Trust Macros from This Publisher is now enabled. Check this box. Click Enable Macros.

From now on, this computer will be able to open your signed macros without any hassle!

In Excel 2007, the process is similar:

Part 3

1. Open Excel. Make sure the macro security is set to Disable All Macros with Notification.

2. Open your workbook. The information bar says Macros Have Been Disabled.

3. Click Options. The next dialog warns that the digital signature is invalid and cannot be trusted. Below that, click Show Signature Details.

4. Click View Certificate.

5. Click Install Certificate.

6. Click Next three times and click OK four times.

7. Close the workbook in Excel.

8. Reopen the workbook in Excel.

9. Click the Options button in the information bar.

10. Choose Always Trust Content from This Publisher.

This computer is now ready to open your signed macros.

Additional Details: The one downside of using this approach is that if a bug arises at your co-worker's computer, you can no longer fix the macro there on the spot. You have to send the macro back to yourself, fix the macro, re-sign the macro, and send it back to your co-worker.

Summary: Self-signing your macros makes it easier for your co-workers to use them.

Source: http://www.mrexcel.com/forum/showthread.php?t=110793

The original post was provided by Greg Truby. The topic was nominated by Joe4.

MAGNIFY A SECTION OF YOUR SCREEN

Challenge: You would like to display 48 months of data across your monitor. When you zoom down to 40%, you can see all the columns, but you cannot make out any numbers on the screen.

Solution: You can use a cool utility written by Ivan F. Moala and Jaafar Tribak and posted at the MrExcel message board. Jaafar started out with a modal user form that would display a magnification of the screen underneath the cursor. Ivan jumped in with improvements to allow the user form to be modeless and to update as you scroll around the worksheet.

The code is shown at the message board and in both Ivan's and Jaafar's versions of the program. They make use of a Windows API to return a stretched version of the screen underneath the cursor.

As you can see in Figure 154, as you move around the screen, an enlarged version of the area around the cell pointer is shown in the form.

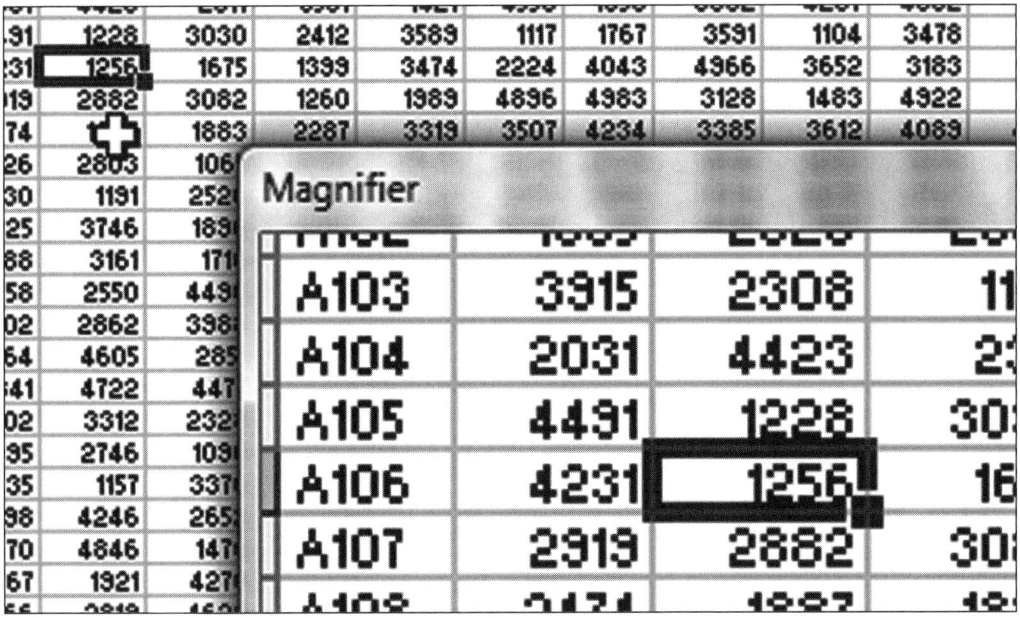

Figure 154. As you move the mouse around the screen, the user form shows a magnified picture of the area under the cursor.

If you move the cursor close to the magnifier, a magnified version of the magnifier appears in the form. In Figure 155, the magnifier appears three times.

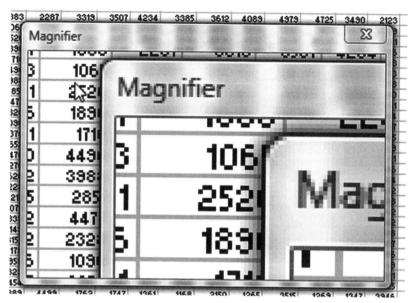

Figure 155. The magnifier even magnifies itself!

Breaking It Down: The user form runs a macro called `GetMagnifiedImageUnderCursor`. This macro loops continuously. To stop the macro from running, a `UserForm_DblClick` procedure sets the value of a global variable to TRUE. When the loop inside `GetMagnifiedImageUnderCursor` sees that this variable is set to TRUE, the loop is allowed to end.

Note: The accessibility options in Windows provide a magnifier. It is not as cool as this one, though.

Summary: You can use a utility to magnify a section of an Excel document.

Source: http://www.mrexcel.com/forum/showthread.php?t=288381

The post was nominated by Greg Truby. Thanks to Ivan F Moala and Jaafar Tribak for collaborating on the code in this topic.

LIST COMBINATIONS OF *N* ITEMS TAKEN *M* AT A TIME

Challenge: You want to list all unique combinations of *m* items from a population set of n items. For example, you might want to generate all possible unique groups of 4 employees from a set of 10.

Solution: There are two ways to go about this: the quick-and-dirty way and the better-but-more-difficult way.

Quick-and-Dirty Solution

An unimaginative (and rather kludgey) approach to solving the problem for `m=3` could be:

```
Sub ClumsyCombin()
    Dim n As Integer
    n = InputBox("Number of items?", "Combinations")
    NumComb = 0
    Range("A:A").ClearContents
    Range("A1").Select
    For i = 1 To n-2
      For j = 2 To n-1
        For k = 3 To n
          If i < j And j < k Then
            ActiveCell = i & " " & j & " " & k
            ActiveCell.Offset(1, 0).Select
            NumComb = NumComb + 1
          End If
        Next k
      Next j
    Next i
    MsgBox (NumComb & " combinations listed")
End Sub
```

A major problem with this approach is that the number of `For...Next` loops is hard-coded in the routine. If you need to find combinations of, say, 4 items at a time, an additional `For...Next` loop has to be inserted, and the condition check needs to be modified. For combinations of 2, a loop would need to be removed or skipped.

A Better Solution

This problem is an ideal candidate for a recursive function. This solution comprises a subroutine to specify the inputs n (population set size) and m (subset size), initialize a combinations counter, and set things up for entry of the combinations in column A of the active worksheet. This routine then calls a recursive function to generate the combinations. After all combinations are generated, the program exits, with a message with information on the number of combinations found.

Copy the following code to a blank module in a workbook:

```
Dim NumComb 'Combinations counter
Sub Combinations()
    Dim n As Integer, m As Integer
    NumComb = 0
    n = InputBox("Number of items?", "Combinations")
    m = InputBox("Taken how many at a time?", "Combinations")
```

```
      'Application.ScreenUpdating = False
      Range("A:A").ClearContents
      Range("A1").Select
      Comb2 n, m, 1, ""
      MsgBox (NumComb & " combinations listed")
End Sub


'Generate  combinations  of  integers  k..n  taken  m  at  a  time,
recursively
Private Function Comb2(ByVal n As Integer, _
ByVal m As Integer, _
ByVal k As Integer, ByVal s As String)
      'Debug.Print m, k, s
      If m > n - k + 1 Then Exit Function
      If m = 0 Then
          ActiveCell = s
          NumComb = NumComb + 1
          ActiveCell.Offset(1, 0).Select
          Exit Function
      End If
      Comb2 n, m - 1, k + 1, s & k & " "
      Comb2 n, m, k + 1, s
End Function
```

The `Sub` procedure is fairly straightforward. The power play begins from the point where the function is called:

```
Comb2 n, m, 1, ""
```

Let's start by analyzing how to logically build the combinations. Let's say you want to generate combinations of 5 items taken 3 at a time (i.e., output 3 characters from 1,2,3,4,5). You would build the strings as follows:

1. Starting with 1, add values sequentially until your subset has a size of 3. The next value is 2, so you get 1,2. The following value is 3, so you get 1,2,3, at which point your subset size of 3 elements is attained. Then you look for other combinations by varying the third value, and you get 1,2,4 and 1,2,5. Thus with 1,2 you get 1,2,3 and 1,2,4 and 1,2,5.

2. Increment the second value to 3 to get the two-piece fragment 1,3. The third value in sequence is 4, so you get 1,3,4, at which point your subset size of 3 elements is attained. Then you look for other combinations by varying the third value, and you get 1,3,5. Thus with 1,3 you get 1,3,4 and 1,3,5.

3. Increment the second value to 4 to get the two-piece fragment 1,4. The third value in sequence is 5, so you get 1,4,5, at which point your subset size of 3 elements is attained. In your quest for other combinations by varying the third value, you find none because 5 is already used. Thus with 1,4 you get 1,4,5 only.

4. Increment the second value to 5 to get 1,5. You find that you have no next value for the third element.

5. Increment the first value to 2, set the second element to 3, and get the combinations 2,3,4 and 2,3,5 and so on to get the remaining combinations 2,4,5 and 3,4,5.

Let's now examine the function `Comb2`. Notice the `ByVals` in the function arguments, which cause arguments to be passed by value. When first called from the subroutine (`Comb2 n, m, 1, ""`), for our example of 5 items taken 3 at a time, the arguments are $n=5$, $m=3$, $k=1$, and a null string indicating that the 3-element string is yet to be built.

At the initial entry point, the two Ifs (which we look at more closely later) are skipped. The line executed is:

```
Comb2 n, m - 1, k + 1, s & k & " "
```

Notice that this is a call to the function itself (which is why it is called a recursive function), with *m* reduced by 1 ($m=2$ now), k incremented by 1 ($k=2$ now), and the string being set to "1 ". The code again skips the two Ifs, and the line `Comb2 n, m - 1, k + 1, s & k & " "` calls the function recursively again, with $m=1$, $k=3$, and $s="1 2 "$ and then with $m=0$, $k=4$, and $s="1 2 3 "$. At this point, you have obtained the first combination.

When the same line calls the function next, the condition $m=0$ is satisfied, and the code enters this block:

```
If m = 0 Then
    ActiveCell = s
    NumComb = NumComb + 1
    ActiveCell.Offset(1, 0).Select
    Exit Function
End If
```

This part of the code enters the combination ('1 2 3 ') in the active cell, activates the next cell, and exits the last call to the function. Remember that the function was last called by:

```
Comb2 n, m - 1, k + 1, s & k & " "
```

The Exit function makes it branch to the next line, `Comb2 n, m, k + 1, s`. At this point, the last value in the string ("1 2 3") is incremented to the extent possible to get "1 2 4" and "1 2 5" in subsequent calls. When "1 2 5" is obtained, the next call by `Comb2 n, m, k + 1, s` is done with `m=1` and `k=6`.

These values of `m` and `k` satisfy the condition for If `m > n - k + 1` Then Exit Function because `1 > 5 - 6 + 1` and the call to the function exits, signifying the end of the loop for combinations for `12*`.

The function thus continues to run, building the combinations for `13*`, `14*`, `23*`, `24*`, and `34*`, and it finally exits to the `Sub Combinations` function from which it was first called, and a message box says that 10 combinations were generated.

An easy way to monitor the flow of calculations is to uncomment the line `Debug.Print m, k, s` in the code for `Comb2` and watch the output in the immediate window:

m	k	s
3	1	
2	2	1
1	3	1 2
0	4	1 2 3
1	4	1 2
0	5	1 2 4
1	5	1 2
0	6	1 2 5
1	6	1 2
2	3	1
1	4	1 3
0	5	1 3 4
1	5	1 3
0	6	1 3 5
1	6	1 3
2	4	1
1	5	1 4
0	6	1 4 5
1	6	1 4
2	5	1
3	2	
2	3	2

1	4	2 3
0	5	2 3 4
1	5	2 3
0	6	2 3 5
1	6	2 3
2	4	2
1	5	2 4
0	6	2 4 5
1	6	2 4
2	5	2
3	3	
2	4	3
1	5	3 4
0	6	3 4 5
1	6	3 4
2	5	3
3	4	

Summary: This topic illustrates how a problem that would otherwise require a variable number of For...Next loops can be efficiently solved using a subroutine/recursive function combination.

Source: http://www.mrexcel.com/forum/showthread.php?t=63064

APPENDIX 1

ALPHABETICAL FUNCTION REFERENCE

While you've seen function references before, this one is different in a couple of ways. First, it is alphabetical, so you don't have to figure out if AVERAGE is considered to be in the math category or the statistics category. Second, I've added guru tips on about a third of the functions. These will often give ideas of how you can use the function.

ABS(number) [Category: Math]

Returns the absolute value of a number. The absolute value of a number is the number without its sign.

ACCRINT(issue,first_interest,settlement,rate,par,frequency,basis) [Category: Financial]*

Returns the accrued interest for a security that pays periodic interest.

ACCRINTM(issue,maturity,rate,par,basis) [Category: Financial]*

Returns the accrued interest for a security that pays interest at maturity.

ACOS(number) [Category: Math]

Returns the arccosine of a number. The arccosine is the angle whose cosine is number. The returned angle is given in radians in the range 0 (zero) to pi.

ACOSH(number) [Category: Math]

Returns the inverse hyperbolic cosine of a number. Number must be greater than or equal to 1. The inverse hyperbolic cosine is the value whose hyperbolic cosine is number, so ACOSH(COSH(number)) equals number.

ADDRESS(row_num,column_num,abs_num,a1,sheet_text) [Category: Lookup & Reference]

Creates a cell address as text, given specified row and column numbers. Guru Tip: Use when you need to generate a cell address for use with INDIRECT, as shown on page 32. In Excel 2007, use =ADDRESS(2^20,2^14) to return $XFD$1048576. Also see page 32.

AMORDEGRC(cost,date_purchased,first_period, salvage, period, rate, basis) [Category: Financial]*

Returns the depreciation for each accounting period. This function is provide for the French accounting system. If an asset is purchased in the middle of the accounting period, the prorated depreciation is taken into account. The function is similar to AMORLINC, except that a depreciation coefficient is applied in the calculation depending on the life of the assets.

AMORLINC(cost,date_purchased,first_period,salvage,period,rate,basis) [Category: Financial]*

Returns the depreciation for each accounting period. This function is provided for the French accounting system. If an asset is purchased in the middle of the accounting period, the prorated depreciation is taken into account.

AND(logical1,logical2, ...) [Category: Logical]

Returns TRUE if all its arguments are TRUE; returns FALSE if one or more arguments is FALSE. Guru Tip: Use the AND function as the first argument in an IF function. To pay a $1000 bonus only when cell F2 is greater than 20000 and cell H2 is greater than 45%, use =IF(AND(F2>20000,H2>0.45),1000,0).

AREAS(reference) [Category: Lookup & Reference]

Returns the number of areas in a reference. An area is a range of contiguous cells or a single cell.

ASC(text) [Category: Text]

Changes full-width (double-byte) English letters or katakana within a character string to half-width (single-byte) characters.

ASIN(number) [Category: Math]

Returns the arcsine of a number. The arcsine is the angle whose sine is number. The returned angle is given in radians in the range -pi/2 to pi/2.

ASINH(number) [Category: Math]

Returns the inverse hyperbolic sine of a number. The inverse hyperbolic sine is the value whose hyperbolic sine is number, so ASINH(SINH(number)) equals number.

ATAN(number) [Category: Math]

Returns the arctangent of a number. The arctangent is the angle whose tangent is number. The returned angle is given in radians in the range -pi/2 to pi/2.

ATAN2(x_num,y_num) [Category: Math]

Returns the arctangent of the specified x- and y-coordinates. The arctangent is the angle from the x-axis to a line containing the origin (0, 0) and a point with coordinates (x_num, y_num). The angle is given in radians between -pi and pi, excluding -pi.

ATANH(number) [Category: Math]

Returns the inverse hyperbolic tangent of a number. Number must be between -1 and 1 (excluding -1 and 1). The inverse hyperbolic tangent is the value whose hyperbolic tangent is number, so ATANH(TANH(number)) equals number.

AVEDEV(number1,number2, ...) [Category: Statistical]]

Returns the average of the absolute deviations of data points from their mean. AVEDEV is a measure of the variability in a data set.

AVERAGE(number1,number2, ...) [Category: Statistical]]

Returns the average (arithmetic mean) of the arguments. Guru Tip: One of the top five functions, right up there with SUM. Annoyingly, the AVERAGE of a range of blank cells returns a division by zero error.

AVERAGEA(value1,value2,...) [Category: Statistical]]

Calculates the average (arithmetic mean) of the values in the list of arguments. In addition to numbers, text and logical values such as TRUE and FALSE are included in the calculation.

AVERAGEIF(range,criteria,average_range) [Category: Statistical]]

Returns the average (arithmetic mean) of all the cells in a range that meet a criteria. New in Excel 2007. Guru Tip: Microsoft added this function in Excel 2007, apparently for people who were tired of using SUMIF()/COUNTIF.

AVERAGEIFS(average_range,criteria_range1,criteria1,[criteria_range2,criteria2,…]) [Category: Statistical]]

Returns the average (arithmetic mean) of all the cells that meet multiple criteria. New in Excel 2007. Guru Tip: One of three "plural" functions added in Excel 2007, designed to increase the number of criteria in SUMIF and COUNTIF from 1 to 127.

BAHTTEXT(number) [Category: Text]

New in Excel XP: Converts a number to Thai text and adds a suffix of "Baht".

BESSELI(x,n) [Category: Engineering]*

Returns the modified Bessel function, which is equivalent to the Bessel function evaluated for purely imaginary arguments. Guru Tip: The BESSEL functions are useful in physics when solving partial differential equations in cylindrical coordinates. It is also useful for getting a laugh in front of a room full of accountants; "the first question ever sent in to MrExcel.com asked me to explain how to use the BESSELJ function".

BESSELJ(x,n) [Category: Engineering]*

Returns the Bessel function.

BESSELK(x,n) [Category: Engineering]*

Returns the modified Bessel function, which is equivalent to the Bessel functions evaluated for purely imaginary arguments.

BESSELY(x,n) [Category: Engineering]*

Returns the Bessel function, which is also called the Weber function or the Neumann function.

BETADIST(x,alpha,beta,A,B) [Category: Statistical]]

Returns the cumulative beta probability density function. The cumulative beta probability density function is commonly used to study variation in the percentage of something across samples, such as the fraction of the day people spend watching television.

BETAINV(probability,alpha,beta,A,B) [Category: Statistical]]

Returns the inverse of the cumulative beta probability density function. That is, if probability = BETADIST(x,...), then BETAINV(probability,...) = x. The cumulative beta distribution can be used in project planning to model probable completion times given an expected completion time and variability.

BIN2DEC(number) [Category: Engineering]*

Converts a binary number to decimal. Guru Tip: Frustratingly, this function only works with numbers up through 511. Otherwise, using BIN2DEC and DEC2BIN might be a great way to code and decode financial statements with bad financial news. See ROMAN.

BIN2HEX(number,places) [Category: Engineering]*

Converts a binary number to hexadecimal.

BIN2OCT(number,places) [Category: Engineering]*

Converts a binary number to octal. Guru Tip: If you are of the age where you learned about alternate numbering systems from Tom Yohe's singing about Little TwelveToes on Saturday mornings, then imagine a planet where everyone only has eight fingers and you've got the concept behind this numbering system. Both Octal and Hexadecimal were popular in the early days of computing.

BINOMDIST(number_s,trials,probability_s,cumulative) [Category: Statistical]]

Returns the individual term binomial distribution probability. Use BINOMDIST in problems with a fixed number of tests or trials, when the outcomes of any trial are only success or failure, when trials are independent, and when the probability of success is constant throughout the experiment. For example, BINOMDIST can calculate the probability that two of the next three babies born are male.

CALL(register_id,argument1,...)

Calls a procedure in a dynamic link library or code resource. Use this syntax only with a previously registered code resource, which uses arguments from the REGISTER function.

CALL(file_text,resource,type_text,argument1,...)

Calls a procedure in a dynamic link library or code resource. Use this syntax to simultaneously register and call a code resource for the Macintosh.

CALL(module_text,procedure,type_text,argument1,...)

Calls a procedure in a dynamic link library or code resource. Use this syntax to simultaneously register and call a code resource for Windows machines.

CEILING(number,significance) [Category: Math]

Returns number rounded up, away from zero, to the nearest multiple of significance. For example, if you want to avoid using pennies in your prices and your product is priced at $4.42, use the formula =CEILING(4.42,0.05) to round prices up to the nearest nickel.

CELL(info_type,reference) [Category: Information]

Returns information about the formatting, location, or contents of the upper-left cell in a reference. (See page 31)

CHAR(number) [Category: Text]

Returns the character specified by a number. Use CHAR to translate code page numbers you might get from files on other types of computers into characters. Guru Tip: character 65 is a capital letter A. Character 90 is a capital letter Z. To fill the letters of the alphabet, select cells A1:A26. Type =CHAR(ROW(A65)) and press Ctrl+Enter.

CHIDIST(x,degrees_freedom) [Category: Statistical]]

Returns the one-tailed probability of the chi-squared distribution. The $\gamma 2$ distribution is associated with a $\gamma 2$ test. Use the $\gamma 2$ test to compare observed and expected values. For example, a genetic experiment might hypothesize that the next generation of plants will exhibit a certain set of colors. By comparing the observed results with the expected ones, you can decide whether your original hypothesis is valid.

CHIINV(probability,degrees_freedom) [Category: Statistical]]

Returns the inverse of the one-tailed probability of the chi-squared distribution. If probability = CHIDIST(x,...), then CHIINV(probability,...) = x. Use this function to compare observed results with expected ones to decide whether your original hypothesis is valid.

CHITEST(actual_range,expected_range) [Category: Statistical]]

Returns the test for independence. CHITEST returns the value from the chi-squared ($\gamma 2$) distribution for the statistic and the appropriate degrees of freedom. You can use $\gamma 2$ tests to determine whether hypothesized results are verified by an experiment.

CHOOSE(index_num,value1,value2,...) [Category: Lookup & Reference]

Uses index_num to return a value from the list of value arguments. Use CHOOSE to select one of up to 29 values based on the index number. For example, if value1 through value7 are the days of the week, CHOOSE returns one of the days when a number between 1 and 7 is used as index_num. See Page 8.

CLEAN(text) [Category: Text]

Removes all nonprintable characters from text. Use CLEAN on text imported from other applications that contains characters that may not print with your operating system. For example, you can use CLEAN to remove some low-level computer code that is frequently at the beginning and end of data files and cannot be printed. Guru Tip: Clean is a great idea that is severely out of date. It removes character codes 1 through 31, 129, 141, 143, 144, and 157. It misses a number of other characters which have become popular due to HTML and web pages. Personally, I wish that CLEAN and TRIM would work with character 160 – the non-breaking space that happens when someone codes   into a web page.

CODE(text) [Category: Text]

Returns a numeric code for the first character in a text string. The returned code corresponds to the character set used by your computer. Guru Tip: Use this to learn the character code for a letter. For example, =CODE("A") will remind you that a capital A is 65. This is good for discovering the character number of an problematic character. In the figure below, someone used Alt+Enter to enter three lines of an address in cell A1. The formula in D11 identifies that the Alt+Enter actually inserts a character code 10 to represent the Alt+Enter. The formula in E1 then uses SUBSTITUTE and CHAR to replace the line feeds with semi-colons. After using paste values in E, you could use Text to Columns to successfully break out a whole column of addresses entered like cell A1.

D11		fx =CODE(MID($B$1,ROW(A11),1))					
	A	C	D	E	F	G	H
1	Bill Jelen PO Box 82 Uniontown OH 44685	B	66	Bill Jelen;PO Box 82;Uniontown OH 44685			
2		i	105				
3		l	108				
4		l	108				
5			32	=SUBSTITUTE(B1,CHAR(10),";")			
6		J	74				
7		e	101				
8		l	108				
9		e	101				
10		n	110				
11			10				
12		P	80				
13		O	79				
14			32				
15		B	66				
16		o	111				
17		x	120				

COLUMN(reference) [Category: Lookup & Reference]

Returns the column number of the given reference. Guru Tip: Writing =COLUMN(B1) is a great way to write the number 2. This is particularly handy when you have to use a similar VLOOKUP to return the 2nd, 3rd, ... 12th columns from a lookup table. Rather than hard-coding 2 as the 3rd argument in the VLOOKUP, specify COLUMN(B1). As you copy this formula to the right, the reference will automatically update to return COLUMN(C1) which is 3, then COLUMN(D1) which is 4, and so on.

B2							fx =VLOOKUP($A2,$H$2:$L$225,COLUMN(B1),FALSE)				
	A	B	C	D	E	F	G	H	I	J	K	L
1	Acct	Q1	Q2	Q3	Q4			Acct	Q1	Q2	Q3	Q4
2	A126	0.317	0.343	0.353	0.32			A101	0.369	0.343	0.347	0.304
3	A117	0.398	0.377	0.369	0.34			A102	0.375	0.334	0.37	0.364
4	A130	0.311	0.395	0.361	0.325			A103	0.332	0.367	0.355	0.373

COLUMNS(array) [Category: Lookup & Reference]

Returns the number of columns in an array or reference.

COMBIN(number,number_chosen) [Category: Math]

Returns the number of combinations for a given number of items. Use COMBIN to determine the total possible number of groups for a given number of items. Guru Tip: You can figure out the probability of your state lottery game using COMBIN. If your lotto drawing draws 6 numbers from a pool of 40 numbers, use =COMBIN(40,6) to show you that there are 3.8 million combinations.

D3		fx =COMBIN(B3,C3)	
	A	B	C	D
1	Game	Number Pool	# Chosen	# of Combinations
2	Lotto	40	6	3,838,380
3	Classic Lotto	49	6	13,983,816
4	Keno	80	10	1,646,492,110,120

COMPLEX(real_num,i_num,suffix) [Category: Engineering]*

Converts real and imaginary coefficients into a complex number of the form x + yi or x + yj.

CONCATENATE(text1,text2,...) [Category: Text]

Joins several text strings into one text string. Guru Tip: Jeff Bissell notes that you can also use the ampersand to join text together: =A2&B2&C2 is equivalent to =CONCATENATE(A2,B2,C2).

CONFIDENCE(alpha,standard_dev,size) [Category: Statistical]]

Returns the confidence interval for a population mean. The confidence interval is a range on either side of a sample mean. For example, if you order a product through the mail, you can determine, with a particular level of confidence, the earliest and latest the product will arrive.

CONVERT(number,from_unit,to_unit) [Category: Engineering]*

Converts a number from one measurement system to another. For example, CONVERT can translate a table of distances in miles to a table of distances in kilometers. Guru Tip: Check out the help topic for this function to get the exact abbreviations for the various measurement units. The function is incredibly versatile, offering conversions of weight, distance, time, pressure, force, energy, power, magnetism, temperature, and liquid measure. Some of the more common abbreviations are shown below.

	D1		▼		f_x =CONVERT(A1,B1,C1)			
	A	B	C	D	E	F	G	H
1	1	kg	lbm	2.204623	pounds mass in a kilogram			
2	1	lbm	ozm	16	ounces in a pound			
3	1	mi	m	1609.344	meters in a mile			
4	1	ft	in	12	inches in a foot			
5	1	yd	in	36	inches in a yard			
6	1	day	hr	24	hours in a day			
7	1	mn	sec	60	seconds in a minute			
8	1	yr	sec	31557600	seconds in a year			
9	1	N	dyn	100000	dynes in a Newton			
10	1	J	e	9999995	ergs in a joule			
11	1	HP	w	745.701	watts in a horsepower			
12	1	T	ga	10000	gauss in a Tesla			
13	68	F	C	20	room temperature in centigrade / farenheit			
14	1	tbs	tsp	3	teaspoons in a tablespoon			
15	1	cup	oz	8	fluid ounces in a cup			
16	1	uk_pt	pt	1.200688	pints in a U.K. pint			
17	1	qt	pt	2	pints in a quart			
18	1	gal	l	3.786235	liters in a gallon			
19	1	Pica	ang	3527778	angstroms in a Pica			
20	1	pica	ang	#N/A	capitalization of the abbreviations matters			

CORREL(array1,array2) [Category: Statistical]]

Returns the correlation coefficient of the array1 and array2 cell ranges. Use the correlation coefficient to determine the relationship between two properties. For example, you can examine the relationship between a location's average temperature and the use of air conditioners.

COS(number) [Category: Math]

Returns the cosine of the given angle. Guru Tip: Although you probably learned about the cosine function in a high school geometry class where the cosine of 360 degrees is 1, the cosine in Excel does not work with degrees, it works with radians. There are 2 x Pi radians in a circle. To convert the degrees shown in column A to radians, use the RADIANS function.

	C6	▼		fx	=COS(RADIANS($A6))		
	A	B	C	D	E	F	G
1	Degrees	Radians	COS	SIN			
2	0	0	1.0	0.0			
3	15	0.261799	0.966	0.259			
4	30	0.523599	0.866	0.5			
5	45	0.785398	0.707	0.707			
6	60	1.047198	0.5	0.866			
7	75	1.308997	0.259	0.966			
8	90	1.570796	0.0	1.0			
9	105	1.832596	-0.259	0.966			
10	120	2.094395	-0.5	0.866			
11	135	2.356194	-0.707	0.707			
12	150	2.617994	-0.866	0.5			
13	165	2.879793	-0.966	0.259			
14	180	3.141593	-1.0	0.0			
15	195	3.403392	-0.966	-0.259			
16	210	3.665191	-0.866	-0.5			
17	225	3.926991	-0.707	-0.707			
18	240	4.18879	-0.5	-0.866			
19	255	4.45059	-0.259	-0.966			
20	270	4.712389	0.0	-1.0			
21	285	4.974188	0.259	-0.966			
22	300	5.235988	0.5	-0.866			
23	315	5.497787	0.707	-0.707			
24	330	5.759587	0.866	-0.5			
25	345	6.021386	0.966	-0.259			
26	360	6.283185	1.0	0.0			
27							

COSH(number) [Category: Math]
Returns the hyperbolic cosine of a number.

COUNT(value1,value2, ...) [Category: Statistical]]
Counts the number of cells that contain numbers and numbers within the list of arguments. Use COUNT to get the number of entries in a number field in a range or array of numbers. Guru Tip: COUNT only counts numeric entries. If you have to count cells in a range that might contain text or TRUE/FALSE values, use COUNTA. If you have to count cells in a vertical range that might contains blanks, use ROWS.

	A	B	C	D	E	F
		#'s	Letters	Logicals	Letters	Empty
1						
2		53	3	41	A	A
3		25	A	FALSE	B	
4		84	60	TRUE	C	C
5		9	B	84	D	
6		30	29	27	E	E
7						
8	COUNT:	5	3	3	0	0
9	COUNTA:	5	5	5	5	3
10	ROWS:	5	5	5	5	5

COUNTA(value1,value2, ...) [Category: Statistical]]
Counts the number of cells that are not empty and the values within the list of arguments. Use COUNTA to count the number of cells that contain data in a range or array.

COUNTBLANK(range) [Category: Information]
Counts empty cells in a specified range of cells. Guru Tip: Use =COUNTA(Range)+COUNTBLANK(Range) to count all the cells in the range. You could also use =ROWS(Range)*COLUMNS(Range). Both seem equally annoying.

COUNTIF(range,criteria) [Category: Math]
Counts the number of cells within a range that meet the given criteria. Guru Tip: Along with SUMIF, added to Excel to prevent people from having to use array formulas. The one drawback is that COUNTIF and SUMIF can only handle a single criteria. Although most people don't realize that the criteria in COUNTIF can be dynamic as shown below. Also see pages 6 & 47.

E3				f_x	=COUNTIF(A6:J30,">"&AVERAGE(A6:J30))					
A	B	C	D	E	F	G	H	I	J	K
1 Question: How can you get most of your students to be above average?										
2			Population:	250						
3		# Above Average:		249	99.6%					
4 Answer: Have one incredibly-below-average student!										
5										
6	96	83	106	101	98	98	95	111	109	101
7	81	118	88	100	114	91	114	91	96	117
8	100	88	111	88	98	113	94	119	83	117
9	86	90	120	89	119	-6000	93	94	114	115
10	97	82	107	110	105	92	82	120	106	81

**COUNTIFS(criteria_range1, criteria1, [criteria_range2, criteria2,...])
[Category: Math]**

Applies criteria to cells across multiple ranges and counts the number of times all criteria are met. Added in Excel 2007. Guru Tip: This is the plural version of COUNTIF. You can specify up to 127 pairs of criteria range and criteria.

COUPDAYBS(settlement,maturity,frequency,basis) [Category: Financial]*

Returns the number of days from the beginning of the coupon period to the settlement date.

COUPDAYS(settlement,maturity,frequency,basis) [Category: Financial]*

Returns the number of days in the coupon period that contains the settlement date.

COUPDAYSNC(settlement,maturity,frequency,basis) [Category: Financial]*

Returns the number of days from the settlement date to the next coupon date.

COUPNCD(settlement,maturity,frequency,basis) [Category: Financial]*

Returns a number that represents the next coupon date after the settlement date. To view the number as a date, click Cells on the Format menu, click Date in the Category box, and then click a date format in the Type box.

COUPNUM(settlement,maturity,frequency,basis) [Category: Financial]*

Returns the number of coupons payable between the settlement date and maturity date, rounded up to the nearest whole coupon.

COUPPCD(settlement,maturity,frequency,basis) [Category: Financial]*

Returns a number that represents the previous coupon date before the settlement date. To view the number as a date, click Cells on the Format menu, click Date in the Category box, and then click a date format in the Type box.

COVAR(array1,array2) [Category: Statistical]]

Returns covariance, the average of the products of deviations for each data point pair. Use covariance to determine the relationship between two data sets. For example, you can examine whether greater income accompanies greater levels of education.

CRITBINOM(trials,probability_s,alpha) [Category: Statistical]]

Returns the smallest value for which the cumulative binomial distribution is greater than or equal to a criterion value. Use this function for quality assurance applications. For example, use CRITBINOM to determine the greatest number of defective parts that are allowed to come off an assembly line run without rejecting the entire lot.

**CUBEKPIMEMBER(connection,kpi_name,kpi_property,[caption])
[Category: Cubel]***

New in Excel 2007. Returns a key performance indicator (KPI) property and displays the KPI name in the cell. Used for OLAP Cubes.

CUBEMEMBER(connection,member_expression,[caption]) [Category: Cube]*

New in Excel 2007. Returns a member or tuple from the cube. Used for OLAP Cubes.

**CUBEMEMBERPROPERTY(connection,member_expression,property)
[Category: Cube]***

New in Excel 2007. Returns the value of a member property from the cube. Use to validate that a member name exists within the cube and to return the specified property for this member. Used for OLAP Cubes.

**CUBERANKEDMEMBER(connection,set_expression,rank,[caption])
[Category: Cube]***

New in Excel 2007. Returns the nth or ranked member in a set. Use to return one or more elements in a set, such as the top sales performer or the top 10 students. Used for OLAP Cubes.

**CUBESET(connection,set_expression,[caption],[sort_order].[sort_by])
[Category: Cube]***

New in Excel 2007. Defines a calculated set of members or tuples by sending a set expression to the cube on the server, which creates the set, and then returns that set to Microsoft Excel. Used for OLAP Cubes.

CUBESETCOUNT(set) [Category: Cube]*

New in Excel 2007. Returns the number of items in a set. Guru Tip: the set argument may be a CUBESET function. Used for OLAP Cubes.

CUBEVALUE(connection,member_expression1) [Category: Cube]*

New in Excel 2007. Returns an aggregated value from the cube. Used for OLAP Cubes.

**CUMIPMT(rate,nper,pv,start_period,end_period,type) [Category:
Financial]***

Returns the cumulative interest paid on a loan between start_period and end_period. Guru Tip: great for calculating how much interest you will pay in each year of your housing mortgage. While I usually use a negative value for the pv argument in the PMT function, this function requires pv to be positive. Note that in the image below, I used a positive value for pv, but preceded the CUMIPMT function with a minus sign. Also, the type argument is no longer optional.

D7		▼		*fx*	=-CUMIPMT($B$3/12,$B$2,$B$1,$B7,$C7,0)	
	A	B	C	D	E	F
1	Principal	175000				
2	Term	180				
3	Rate	6%				
4	First payment	Aug-2000				
5						
6	Year	Starting Payment	Last Payment	Interest Paid	Principal Paid	Total Paid
7	2000	1	5	4,345	3,039	7,384
8	2001	6	17	10,111	7,610	17,721
9	2002	18	29	9,641	8,080	17,721
10	2003	30	41	9,143	8,578	17,721
11	2004	42	53	8,614	9,107	17,721
12	2005	54	65	8,052	9,669	17,721
13	2006	66	77	7,456	10,265	17,721
14	2007	78	89	6,823	10,898	17,721
15	2008	90	101	6,150	11,571	17,721
16	2009	102	113	5,437	12,284	17,721
17	2010	114	125	4,679	13,042	17,721
18	2011	126	137	3,875	13,846	17,721
19	2012	138	149	3,021	14,700	17,721
20	2013	150	161	2,114	15,607	17,721
21	2014	162	173	1,151	16,570	17,721
22	2015	174	180	204	10,134	10,337

CUMPRINC(rate,nper,pv,start_period,end_period,type) [Category: Financial]*

Returns the cumulative principal paid on a loan between start_period and end_period. Guru Tip: See the example shown for CUMIPMT, above.

DATE(year,month,day) [Category: Date & Time]

Returns the serial number that represents a particular date. Guru Tip: Say that you have a date entered in D2. To find the first of that month, use =DATE(YEAR(D2),MONTH(D2),1). To find the last of the month, use =DATE(YEAR(D2), MONTH(D2)+1,0). Amazingly, the DATE function has no problem with months in excess of 12. If you ask for the 45th day of the 17th month of 2009 with =DATE(2009,17,45), Excel will correctly report June 14, 2010.

DATEDIF(start_date,end_date,unit) [Category: Date & Time]

Calculates the number of days, months, or years between two dates. This function is provided for compatibility with Lotus 1-2-3. Guru Tip: DATEDIF has only been documented in Excel 2000. The trick is to figure out the proper code for unit. Column C below shows the valid units for DATEDIF. Using these codes, you can express an age in years, months, day or years, days, or even decimal years.

D3   fx =DATEDIF(A3,B3,C3)

	A	B	C	D	E	F	G	H	I	J
1										
2	**Start**	**End**	**Unit**	**DateDif**	**meaning of unit code**					
3	2/17/1965	7/4/2010	y	45	years					
4	2/17/1965	7/4/2010	ym	4	months in excess of years					
5	2/17/1965	7/4/2010	md	17	days in excess of months					
6	2/17/1965	7/4/2010	m	544	pure # of months					
7	2/17/1965	7/4/2010	d	16,573	pure # of days					
8	2/17/1965	7/4/2010	yd	137	days in excess of years					
9										
10	Other examples:									
11										
12	45 years, 4 months, 17 days.									
13	=DATEDIF(A3,B3,"y")&" years, "&DATEDIF(A3,B3,"ym")&" months, "&DATEDIF(A3,B3,"md")&" days. "									
14										
15	45 years, 137 days									
16	=DATEDIF(A3,B3,"y")&" years, "&DATEDIF(A3,B3,"yd")&" days"									
17										
18	45.375 years									
19	=TEXT(DATEDIF(A3,B3,"y")+DATEDIF(A3,B3,"yd")/365,"0.000")&" years"									
20										
21	45.374 years									
22	=TEXT((B3-A3)/365.25,"0.000")&" years"									

B3   fx =DATEVALUE(A3)

	A	B	C	D	E
1	TEXT	DATEVALUE	Comment		
2	07/04/10	40363	works as expected		
3	07/04/2010	40363	"		
4	7/4/10	40363	"		
5	7/4/2010	40363	"		
6	7-4-2010	40363	"		
7	4-Jul-2010	40363	"		
8	Jul-4-2010	#VALUE!	strange, given row 7		
9	July-4-2010	#VALUE!	strange, given row 7		
10	Jul 4, 2010	40363	works as expected		
11	July 04, 2010	40363	"		
12	4/7/2010	40275	hope this isnt a d/m/yyyy format		
13	07042010	#VALUE!	COBOL data is out of luck		
14	20100704	#VALUE!	COBOL data is out of luck		
15	2010/07/04	40363	If only COBOL used 2more bytes...		
16	2010-07-04	40363	"		
17	July 2010	40360	July 1, 2010		
18	Jul 2010	40360	July 1, 2010		
19	Jul 10	40004	July 10 of the current year		
20	Jul 99	36342	July 1, 1999		
21	Jul 32	11871	July 1, 1932		
22	31/12/2010	#VALUE!	Fails even when obviously d/m/yyyy		
23					
24	Results based on US setting in Regional and				
25	Language Options of the Vista Control Panel				

DATEVALUE(date_text) [Category: Date & Time]

Returns the serial number of the date represented by date_text. Use DATEVALUE to convert a date represented by text to a serial number. Guru Tip: Use DATEVALUE to correct a spreadsheet where all of the dates have been entered as text. If you don't format the cell that contains DATEVALUE, you will see the serial number used to represent the date. In the image below, you can format column B as a date to display the results as a date. On a Windows PC, 40363 is the serial number for July 4, 2010. Note that DATEVALUE works with some surprising abbreviations such as 4-Jul-2010, but then fails with others such as Jul-4-2010. The result of DATEVALUE will change based on the Regional and Language option of your computer. In many countries, the DATEVALUE("07/04/2010") will return April 7, 2010.

DAVERAGE(database,field,criteria) [Category: Database]

Averages the values in a column in a list or database that match conditions that you specify. Guru Tip: See DSUM.

DAY(serial_number) [Category: Date & Time]

Returns the day of a date, represented by a serial number. The day is given as an integer ranging from 1 to 31.

DAYS360(start_date,end_date,method) [Category: Date & Time]

Returns the number of days between two dates based on a 360-day year (twelve 30-day months), which is used in some accounting calculations. Use this function to help compute payments if your accounting system is based on twelve 30-day months.

DB(cost,salvage,life,period,month) [Category: Financial]

Returns the depreciation of an asset for a specified period using the fixed-declining balance method. Guru Tip: VDB seems to run circles around this function.

DCOUNT(database,field,criteria) [Category: Database]

Counts the cells that contain numbers in a column in a list or database that match conditions that you specify. Guru Tip: See DSUM.

DCOUNTA(database,field,criteria) [Category: Database]

Counts all of the nonblank cells in a column in a list or database that match conditions that you specify. Guru Tip: See DSUM.

DDB(cost,salvage,life,period,factor) [Category: Financial]

Returns the depreciation of an asset for a specified period using the double-declining balance method or some other method you specify. Guru Tip: VDB seems to run circles around this function.

DEC2BIN(number,places) [Category: Engineering]*

Converts a decimal number to binary. Guru Tip: Returns up to a 10 character result. Since each character holds a single bit, you have one sign bit and 9 magnitude bits. This means that DEC2BIN works with numbers from -512 to +511.

B6		f_x =DEC2BIN($A6)		
	A	B	C	D
1	# in Decimal	DEC2BIN	DEC2OCT	DEC2HEX
2	0	0	0	0
3	1	1	1	1
4	2	10	2	2
5	3	11	3	3
6	4	100	4	4
7	7	111	7	7
8	8	1000	10	8
9	9	1001	11	9
10	15	1111	17	F
11	16	10000	20	10
12	256	100000000	400	100
13	Limits of DEC2BIN:			
14	511	111111111	777	1FF
15	512	#NUM!	1000	200
16	-1	1111111111	7777777777	FFFFFFFFFF
17	-512	1000000000	7777777000	FFFFFFFE00
18	-513	#NUM!	7777776777	FFFFFFFDFF
19	Limits of DEC2OCT:			
20	536,870,911	#NUM!	3777777777	1FFFFFFF
21	536,870,912	#NUM!	#NUM!	20000000
22	-536,870,912	#NUM!	4000000000	FFE0000000
23	Limits of DEC2HEX:			
24	549,755,813,887	#NUM!	#NUM!	7FFFFFFFFF
25	549,755,813,888	#NUM!	#NUM!	#NUM!
26	-549,755,813,888	#NUM!	#NUM!	8000000000

DEC2HEX(number,places) [Category: Engineering]*

Converts a decimal number to hexadecimal. Guru Tip: Returns up to a 10 character result. Since each character holds 4 bits (2^4=16), the function can represent one sign bit and 39 magnitude bits. This means that DEC2HEX works with numbers in the range of -549,755,813,888 to +549,755,813,887. A real-life use for DEC2HEX is converting RGB values to color codes for use in web page design.

E4			fx =DEC2HEX(B4,2)&DEC2HEX(C4,2)&DEC2HEX(D4,2)			
A	B	C	D	E	F	G
1 Converting RGB to Hex using DEC2HEX:						
2						
3	Red	Green	Blue	Hex		
4 MrExcel.com Orange:	255	144	7	FF9007		
5 MrExcel.com Green:	76	152	115	4C9873		
6 MrExcel.com Blue:	210	100	42	D2642A		
7						
8 Converting Hex to RGB using HEX2DEC:						
9						
10	Hex	Red	Green	Blue		
11 MrExcel.com Orange:	FF9007	255	144	7		
12 MrExcel.com Green:	4C9873	76	152	115		
13 MrExcel.com Blue:	D2642A	210	100	42		

DEC2OCT(number,places) [Category: Engineering]*

Converts a decimal number to octal. Guru Tip: Since each character in the result holds 3 bits (2^3), the 10 character result can hold up to 29 bits plus a sign bit as the most significant bit. The result is that DEC2OCT can work with positive numbers up to 536,870,911 and negative numbers (expressed in two's complement notation) to -536,870,912. If the places argument is omitted, Excel will return only as many characters as necessary.

DEGREES(angle) [Category: Math]

Converts radians into degrees. Guru Tip: Cosine and sine functions in Excel work with radians instead of degrees. There are 2 x Pi radians in a circle and 360 degrees in a circle. You can convert radians to degrees by dividing the radians by (PI()/180) or instead use this handy function.

DELTA(number1,number2) [Category: Engineering]*

Tests whether two values are equal. Returns 1 if number1 = number2; returns 0 otherwise. Use this function to filter a set of values. For example, by summing several DELTA functions you calculate the count of equal pairs. This function is also known as the Kronecker Delta function.

DEVSQ(number1,number2,...) [Category: Statistical]]

Returns the sum of squares of deviations of data points from their sample mean.

DGET(database,field,criteria) [Category: Database]

Extracts a single value from a column in a list or database that matches conditions you specify. Guru Tip: Please read and understand DSUM first. This is the one unique function amongst the database functions. It will return a single value at the intersection of many criteria. In the figure for DSUM, the formula in cell J18 is =DGET($A$3:$D$15,"Revenue",F18:H19) and will find the single cell which matches all three criteria.

DISC(settlement,maturity,pr,redemption,basis) [Category: Financial]*

Returns the discount rate for a security.

DMAX(database,field,criteria) [Category: Database]

Returns the largest number in a column in a list or database that matches conditions you specify. Guru Tip: See DSUM.

DMIN(database,field,criteria) [Category: Database]

Returns the smallest number in a column in a list or database that matches conditions you specify. Guru Tip: See DSUM.

DOLLAR(number,decimals) [Category: Text]

Converts a number to text using currency format, with the decimals rounded to the specified place. The format used is $#,##0.00_);($#,##0.00).

DOLLARDE(fractional_dollar,fraction) [Category: Financial]*

Converts a dollar price expressed as a fraction into a dollar price expressed as a decimal number. Use DOLLARDE to convert fractional dollar numbers, such as securities prices, to decimal numbers. Guru Tip: This function is pretty much obsolete since Wall Street switched to decimal prices for stock quotes in 2001.

DOLLARFR(decimal_dollar,fraction) [Category: Financial]*

Converts a dollar price expressed as a decimal number into a dollar price expressed as a fraction. Use DOLLARFR to convert decimal numbers to fractional dollar numbers, such as securities prices.

DPRODUCT(database,field,criteria) [Category: Database]

Multiplies the values in a column in a list or database that match conditions that you specify. Guru Tip: See DSUM.

DSTDEV(database,field,criteria) [Category: Database]

Estimates the standard deviation of a population based on a sample, using the numbers in a column in a list or database that match conditions that you specify. Guru Tip: See DSUM.

DSTDEVP(database,field,criteria) [Category: Database]

Calculates the standard deviation of a population based on the entire population, using the numbers in a column in a list or database that match conditions that you specify. Guru Tip: See DSUM.

DSUM(database,field,criteria) [Category: Database]

Adds the numbers in a column in a list or database that match conditions that you specify. Guru Tip: Before pivot tables, most analysts made frequent use of DSUM and the similar database functions such as DAVERAGE, DCOUNT, etc. If you have the space to enter a criteria range, this function certainly did SUMIFS before there was a SUMIFS. It also replaces the need for AVERAGEIF, STDDEVIF, VARIANCEIF, COUNTAIF, etc. The figure below shows the DSUM result for several types of criteria ranges. In J4, the DSUM adds up all records where the region is East. In J7, the criteria range finds East & Central region sales of product A. In J11, the formula adds up Joe's sales of product A in the East and West. Notice the criteria range in F14:F15. The heading in F14 is left blank and cell F15 contains a formula which points to the first data row of the database. In this image, the formula is =D4<32 and causes Excel to pull all of the records where column D is less than 32. You can use complex formula here such as =NOT(ISNA(VLOOKUP())) to find records that match a list.

	J11					fx	=DSUM($A$3:$D$15,"Revenue",F10:H12)			
	A	B	C	D	E	F	G	H	I	J
1		Database					Criteria			DSUM
2										
3	Region	Product	Rep	Revenue		Region				
4	East	A	Joe	1		East				15
5	East	A	Bob	2						
6	East	B	Joe	4		Region	Product			
7	East	B	Bob	8		East	A			51
8	Central	A	Joe	16		Central	A			
9	Central	A	Bob	32						
10	Central	B	Joe	64		Region	Product	Rep		
11	Central	B	Bob	128		East	A	Joe		257
12	West	A	Joe	256		West	A	Joe		
13	West	A	Bob	512						
14	West	B	Joe	1024						
15	West	B	Bob	2048		TRUE				31
16										
17										DGET
18						Region	Product	Rep		128
19						Central	B	Bob		

DURATION(settlement,maturity,coupon yld,frequency,basis) [Category: Financial]*

Returns the Macauley duration for an assumed par value of $100. Duration is defined as the weighted average of the present value of the cash flows and is used as a measure of a bond price's response to changes in yield.

DVAR(database,field,criteria) [Category: Database]

Estimates the variance of a population based on a sample, using the numbers in a column in a list or database that match conditions that you specify. Guru Tip: See DSUM.

DVARP(database,field,criteria) [Category: Database]

Calculates the variance of a population based on the entire population, using the numbers in a column in a list or database that match conditions that you specify. Guru Tip: See DSUM.

EDATE(start_date,months) [Category: Date & Time]*

Returns the serial number that represents the date that is the indicated number of months before or after a specified date (the start_date). Use EDATE to calculate maturity dates or due dates that fall on the same day of the month as the date of issue. See page 51

EFFECT(nominal_rate,npery) [Category: Financial]*

Returns the effective annual interest rate, given the nominal annual interest rate and the number of compounding periods per year.

EOMONTH(start_date,months) [Category: Date & Time]*

Returns the serial number for the last day of the month that is the indicated number of months before or after start_date. Use EOMONTH to calculate maturity dates or due dates that fall on the last day of the month. Guru Tip: =EOMONTH(TODAY(),1) will return the last date of this month. This is a function which returns the correct result in the wrong format. Always format the cell as a date.

ERF(lower_limit,upper_limit) [Category: Engineering]*

Returns the error function integrated between lower_limit and upper_limit.

ERFC(x) [Category: Engineering]*

Returns the complementary ERF function integrated between x and infinity.

ERROR.TYPE(error_val) [Category: Information]*

Returns a number corresponding to one of the error values in Microsoft Excel or returns the #N/A error if no error exists. You can use ERROR.TYPE in an IF function to test for an error value and return a text string, such as a message, instead of the error value. Guru Tip: Here are the 7 types of errors and the result from ERROR.TYPE:

C2				*fx* =SUM(A15:A20 E6:H6)			
	C	D	E	F	G		H
1	Result	Error Type	ISERROR	ISERR	ISNA		Common cause:
2	#NULL!	1	TRUE	TRUE	FALSE		When using a space as an intersection operator and the two areas do not intersect
3	#DIV/0!	2	TRUE	TRUE	FALSE		Division by zero
4	#VALUE!	3	TRUE	TRUE	FALSE		Using text when a formula requires a number. Forgetting CSE with array formula
5	#REF!	4	TRUE	TRUE	FALSE		Deleting cells referred to by this formula
6	#NAME?	5	TRUE	TRUE	FALSE		Misspelling a function or range name
7	#NUM!	6	TRUE	TRUE	FALSE		Number out of range
8	#N/A	7	TRUE	FALSE	TRUE		Lookup function fails

EUROCONVERT(number,source,target,full_precision,triangulation_precision)

New in Excel XP - Converts a number to euros, converts a number from euros to a euro member currency, or converts a number from one euro member currency to another by using the euro as an intermediary (triangulation). The currencies available for conversion are those of the European Union (EU) members that have adopted the euro.

EVEN(number) [Category: Math]

Returns number rounded up to the nearest even integer. You can use this function for processing items that come in twos. For example, a packing crate accepts rows of one or two items. The crate is full when the number of items, rounded up to the nearest two, matches the crate's capacity. Guru Tip: I've been waiting most of my Excel career to find a product that comes in crates of two so that I can use this function. It has never happened yet. The book that you are holding comes in crates of 24. Sigh.

EXACT(text1,text2) [Category: Text]

Compares two text strings and returns TRUE if they are exactly the same, FALSE otherwise. EXACT is case-sensitive but ignores formatting differences. Use EXACT to test text being entered into a document. Guru Tip: Excel will generally ignore case of text. In the image below A1 and B1 are considered equal. In the VLOOKUP in cell A4, the lower case "hello" is considered a match for "HELLO". While this is mostly convenient, you might need to really know if two cells have the exact same capitalization. In that case, use EXACT.

	A5	▼		fx	=EXACT(A1,B1)	
	A	B	C	D	E	
1	HELLO	Hello				
2						
3	TRUE	=A1=B1				
4		10	=VLOOKUP(A1,$A$8:$B$10,2,FALSE)			
5	FALSE	=EXACT(A1,B1)				
6						
7						
8	hello	10				
9	Hello	20				
10	HELLO	40				

EXP(number) [Category: Math]

Returns raised to the power of number. The constant equals 2.71828182845904, the base of the natural logarithm.

EXPONDIST(x,lambda,cumulative) [Category: Statistical]]

Returns the exponential distribution. Use EXPONDIST to model the time between events, such as how long an automated bank teller takes to deliver cash. For example, you can use EXPONDIST to determine the probability that the process takes at most 1 minute.

FACT(number) [Category: Math]

Returns the factorial of a number. The factorial of a number is equal to 1*2*3*...* number.

FACTDOUBLE(number) [Category: Math]*

Returns the double factorial of a number. Guru Tip: The double factorial of a number is the product of every other number. For example, the double factorial of 9 is 9 x 7 x 5 x 3 x 1. It is fairly difficult to find real-life examples for this function. It does something mathematically interesting when you chart the double factorial from -2 to -1, but Excel won't calculate double factorial for negative numbers. So – the two examples that I have found: used to calculate the number of permutations of the five-card board that can be dealt in a game of Texas Hold-em (the formula involved the FACTDOUBLE of the number of players sitting at the table) and the number of games in a round-robin tennis match.

FALSE( ) [Category: Logical]

Returns the logical value FALSE. Guru Tip: This seems redundant. Any place where I might want to use =FALSE(), I could simply type FALSE. Am I missing something?

FDIST(x,degrees_freedom1,degrees_freedom2) [Category: Statistical]]

Returns the F probability distribution. You can use this function to determine whether two data sets have different degrees of diversity. For example, you can examine test scores given to men and women entering high school and determine if the variability in the females is different from that found in the males.

FIND(find_text,within_text,start_num) [Category: Text]

FIND finds one text string (find_text) within another text string (within_text), and returns the number of the starting position of find_text, from the first character of within_text. You can also use SEARCH to find one text string within another, but unlike SEARCH, FIND is case sensitive and doesn't allow wildcard characters. Guru Tip: I frequently use FIND when I need to categorize data. For example, say I have 800 rows of data and each record contains a paragraph of description for an episode of the MrExcel podcast. A formula of =FIND("pivot",lower(D2)) will mostly return a #VALUE! error. (first figure below) However, sort the FIND column ascending and all of the episodes which mention a pivot will sort to the top. (second figure below).

	E2	▼		f_x	=FIND($G$1,LOWER(D2))		
	B	C	D	E	F	G
1	Episode	Title	Description	There?		pivot
2	101	Show Full Menus	Why does Micro⊕ h	#VALUE!		
3	102	Excel Standard &	Move these two impor	#VALUE!		
4	103	New Icons	Add new icons to you	#VALUE!		
5	104	Secret Menu Item	Secret Menu Items- Ep	#VALUE!		
6	105	Recent Files	Double the Power of R	#VALUE!		

Note that in the second figure the episodes are sorted by how early in the description the pivot table is mentioned. If I wanted them to be sorted in episode sequence, I could have used =NOT(ISERROR(FIND("pivot",LOWER(D2)))). Also note that instead of hard-coding "pivot" in the function, I refer to cell $G$1 instead. This way, I can enter subtotal in G1 and re-sort by column E to find items that contain the word subtotal.

E2				ƒx =FIND($G$1,LOWER(D2))	
	A	B	C	D	E
1	Date	Episode	Title	Description	There?
2	6/2/06	267	Pivot Update	Pivot tables don't auto:	1
3	6/21/06	280	Multiple Data Fie	Pivot Tables look horri	1
4	6/28/06	285	Formatting Pivot:	While pivot tables are i	7
5	3/10/08	311	Show Filter Page:	Make a pivot table for :	8
6	6/9/06	272	AutoSort	Why are pivot tables a:	9
7	6/22/06	281	Daily to Monthly	If your pivot table shou	9
8	6/19/06	278	Pivot Average	All of the pivot tables 1	12

Note that people frequently ask me why I go to all this trouble when I could use a custom AutoFilter of *pivot* as shown here. Well...I guess it is because old habits are hard to break. Based on the first paragraph, I really should be using SEARCH instead of FIND.

FINDB(find_text,within_text,start_num) [Category: Text]

FINDB finds one text string (find_text) within another text string (within_text), and returns the number of the starting position of find_text, based on the number of bytes each character uses, from the first character of within_text. This function is for use with double-byte characters. You can also use SEARCHB to find one text string within another.

FINV(probability,degrees_freedom1,degrees_freedom2) [Category: Statistical]]

Returns the inverse of the F probability distribution. If p = FDIST(x,...), then FINV(p,...) = x.

FISHER(x) [Category: Statistical]]

Returns the Fisher transformation at x. This transformation produces a function that is approximately normally distributed rather than skewed. Use this function to perform hypothesis testing on the correlation coefficient.

FISHERINV(y) [Category: Statistical]]

Returns the inverse of the Fisher transformation. Use this transformation when analyzing correlations between ranges or arrays of data. If y = FISHER(x), then FISHERINV(y) = x.

FIXED(number,decimals,no_commas) [Category: Text]

Rounds a number to the specified number of decimals, formats the number in decimal format using a period and commas, and returns the result as text. Guru Tip: =TEXT(number,"0.00") would do the same thing, with additional flexibility.

FLOOR(number,significance) [Category: Math]

Rounds number down, toward zero, to the nearest multiple of significance. Guru Tip: CEILING will round up to the nearest nickel, which seems a more likely scenario.

FORECAST(x,known_y's,known_x's) [Category: Statistical]]

Calculates, or predicts, a future value by using existing values. The predicted value is a y-value for a given x-value. The known values are existing x-values and y-values, and the new value is predicted by using linear regression. You can use this function to predict future sales, inventory requirements, or consumer trends. Guru Tip: FORECAST is used with linear progression. Cells B25:B29 of this image use FORECAST to predict future sales. This is theoretically easier than calculating =INTERCEPT()+SLOPE()*A25. Also see LINEST, INTERCEPT, SLOPE.

	B29	▼		fx	=FORECAST(A29,$B$2:$B$23,$A$2:$A$23)			
	A	B	C	D	E	F	G	H
1		Sales						
2	1	100						
3	2	107						
4	3	117			$y = 9.7307x + 90.597$			
5	4	127						
6	5	139						
7	6	147						
8	7	158						
9	8	169						
10	9	179						
11	10	190						
12	11	201						
13	12	211						
14	13	222						
15	14	230						
16	15	239						
17	16	248						
18	17	259		Slope	9.730661	=SLOPE(B2:B23,A2:A23)		
19	18	266		Intercept	90.5974	=INTERCEPT(B2:B23,A2:A23)		
20	19	274						
21	20	282		9.730661	90.5974	=LINEST(B2:B23,A2:A23)		
22	21	289						
23	22	301						
24								
25	23	314.4026	=FORECAST(A25,$B$2:$B$23,$A$2:$A$23)					
26	24	324.1333						
27	25	333.8639						
28	26	343.5946						
29	27	353.3252						

Note that if you create a line chart from A1:B23, you can right-click the line, choose Add Trendline. In the Options tab of the dialog, ask for Excel to add the equation to the chart. This will describe the slope and y-intercept.

FREQUENCY(data_array,bins_array) [Category: Statistical]]

Calculates how often values occur within a range of values, and then returns a vertical array of numbers. For example, use FREQUENCY to count the number of test scores that fall within ranges of scores. Because FREQUENCY returns an array, it must be entered as an array formula. Guru Tip: This is a tough function to set up. In my example, I have 1000 test results in A2:A1001. In D2:D11, I enter a series of bin values. To see scores less than 10, I enter 10 in D2. To see scores between 10 and 20, I enter 20 in D3, and so on down to 100 in D11. Then, to compute the frequency distribution, select E2:E12 (one more row than you have in the bins range). Type =FREQUENCY($A$2:$A$1001,$D$2:$

D$12) and press Ctrl+Shift+Enter. This one function returns an entire range of results. In the image below, I've added a comment about the meaning of each result. Note that any entries in the last row are for scores above the largest bin value.

	E2		▼		fx {=FREQUENCY($A$2:$A$1001,$D$2:$D$12)}				
	A	B	C	D	E	F	G	H	I
1	Result			Bin	Frequency	What this means			
2	57			10	70	70 results are <= 10			
3	17			20	48	48 results are >10 and <=20			
4	50			30	72	72 results are >20 and <=30			
5	87			40	82	82 results are >30 and <=40			
6	52			50	100	100 results are >40 and <=50			
7	77			60	208	208 results are >50 and <=60			
8	101			70	133	133 results are >60 and <=70			
9	55			80	120	120 results are >70 and <=80			
10	47			90	64	64 results are >80 and <=90			
11	63			100	94	94 results are >90 and <=100			
12	60				9	9 results are >100			
13	66								
14	71								

If you don't need a "live" formula, it is faster to create the frequency distribution using a pivot table. Create a pivot table from A1:A1001. Put Result down the row area. Put Count of Result in the data area. Right-click the first result in the row area of your pivot table and choose Group and Show Detail, Group. In the Grouping dialog, choose to group from 1 to 110 in groups of 10. The result is shown below.

Count of Re	
Result ▼	Total
1-10	70
11-20	48
21-30	72
31-40	82
41-50	100
51-60	208
61-70	133
71-80	120
81-90	64
91-100	94
101-110	9
Grand Total	1000

Grouping   X

Auto

☐ Starting at: 1

☐ Ending at: 110

By: 10

OK   Cancel

FTEST(array1,array2) [Category: Statistical]]

Returns the result of an F-test. An F-test returns the one-tailed probability that the variances in array1 and array2 are not significantly different. Use this function to determine whether two samples have different variances. For example, given test scores from public and private schools, you can test whether these schools have different levels of diversity.

FV(rate,nper,pmt,pv,type) [Category: Financial]

Returns the future value of an investment based on periodic, constant payments and a constant interest rate.

FVSCHEDULE(principal,schedule) [Category: Financial]*

Returns the future value of an initial principal after applying a series of compound interest rates. Use FVSCHEDULE to calculate future value of an investment with a variable or adjustable rate.

GAMMADIST(x,alpha,beta,cumulative) [Category: Statistical]]

Returns the gamma distribution. You can use this function to study variables that may have a skewed distribution. The gamma distribution is commonly used in queuing analysis.

GAMMAINV(probability,alpha,beta) [Category: Statistical]]

Returns the inverse of the gamma cumulative distribution. If p=GAMMADIST(x,...), then GAMMAINV(p,...) = x.

GAMMALN(x) [Category: Statistical]]

Returns the natural logarithm of the gamma function, $\Gamma(x)$.

GCD(number1,number2, ...) [Category: Math]*

Returns the greatest common divisor of two or more integers. The greatest common divisor is the largest integer that divides both number1 and number2 without a remainder. Guru Tip: With all due respect to Nick Irwin, my 7th grade math teacher, Excel just made the need for one month of your math class disappear.

GEOMEAN(number1,number2, ...) [Category: Statistical]]

Returns the geometric mean of an array or range of positive data. For example, you can use GEOMEAN to calculate average growth rate given compound interest with variable rates.

GESTEP(number,step) [Category: Engineering]*

Returns 1 if number ≥ step; returns 0 (zero) otherwise. Use this function to filter a set of values. For example, by summing several GESTEP functions, you calculate the count of values that exceed a threshold.

GETPIVOTDATA(pivot_table,name) [Category: Database]

Returns data stored in a PivotTable report. You can use GETPIVOTDATA to retrieve summary data from a PivotTable report, provided the summary data is visible in the report. Guru Tip: While a few people swear by this function, most swear at it, when Microsoft automatically inserts it in any formula outside of a pivot table that points inside the pivot table. To enter a formula without getting GETPIVOTDATA, type the cell references rather than using the mouse or arrow keys. To turn it off permanently in Excel 2007, go to PivotTable Tools Options. Open the Options dropdown and uncheck Generate GetPivotData. In Excel 2003, there is an icon available, but you have to add it to a toolbar. Use Tools, Customize. Go to the Commands tab. On the left side choose Data. On the right side, scroll almost to the bottom. Drag the Generate GetPivotData icon onto any toolbar (even the Pivot Table Toolbar). Click the icon to turn off the annoying feature.

GROWTH(known_y's,known_x's,new_x's,const) [Category: Statistical]]

Calculates predicted exponential growth by using existing data. GROWTH returns the y-values for a series of new x-values that you specify by using existing x-values and y-values. You can also use the GROWTH worksheet function to fit an exponential curve to existing x-values and y-values.

HARMEAN(number1,number2, ...) [Category: Statistical]]

Returns the harmonic mean of a data set. The harmonic mean is the reciprocal of the arithmetic mean of reciprocals.

HEX2BIN(number,places) [Category: Engineering]*

Converts a hexadecimal number to binary.

HEX2DEC(number) [Category: Engineering]*

Converts a hexadecimal number to decimal. Guru Tip: Useful for converting Hex color codes from a web page into RGB values. See DEC2HEX for an example.

HEX2OCT(number,places) [Category: Engineering]*

Converts a hexadecimal number to octal.

HLOOKUP(lookup_value,table_array,row_index_num,range_lookup) [Category: Lookup & Reference]

Searches for a value in the top row of a table or an array of values, and then returns a value in the same column from a row you specify in the table or array. Use HLOOKUP when your comparison values are located in a row across the top of a table of data, and you want to look down a specified number of rows. Use VLOOKUP when your comparison values are located in a column to the left of the data you want to find. Guru Tip: If you can use VLOOKUP, you know how to use HLOOKUP. If you know how to use VLOOKUP and also Paste Special Transpose, then you never have to use HLOOKUP!

HOUR(serial_number) [Category: Date & Time]

Returns the hour of a time value. The hour is given as an integer, ranging from 0 (12:00 A.M.) to 23 (11:00 P.M.).

HYPERLINK(link_location,friendly_name) [Category: Lookup & Reference]

Creates a shortcut or jump that opens a document stored on a network server, an intranet, or the Internet. When you click the cell that contains the HYPERLINK function, Microsoft Excel opens the file stored at link_location. Guru Tip: These hyperlinks are not as good as the ones created by the Insert Hyperlink dialog. Yes, I understand that you are using this function because you have the web page URL right over there in column C. If you want to add a bunch of hyperlinks, select the range where the hyperlinks to be and run this three line macro:

```
Sub AddRealHyperlinks()
For Each cell In Selection
    ActiveSheet.Hyperlinks.Add Anchor:=cell, Address:=cell.Offset(0, 1).Value
Next cell
End Sub
```

B	C	D	E
Site Name	URL		
MrExcel	http://www.mrexcel.com		
Office Experts	http://www.theofficeexperts.com		
Utter Access	http://www.utteraccess.com		

HYPGEOMDIST(sample_s,number_sample,population_s,number_population) [Category: Statistical]]

Returns the hypergeometric distribution. HYPGEOMDIST returns the probability of a given number of sample successes, given the sample size, population successes, and population size. Use HYPGEOMDIST for problems with a finite population, where each observation is either a success or a failure, and where each subset of a given size is chosen with equal likelihood.

IF(logical_test,value_if_true,value_if_false) [Category: Logical]

Returns one value if a condition you specify evaluates to TRUE and another value if it evaluates to FALSE. Guru Tip: To make this function more powerful, replace the logical_test argument with a combination of AND, OR, NOT functions. See page 17

IFERROR(value,value_if_error) [Category: Logical]

Returns a value you specify if a formula evaluates to an error; otherwise, returns the result of the formula. New in Excel 2007. Use the IFERROR function to trap and handle errors in a formula. Guru Tip: IFERROR is designed to speed your worksheet calculation. Many gurus routinely have their spreadsheets calculate every VLOOKUP twice with =IF(ISNA(VLOOKUP(A2,MyTable,2,False)),0, VLOOKUP(A2,MyTable,2,False)). The problem with this long formula is that Excel first does the VLOOKUP to see if the result is #N/A. If the result is not #N/A, the formula then makes Excel do the VLOOKUP a second time to use the result in the value_if_false portion of the formula. If you are doing this in 500,000 cells, calculation time will slow dramatically. The IFERROR function first calculates the formula in the value argument. If that formula does not evaluate to an error, calculation stops and the result of the first argument is used in the cell. If the calculation results in any error such as #N/A or #DIV/0, the function will use the 2nd argument instead. This means that time-consuming calculations only have to be performed once per cell. =IFERROR(VLOOKUP(A2,Table,2,False),0).

IMABS(inumber) [Category: Engineering]*

Returns the absolute value (modulus) of a complex number in x + yi or x + yj text format.

IMAGINARY(inumber) [Category: Engineering]*

Returns the imaginary coefficient of a complex number in x + yi or x + yj text format.

IMARGUMENT(inumber) [Category: Engineering]*

Returns the argument

(theta) an angle expressed in radians, such that:

IMCONJUGATE(inumber) [Category: Engineering]*

Returns the complex conjugate of a complex number in x + yi or x + yj text format.

IMCOS(inumber) [Category: Engineering]*

Returns the cosine of a complex number in x + yi or x + yj text format.

IMDIV(inumber1,inumber2) [Category: Engineering]*

Returns the quotient of two complex numbers in x + yi or x + yj text format.

IMEXP(inumber) [Category: Engineering]*

Returns the exponential of a complex number in x + yi or x + yj text format.

IMLN(inumber) [Category: Engineering]*

Returns the natural logarithm of a complex number in x + yi or x + yj text format.

IMLOG10(inumber) [Category: Engineering]*

Returns the common logarithm (base 10) of a complex number in x + yi or x + yj text format.

IMLOG2(inumber) [Category: Engineering]*

Returns the base-2 logarithm of a complex number in x + yi or x + yj text format.

IMPOWER(inumber,number) [Category: Engineering]*

Returns a complex number in x + yi or x + yj text format raised to a power.

IMPRODUCT(inumber1,inumber2,...) [Category: Engineering]*

Returns the product of 2 to 29 complex numbers in x + yi or x + yj text format.

IMREAL(inumber) [Category: Engineering]*

Returns the real coefficient of a complex number in x + yi or x + yj text format.

IMSIN(inumber) [Category: Engineering]*

Returns the sine of a complex number in x + yi or x + yj text format.

IMSQRT(inumber) [Category: Engineering]*

Returns the square root of a complex number in x + yi or x + yj text format.

IMSUB(inumber1,inumber2) [Category: Engineering]*

Returns the difference of two complex numbers in x + yi or x + yj text format.

IMSUM(inumber1,inumber2,...) [Category: Engineering]*

Returns the sum of two or more complex numbers in x + yi or x + yj text format.

INDEX(array,row_num,column_num) [Category: Lookup & Reference]

Returns the value of a specified cell or array of cells within array. Guru Tip: INDEX is often paired with the MATCH function to do a lookup which is more flexible than VLOOKUP (see page 54 for an example). Column_num is optional if you have only a single column of data in the array. If you want to select a random item from J1:J20, use =INDEX($J$1:$J$20,RANDBETWEEN(1,20)). To turn a range on its side, use INDEX and ROW as shown below:

	B5				f_x	=INDEX($C$3:$N$3,1,ROW(A1))			
	A	**B**	**C**	**D**	**E**	**F**	**G**	**H**	**I**	**J**
1			Rates							
2			Jan	Feb	Mar	Apr	May	Jun	Jul	Aug
3			3.0%	1.8%	3.0%	2.0%	2.0%	4.0%	4.0%	3.0%
4										
5	Jan	3.0%								
6	Feb	1.8%								
7	Mar	3.0%								
8	Apr	2.0%								
9	May	2.0%								
10	Jun	4.0%								
11	Jul	4.0%								
12	Aug	3.0%								
13	Sep	4.0%	Transpose with							
14	Oct	2.0%	a formula!							
15	Nov	2.0%								
16	Dec	3.0%								
17										

INDEX(reference,row_num,column_num,area_num) [Category: Lookup & Reference]

Returns a reference to a specified cell or cells within reference. See MATCH for an example. Also see page 2.

INDIRECT(ref_text,a1) [Category: Lookup & Reference]

Returns the reference specified by a text string. References are immediately evaluated to display their contents. Use INDIRECT when you want to change the reference to a cell within a formula without changing the formula itself. Guru Tip: Guru Asad Ali calls this his favorite function. There are many uses for INDIRECT. It can be used to point to another worksheet, but fails when you need to point to another workbook. Some examples: =INDIRECT("A2") will always point to A2. See pages 5, 20, 27, 30-38, and 130 for more examples.

INFO(type_text) [Category: Information]

Returns information about the current operating environment. Guru Tip: British Guru Bryony Stewart-Seume uses =INFO("directory") to put the current folder in a cell. She also uses it in combination with INDIRECT and CONCATENATE to build complicated lookups and references to other documents.

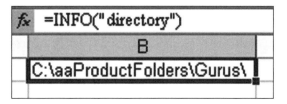

INT(number) [Category: Math]

Rounds a number down to the nearest integer. Guru Tip: Often used with RAND to generate random integers: =INT(RAND()*100)+1 will generate a random integer between 1 and 100. Also, note that INT might not act as you would expect for negative numbers. The INT(-3.1) is -4. See TRUNC.

INTERCEPT(known_y's,known_x's) [Category: Statistical]]

Calculates the point at which a line will intersect the y-axis by using existing x-values and y-values. The intercept point is based on a best-fit regression line plotted through the known x-values and known y-values. Use the intercept when you want to determine the value of the dependent variable when the independent variable is 0 (zero). For example, you can use the INTERCEPT function to predict a metal's electrical resistance at 0°C when your data points were taken at room temperature and higher. Guru Tip: See image under FORECAST. Use with SLOPE to describe the linear regression line. The intercept value is also the second value returned from the LINEST function.

INTRATE(settlement,maturity,investment,redemption,basis) [Category: Financial]*

Returns the interest rate for a fully invested security.

IPMT(rate,per,nper,pv,fv,type) [Category: Financial]

Returns the interest payment for a given period for an investment based on periodic, constant payments and a constant interest rate. For a more complete description of the arguments in IPMT and for more information about annuity functions, see Excel help for PV. Guru Tip: See ROW for an example of building an amortization table using IPMT and PPMT.

IRR(values,guess) [Category: Financial]

Returns the internal rate of return for a series of cash flows represented by the numbers in values. These cash flows do not have to be even, as they would be for an annuity. However, the cash flows must occur at regular intervals, such as monthly or annually. The internal rate of return is the interest rate received for an investment consisting of payments (negative values) and income (positive values) that occur at regular periods. Guru Tip: IRR is related to NPV. The IRR is the interest rate at which a series of cash flows would generate a NPV of zero. For an example of IRR, see the image after NPV.

ISBLANK(value) [Category: Information]

Returns TRUE if Value refers to an empty cell. Guru Tip: This is an unfortunate name for this function. It really is testing for an empty cell. An empty cell has nothing in the cell. If you type some spaces in a cell, it is no longer blank. If you type a leading apostrophe in a cell, it is no longer blank. The net result is that you will have a lot of cells that might appear to be blank and ISBLANK will not report them as blank. Also see page 2.

ISERR(value) [Category: Information]

Returns TRUE if Value refers to any error value except #N/A. Guru Tip: Unless you have some reason to accept #N/A in your worksheet, use ISERROR instead.

ISERROR(value) [Category: Information]

Returns TRUE if Value refers to any error value (#N/A, #VALUE!, #REF!, #DIV/0!, #NUM!, #NAME?, or #NULL!). Guru Tip: ISERROR checks for all 7 of the possible error results. To test for a specific error result, see the ERROR.TYPE function. ISERROR is more comprehensive than the older ISERR function. ISERR does not recognize #N/A as an error.

ISEVEN(number) [Category: Information]*

Returns TRUE if number is even, or FALSE if number is odd.

ISLOGICAL(value) [Category: Information]

Returns TRUE if Value refers to a logical value.

ISNA(value) [Category: Information]

Returns TRUE if Value refers to the #N/A (value not available) error value. Guru Tip: Specifically tests for #N/A error results. Good for preventing errors as the result of VLOOKUP: =IF(ISNA(VLOOKUP(A2,MyTable,2,False)),0, VLOOKUP

(A2,MyTable,2,False)). If you've upgraded to Excel 2007 and everyone who might open your workbook has upgraded to Excel 2007, check out the new IFERROR function instead.

ISNONTEXT(value) [Category: Information]

Returns TRUE if Value refers to any item that is not text. (Note that this function returns TRUE if value refers to a blank cell.)

ISNUMBER(value) [Category: Information]

Returns TRUE if Value refers to a number.

ISODD(number) [Category: Information]*

Returns TRUE if number is odd, or FALSE if number is even. Guru Tip: You could also use =MOD(Number,2)=1 to replace this function.

ISPMT(rate,per,nper,pv) [Category: Financial]

Calculates the interest paid during a specific period of an investment. This function is provided for compatibility with Lotus 1-2-3.

ISREF(value) [Category: Information]

Returns TRUE if Value refers to a reference. Guru Tip: If you don't want your INDIRECT functions to return errors, you can check to see if it is a reference with ISREF first.

ISTEXT(value) [Category: Information]

Returns TRUE if Value refers to text.

JIS(text) [Category: Text]

Changes half-width (single-byte) English letters or katakana within a character string to full-width (double-byte) characters.

KURT(number1,number2, ...) [Category: Statistical]]

Returns the kurtosis of a data set. Kurtosis characterizes the relative peakedness or flatness of a distribution compared with the normal distribution. Positive kurtosis indicates a relatively peaked distribution. Negative kurtosis indicates a relatively flat distribution.

LARGE(array,k) [Category: Statistical]]

Returns the k-th largest value in a data set. You can use this function to select a value based on its relative standing. For example, you can use LARGE to return the highest, runner-up, or third-place score. Guru Tip: while =MAX returns the largest value, =LARGE(range,2) will return the 2nd largest value. Great for throwing out outliers. Also see PERCENTILE. Also see page 49.

LCM(number1,number2, ...) [Category: Math]*

Returns the least common multiple of integers. The least common multiple is the smallest positive integer that is a multiple of all integer arguments number1, number2, and so on. Use LCM to add fractions with different denominators.

Guru Tip: If you have kids in middle school math, they can check their homework using this function.

LEFT(text,num_chars) [Category: Text]

LEFT returns the first character or characters in a text string, based on the number of characters you specify. Guru Tip: In the image below, the item # predictably has a 3 character prefix. To isolate the prefix, use =LEFT(A4,3). To get the number after the dash, use =MID(A4,5,3) or =RIGHT(A4,3).

B4			ƒ× =LEFT(A4,3)
	A	B	C	D
1		LEFT(,3)	MID(,5,3)	RIGHT(,3)
3	Item #	Prefix	Suffix	Suffix
4	BFL-304	BFL	304	304
5	BHV-762	BHV	762	762
6	DHJ-757	DHJ	757	757

If the dash does not reliably occur in the 4th position in every value, use FIND to locate the position of the dash and then subtract 1: =LEFT(F4,FIND("-",F4)-1

H4			ƒ× =LEFT(F4,FIND("-",F4)-1)			
	F	G	H	I	J	K
1			LEFT	MID	MID	RIGHT
3	Item #	Find -	Prefix	Suffix	Suffix	Suffix
4	U-2	2	U	2	2	2
5	CCNC-69	5	CCNC	69	69	69
6	NNN-75	4	NNN	75	75	75
7	TRT-53	4	TRT	53	53	53
8	FAS-87	4	FAS	87	87	87
9	QRSTQ-70	6	QRSTQ	70	70	70

LEFTB(text,num_bytes) [Category: Text]

LEFTB returns the first character or characters in a text string, based on the number of bytes you specify. This function is for use with double-byte characters.

LEN(text) [Category: Text]

LEN returns the number of characters in a text string. Guru Tip: See an example under RIGHT where LEN is used in conjunction with RIGHT.

LENB(text) [Category: Text]

LENB returns the number of bytes used to represent the characters in a text string. This function is for use with double-byte characters.

LINEST(known_y's,known_x's,const,stats) [Category: Statistical]]

Calculates the statistics for a line by using the "least squares" method to calculate a straight line that best fits your data, and returns an array that describes the line. Because this function returns an array of values, it must be entered as an array formula. Guru Tip: See image under FORECAST. For a simple straight-line regression, you should select a 1 row x 2 column area and type the LINEST function. Do not press Enter. Instead, press Ctrl+Shift+Enter. The first value is the slope and the second value is the intercept.

For multiple regression, you might have several columns of causal variables and one dependent variable. In the image below, daily sales are in column G. Several drivers of sales are in A:F.

	A	B	C	D	E	F	G
1	Friday	Weekend	ValDay	Easter	MothersDay	Christmas	Sales
2	0	0	0	0	0	0	547.34
3	0	0	0	0	0	0	919.36
4	1	0	0	0	0	0	1437.36
5	0	1	0	0	0	0	1491.87
6	0	1	0	0	0	0	1476.35
7	0	0	0	0	0	0	515.92
8	0	0	0	0	0	0	1337.81
9	0	0	0	0	0	0	743.86
10	0	0	0	0	0	0	1686.26

To calculate multiple regression, select a range of blank cells that is five rows tall and several columns wide. You will need one column for every causal variable (in this case, six) and one extra column to hold the intercept. Select 7 columns by 5 rows. Type =LINEST(G2:G363,A2:F363,FALSE,TRUE) and press Ctrl+Shift+Enter. You then need to label the columns and rows. The first column in the result corresponds to the final causal variable. I always type the values from F1 to A1 backwards starting in the first column above the LINEST formula. (Type Cell F1 in J5. Type cell E1 in K5, and so on until you type cell A1

f_x {=LINEST(G2:G363,A2:F363,FALSE,TRUE)}

I	J	K	L	M	N	O	P
	Christmas	Mothers	Easter	Val	WkEnd	Friday	Intercept
Slopes	5010.46922	3010.14822	976.4596	1432.2967	1725.2356	1867.7015	0
Std Error	286.140555	733.067333	554.45733	554.45733	145.94371	204.86172	#N/A
R-Squared	0.6618511	460.5868	#N/A	#N/A	#N/A	#N/A	#N/A
F	116.131774	356	#N/A	#N/A	#N/A	#N/A	#N/A
SSReg	1486473102	7.59E+08	#N/A	#N/A	#N/A	#N/A	#N/A
	Std Error of Y		ss Residual				
	Degrees of Freedom						

in O5). The final column is the intercept. The first row of values is the slope. The second line is the standard error. I always pay attention to line 3, column 1 as this is the R-Squared. This ranges from 0 to 1. The closer you are to 1, the better your regression is at predicting sales. In the present example, I would probably go back and try to find some other causal variables since an R-squared of 0.66 means that my current variables aren't doing a good job of predicting sales. They are better than random, but not perfect.

LN(number) [Category: Math]

Returns the natural logarithm of a number. Natural logarithms are based on the constant e (2.71828182845904).

LOG(number,base) [Category: Math]

Returns the logarithm of a number to the base you specify.

LOG10(number) [Category: Math]

Returns the base-10 logarithm of a number.

LOGEST(known_y's,known_x's,const,stats) [Category: Statistical]]

In regression analysis, calculates an exponential curve that fits your data and returns an array of values that describes the curve. Because this function returns an array of values, it must be entered as an array formula.

LOGINV(probability,mean,standard_dev) [Category: Statistical]]

Returns the inverse of the lognormal cumulative distribution function of x, where ln(x) is normally distributed with parameters mean and standard_dev. If p = LOGNORMDIST(x,...) then LOGINV(p,...) = x.

LOGNORMDIST(x,mean,standard_dev) [Category: Statistical]]

Returns the cumulative lognormal distribution of x, where ln(x) is normally distributed with parameters mean and standard_dev. Use this function to analyze data that has been logarithmically transformed.

LOOKUP(lookup_value,lookup_vector,result_vector) [Category: Lookup & Reference]

Returns a value either from a one-row or one-column range. This vector form of LOOKUP looks in a one-row or one-column range (known as a vector) for a value and returns a value from the same position in a second one-row or one-column range. Included for compatibility with other worksheets. Use VLOOKUP instead.

LOOKUP(lookup_value,array) [Category: Lookup & Reference]

Returns a value from an array. The array form of LOOKUP looks in the first row or column of an array for the specified value and returns a value from the same position in the last row or column of the array. Included for compatibility with other spreadsheet programs. Use VLOOKUP instead.

LOWER(text) [Category: Text]

Converts all uppercase letters in a text string to lowercase. Guru Tip: great function for eliminating case differences between values. Also see UPPER and PROPER.

MATCH(lookup_value,lookup_array,match_type) [Category: Lookup & Reference]

Returns the relative position of an item in an array that matches a specified value in a specified order. Use MATCH instead of one of the LOOKUP functions when you need the position of an item in a range instead of the item itself. Guru Tip: If the final argument of MATCH is 0, then it finds an exact match from an unsorted list, similar to using FALSE in VLOOKUP. If the final argument is 1, then MATCH will find the value equal to or just larger the lookup value from a sorted list, the same as using TRUE in VLOOKUP. MATCH offers further functionality in that you can specify -1 as the final argument and MATCH will find a value equal to or just smaller than the lookup value from an unsorted list. This option is beyond the powers of VLOOKUP. Also, the function can find a value from a single column lookup-array like VLOOKUP or from a single-row lookup_array like HLOOKUP. The one strange thing about MATCH is that it returns the relative position of the match within the list. In the image below, Green Bay is the 7th city in A10:A19 so the formula in E5 returns a 7. For a long time, I could never figure out why I would care to know that an item is the nth item in a list. My managers never ask me, "Hey Bill, what relative row is that account found on?". The power is to

`=INDEX(C10:G19,MATCH(C2,B10:B19,0),MATCH(C1,C9:G9,0))`

	A	B	C	D	E	F	G	H
1		Choose a product:	C457					
2		Choose a market:	Green Bay					
3								
4		Position of this product within C9:G9:			3	=MATCH(C1,C9:G9,0)		
5		Position of this market within B10:B19:			7	=MATCH(C2,B10:B19,0)		
6				Intersection:	38378	=INDEX(C10:G19,E5,E4)		
7				Single formula:	38378			
8								
9			A101	B714	C457	D784	H593	
10		Akron	5148	12729	29378	48905	76696	
11		Birmingham	6700	13215	31868	49748	77293	
12		Canton MO	7074	16760	32821	51229	79508	
13		Columbus IN	7980	20665	32902	52054	80364	
14		Dublin	9234	22634	35653	54391	87004	
15		Falls Church	9879	23547	36013	56917	87681	
16		Green Bay	10909	24977	38378	59601	91168	
17		Kansas City	11797	26789	40223	60839	93459	
18		Laguna Beach	12449	28188	41228	61165	98566	
19		Madison	12627	29006	47017	74666	99767	

use the result of the MATCH as the row and/or column argument in an INDEX function. In the image below, a horizontal MATCH in E4 does a lookup to find which column has the selected product. A vertical match in E5 does a lookup to find which row has the selected city. The INDEX function in E6 grabs the appropriate value at the intersection of the selected row and column.

If you have to do a dozen columns of VLOOKUP, you might consider replacing that with a single MATCH column and then 12 columns of INDEX. While VLOOKUP and MATCH take a long time to calculate, the INDEX function calculates very rapidly. Also see page 2.

MAX(number1,number2,...) [Category: Statistical]]

Returns the largest value in a set of values. Guru Tip: You use MAX all the time to find the largest value in a list. Also check out LARGE which can find the 2nd, 3rd, and 4th largest values.

MAXA(value1,value2,...) [Category: Statistical]]

Returns the largest value in a list of arguments. Text and logical values such as TRUE and FALSE are compared as well as numbers.

MDETERM(array) [Category: Math]

Returns the matrix determinant of an array.

MDURATION(settlement,maturity,coupon,yld,frequency,basis) [Category: Financial]*

Returns the modified duration for a security with an assumed par value of $100.

MEDIAN(number1,number2, ...) [Category: Statistical]]

Returns the median of the given numbers. The median is the number in the middle of a set of numbers; that is, half the numbers have values that are greater than the median, and half have values that are less. Guru Tip: For those of you

=MID(F4,FIND("-",F4)+1,LEN(F4)-FIND("-",F4))

	F	I	J	K	
1		MID	MID	RIGHT	
3	Item #	Suffix	Suffix	Suffix	
4	U-2	2	2	2	
5	CCNC-69	69	69	69	
6	NNN-75	75	75	75	
7	TRT-53	53	53	53	
8	FAS-87	87	87	87	
9	QRSTQ-70	70	70	70	

who know Juan Pablo Gonzalez, he once wrote a macro which would simulate having MEDIAN in a pivot table. Ask him how he did it.

MID(text,start_num,num_chars) [Category: Text]

MID returns a specific number of characters from a text string, starting at the position you specify, based on the number of characters you specify. Guru Tip: See an example under LEFT. You might sometimes need to use FIND and/or LEN to find the starting position or the number of characters. In the figure above, the starting position is calculated using the FIND function. The number of characters is calculated using LEN to get the length of the part number and then subtracting the position of the dash. Instead of explicitly calculating the number of characters in this case you could simply ask for a large number. Excel will not pad the result with spaces: =MID(F4,FIND("-",F4)+1,50). Also see page 120

MIDB(text,start_num,num_bytes) [Category: Text]

MIDB returns a specific number of characters from a text string, starting at the position you specify, based on the number of bytes you specify. This function is for use with double-byte characters.

MIN(number1,number2, ...) [Category: Statistical]]

Returns the smallest number in a set of values. Guru Tip: Check out SMALL as well.

MINA(value1,value2,...) [Category: Statistical]]

Returns the smallest value in the list of arguments. Text and logical values such as TRUE and FALSE are compared as well as numbers.

MINUTE(serial_number) [Category: Date & Time]

Returns the minutes of a time value. The minute is given as an integer, ranging from 0 to 59. Guru Tip: If you ask for the minute of 1:30, the answer will be 30. If you expect to find the total number of minutes, use =TEXT(A2,"[m]") instead.

MINVERSE(array) [Category: Math]

Returns the inverse matrix for the matrix stored in an array.

MIRR(values,finance_rate,reinvest_rate) [Category: Financial]

Returns the modified internal rate of return for a series of periodic cash flows. MIRR considers both the cost of the investment and the interest received on reinvestment of cash.

MMULT(array1,array2) [Category: Math]

Returns the matrix product of two arrays. The result is an array with the same number of rows as array1 and the same number of columns as array2. Guru Tip: You can use this to solve simultaneous equations in Excel. For an example, check out Excel 2007 Miracles Made Easy.

MOD(number,divisor) [Category: Math]

Returns the remainder after number is divided by divisor. The result has the same sign as divisor. Guru Tip: Remember back to when you first started to learn division? 22 divided by 4 would be listed as 5 R 2? This function returns the remainder. You could use this to count off by 3's (as in gym class): =MOD(ROW(),3) will classify a data set into groups numbered 0, 1, and 2. Guru Dave Goodman suggests using =MOD(ROW(),2) as the formula in conditional formatting to highlight every other row. Also see QUOTIENT. Also see page 11

MODE(number1,number2, ...) [Category: Statistical]]

Returns the most frequently occurring, or repetitive, value in an array or range of data. Like MEDIAN, MODE is a location measure.

MONTH(serial_number) [Category: Date & Time]

Returns the month of a date represented by a serial number. The month is given as an integer, ranging from 1 (January) to 12 (December).

MROUND(number,multiple) [Category: Math]*

Returns a number rounded to the desired multiple. Guru Tip: If you need to round a price to the nearest nickel, use MROUND. If you price calculation is =C2/0.45, then use =MROUND(C2/0.45,0.05).

MULTINOMIAL(number1,number2, ...) [Category: Math]*

Returns the ratio of the factorial of a sum of values to the product of factorials.

N(value) [Category: Information]

Returns a value converted to a number. Guru Tip: If value is numeric, then N returns the value. If value is text, then N returns zero. I've seen people use this to add a comment to a formula. At the end of the formula, type +N("this is how the formula is working....."). Since the argument is text, N adds zero to the formula.

NA( ) [Category: Information]

Returns the error value #N/A. #N/A is the error value that means "no value is available." Use NA to mark empty cells. By entering #N/A in cells where you are missing information, you can avoid the problem of unintentionally including empty cells in your calculations. (When a formula refers to a cell containing #N/A, the formula returns the #N/A error value.)

NEGBINOMDIST(number_f,number_s,probability_s) [Category: Statistical]]

Returns the negative binomial distribution. NEGBINOMDIST returns the probability that there will be number_f failures before the number_s-th success, when the constant probability of a success is probability_s. This function is similar to the binomial distribution, except that the number of successes is fixed, and the number of trials is variable. Like the binomial, trials are assumed to be independent.

NETWORKDAYS(start_date,end_date,holidays) [Category: Date & Time]*

Returns the number of whole working days between start_date and end_date. Working days exclude weekends and any dates identified in holidays. Use NETWORKDAYS to calculate employee benefits that accrue based on the number of days worked during a specific term. Guru Tip: This function assumes that you work Monday through Friday. For other work weeks, see page 4. You can optionally specify a range of company holidays as the third argument in the function. See page 4

=NETWORKDAYS(B1,B2,F2:F9)						
	A	B	C	D	E	F	G
1	Today:	2/27/2009	=TODAY()			Company Holidays	
2	Project Due Date:	10/15/2009				5/25/2009	
3						7/4/2009	
4	Workdays	163				9/7/2009	
5						11/26/2009	
6						11/27/2009	
7						12/24/2009	
8						12/25/2009	
9						1/1/2010	
10							

NOMINAL(effect_rate,npery) [Category: Financial]*

Returns the nominal annual interest rate, given the effective rate and the number of compounding periods per year.

NORMDIST(x,mean,standard_dev,cumulative) [Category: Statistical]]

Returns the normal cumulative distribution for the specified mean and standard deviation. This function has a very wide range of applications in statistics, including hypothesis testing.

NORMINV(probability,mean,standard_dev) [Category: Statistical]]

Returns the inverse of the normal cumulative distribution for the specified mean and standard deviation.

NORMSDIST(z) [Category: Statistical]]

Returns the standard normal cumulative distribution function. The distribution has a mean of 0 (zero) and a standard deviation of one. Use this function in place of a table of standard normal curve areas.

NORMSINV(probability) [Category: Statistical]]

Returns the inverse of the standard normal cumulative distribution. The distribution has a mean of zero and a standard deviation of one.

NOT(logical) [Category: Logical]

Reverses the value of its argument. Use NOT when you want to make sure a value is not equal to one particular value. Guru Tip: Sometimes you write a logical expression that is returning TRUE when it should be returning FALSE. Reverse the TRUE/FALSE by using NOT. Also great for creating NAND logic; =NOT(AND(condition 1, condition 2)).

NOW( ) [Category: Date & Time]

Returns the serial number of the current date and time. Guru Tip: =NOW() will return the date and time of the last calculation of the worksheet. The cell does not update every second unless you are pressing F9 to recalculate every second (or entering numbers in other cells every second). While NOW is popular, you should consider =TODAY() instead if you need to calculate the number of days from now until a due date.

NPER(rate, pmt, pv, fv, type) [Category: Financial]

Returns the number of periods for an investment based on periodic, constant payments and a constant interest rate.

=NPV(B3,B5:B9)+B4			
A	**B**	**C**	**D**
1			
2			
3 Discount Rate	2.80%		
4 Buy a business:	-450000		
5 Loss in year 1:	-22000		
6 Profit in year 2:	33000		
7 Profit in year 3:	129000		
8 Profit in year 4:	278000		
9 Profit in year 5:	389000		
10			
11 NPV	266,329	=NPV(B3,B5:B9)+B4	
12			
13 Internal Rates of Return:			
14 After year 2	-75%	=IRR(B$4:B6,-0.95)	
15 After year 3	-32%	=IRR(B$4:B7,-0.5)	
16 After year 4	-2%	=IRR(B$4:B8)	
17 After year 5	15%	=IRR(B$4:B9)	

NPV(rate,value1,value2, ...) [Category: Financial]

Calculates the net present value of an investment by using a discount rate and a series of future payments (negative values) and income (positive values). Guru Tip: Unlike PV, the payments don't have to be identical with NPV. In the image below, you buy a business for $450,000 as represented by cell B4. Future annual cash flows are shown in B5:B9. In the opinion of many, Excel doesn't calculate NPV correctly. Rather than including the cost of the business, run NPV using the discount rate shown in B3 and then the cash flows in B5:B9. Excel will report that the NPV is 716,329 which is not exactly right. To get what most people would call Net Present Value, you have to add in the initial cash outlay. Adding negative 450,000 to 716329 gives you the true Net Present Value of 266,329. The discount rate is the cost of capital. Think of it as the interest rate you could get with that money if you did not invest it in this business.

OCT2BIN(number,places) [Category: Engineering]*

Converts an octal number to binary.

OCT2DEC(number) [Category: Engineering]*

Converts an octal number to decimal.

OCT2HEX(number,places) [Category: Engineering]

Converts an octal number to hexadecimal.

ODD(number) [Category: Math]

Returns number rounded up to the nearest odd integer.

ODDFPRICE(settlement,maturity,issue,first_coupon,rate,yld,redemption,frequency,basis) [Category: Financial]*

Returns the price per $100 face value of a security having an odd (short or long) first period.

ODDFYIELD(settlement,maturity,issue,first_coupon,rate,pr,redemption,frequency,basis) [Category: Financial]*

Returns the yield of a security that has an odd (short or long) first period.

ODDLPRICE(settlement,maturity,last_interest,rate,yld,redemption,frequency,basis) [Category: Financial]*

Returns the price per $100 face value of a security having an odd (short or long) last coupon period.

ODDLYIELD(settlement,maturity,last_interest,rate,pr,redemption,frequency,basis) [Category: Financial]*

Returns the yield of a security that has an odd (short or long) last period.

OFFSET(reference,rows,cols,height,width) [Category: Lookup & Reference]

Returns a reference to a range that is a specified number of rows and columns from a cell or range of cells. The reference that is returned can be a single cell or a range of cells. You can specify the number of rows and the number of columns to be returned. Guru Tip: OFFSET is a powerful function for returning a dynamic range. In the example below, OFFSET starts at cell B12. It goes down 5 rows and right 4 columns to get to the starting point of the range. The range is then 5 rows tall and 2 columns wide. Because OFFSET is returning multiple values in this case, you will often use OFFSET as an argument in another function. In this example, the result of the OFFSET is calculated with the SUM function. In other cases, OFFSET might be used to describe a dynamic range for a VLOOKUP lookup range.

	D8			*fx* =SUM(OFFSET($B$12,D4,D5,D6,D7))							
	A	B	C	D	E	F	G	H	I	J	K
1	Choose a month (1-12):	7									
2	Choose a product line:	B									
3											
4	1st record for this month?			5	=MATCH(D1,B13:B29,0)						
5	1st col for this product?			4	=MATCH(D2,C11:K11,0)						
6	# rows this month:			5	=COUNTIF($B$13:$B$29,D1)						
7	# cols this product:			2	=COUNTIF(C11:K11,D2)						
8			Total:	1437	=SUM(OFFSET($B$12,D4,D5,D6,D7))						
9			Combined:	1437							
10											
11			A	A	A	B	B	C	C	C	C
12	Date		Month A1	A2	A5	B3	B4	C6	C7	C8	C9
13	6/4/2010		6	11	46	79	112	147	184	214	245	279
14	6/11/2010		6	14	48	81	115	150	185	217	246	282
15	6/18/2010		6	17	50	83	117	152	187	218	249	283
16	6/25/2010		6	20	53	84	120	155	188	219	251	285
17	7/2/2010		7	21	55	85	122	156	189	220	254	286
18	7/9/2010		7	23	58	88	125	157	192	221	255	288
19	7/16/2010		7	26	59	91	128	159	194	224	257	291
20	7/23/2010		7	27	61	94	130	162	195	225	260	294
21	7/30/2010		7	30	63	96	133	165	196	227	263	295
22	8/6/2010		8	32	65	98	134	167	197	229	266	297
23	8/13/2010		8	35	67	100	135	170	198	231	268	300
24	8/20/2010		8	36	68	103	136	171	201	233	269	302

OR(logical1,logical2,...) [Category: Logical]

Returns TRUE if any argument is TRUE; returns FALSE if all arguments are FALSE. Guru Tip: Use the OR function in place of a logical_test as the first argument of the IF function.

PEARSON(array1,array2) [Category: Statistical]]

Returns the Pearson product moment correlation coefficient, r, a dimensionless index that ranges from -1.0 to 1.0 inclusive and reflects the extent of a linear relationship between two data sets. Guru Tip: When the Microsoft MVP's get together in Seattle for the annual MVP Summit, only Chip Pearson can claim that he has an Excel function named after him. If you haven't done so already, check out the great articles at cpearson.com.

PERCENTILE(array,k) [Category: Statistical]]

Returns the k-th percentile of values in a range. You can use this function to establish a threshold of acceptance. For example, you can decide to examine candidates who score above the 90th percentile. Guru Tip: the second argument needs to be a percentage or a decimal. Use 0.1 for the 10th percentile. Also be aware that the percentiles are extrapolated and often will be a number which does not appear in the data set.

`=PERCENTILE(A2:$A$21,C3)`

	A	B	C	D	
1	Data Set				
2	125				
3	126		10%	129.6	
4	130		50%	150	
5	131		90%	166.3	
6	132				
7	133				
8	135				
9	139				
10	146				
11	150				
12	150				
13	158				
14	159				
15	161				
16	162				
17	164				
18	165				
19	166				
20	167				
21	170				
22					

PERCENTRANK(array,x,significance) [Category: Statistical]]

Returns the rank of a value in a data set as a percentage of the data set. This function can be used to evaluate the relative standing of a value within a data set. For example, you can use PERCENTRANK to evaluate the standing of an aptitude test score among all scores for the test. Guru Tip: Unlike RANK, this function always assumes that the largest score is at the 100th percentile. You can't specify that lower scores are better, although you could subtract the result from 100% to reverse the sequence. If significance is omitted, a value of 3 is used, meaning that the result will contain 3 significant digts. A result of 0.123 will appear at 12.3% when properly formatted as a percentage.

PERMUT(number,number_chosen) [Category: Statistical]]

Returns the number of permutations for a given number of objects that can be selected from number objects. A permutation is any set or subset of objects or events where internal order is significant. Permutations are different from combinations, for which the internal order is not significant. Guru Tip: Use COMBIN for lottery probabilities where the order of the numbers drawn does not matter. Use PERMUT when the order of the results matter. To find out how many possible ways that 8 greyhounds can finish in first-second-third, use =PERMUT(8,3).

=PERMUT(8,4)

	A	B	C	D
1	Trifecta	336	=PERMUT(8,3)	
2	Superfecta	1680	=PERMUT(8,4)	

PHONETIC(reference) [Category: Text]

Extracts the phonetic (furigana) characters from a text string.

PI( ) [Category: Math]

Returns the number 3.14159265358979, the mathematical constant pi, accurate to 15 digits. Guru Tip: Useful for figuring out which pizza deal is best for the office staff meeting. The area of a circle is PI()*Radius^2. A 16" pie has a radius of 8" and contains 201 square inches of piizza. A 12" pie has a radius of 6" and contains 113 square inches of pizza. To compare these round pizzas to square pizzas, see SQRTPI.

=PI()*B2^2

	A	B	C
1	Pizza Diameter	Radius	Area
2	8	4	50.3
3	12	6	113.1
4	13	6.5	132.7
5	15	7.5	176.7
6	16	8	201.1

PMT(rate,nper,pv,fv,type) [Category: Financial]

Calculates the payment for a loan based on constant payments and a constant interest rate. Guru Tip: there are several gotchas in this function. The rate is the percentage rate per period of the loan. So, while your car loan might have a 5.25% interest rate, the monthly interest rate is 5.25%/12. Also, the present value argument should be negative, as this is money coming out of the bank.

=PMT(B3/12,B2,-B1)

	A	B
1	Car Price	25995
2	Term	60
3	Rate	5.25%
4		
5	Payment	$493.54
6		

POISSON(x,mean,cumulative) [Category: Statistical]]

Returns the Poisson distribution. A common application of the Poisson distribution is predicting the number of events over a specific time, such as the number of cars arriving at a toll plaza in 1 minute.

POWER(number,power) [Category: Math]

Returns the result of a number raised to a power. Guru Tip: this function seems irrelevant given the carat operator. =POWER(8,7) returns the same result as =8^7.

=POWER(A2,B2)

	A	B	C	D
1	Number	Power	Power	=A^B
2	8	7	2097152	2097152
3	7	4	2401	2401
4	10	6	1000000	1000000
5	6	7	279936	279936
6	4	5	1024	1024
7	2	4	16	16

PPMT(rate,per,nper,pv,fv,type) [Category: Financial]

Returns the payment on the principal for a given period for an investment based on periodic, constant payments and a constant interest rate. Guru Tip: Column C of the image for the ROW function is built using PPMT.

PRICE(settlement,maturity,rate,yld,redemption,frequency,basis) [Category: Financial]*

Returns the price per $100 face value of a security that pays periodic interest.

PRICEDISC(settlement,maturity,discount,redemption,basis) [Category: Financial]*

Returns the price per $100 face value of a discounted security.

PRICEMAT(settlement,maturity,issue,rate,yld,basis) [Category: Financial]*

Returns the price per $100 face value of a security that pays interest at maturity.

PROB(x_range,prob_range,lower_limit,upper_limit) [Category: Statistical]]

Returns the probability that values in a range are between two limits. If upper_limit is not supplied, returns the probability that values in x_range are equal to lower_limit. Guru Tip: Used frequently in statistics. I had an opportunity to use it once, when I was in a statistics class.

PRODUCT(number1,number2, ...) [Category: Math]

Multiplies all the numbers given as arguments and returns the product.

PROPER(text) [Category: Text]

Capitalizes the first letter in a text string and any other letters in text that follow any character other than a letter. Converts all other letters to lowercase letters. Guru Tip: PROPER is great for putting upper case names into proper case. Although, watch out for names where an interior letter is supposed to be capitalized. =PROPER("MCCARTNEY") is going to return Mccartney.

PV(rate,nper,pmt,fv,type) [Category: Financial]

Returns the present value of an investment. The present value is the total amount that a series of future payments is worth now. For example, when you borrow money, the loan amount is the present value to the lender.

QUARTILE(array,quart) [Category: Statistical]]

Returns the quartile of a data set. Quartiles often are used in sales and survey data to divide populations into groups. For example, you can use QUARTILE to find the top 25 percent of incomes in a population.

QUOTIENT(numerator,denominator) [Category: Math]*

Returns the integer portion of a division. Use this function when you want to discard the remainder of a division. Guru Tip: For the opposite of QUOTIENT, see MOD.

RADIANS(angle) [Category: Math]

Converts degrees to radians. Guru Tip: See COS.

RAND( ) [Category: Math]

Returns an evenly distributed random number greater than or equal to 0 and less than 1. A new random number is returned every time the worksheet is calculated. Guru Tip: To generate random numbers between 1 and 10, use =INT(RAND()*10)+1

RANDBETWEEN(bottom,top) [Category: Math]*

Returns a random number between the numbers you specify. A new random number is returned every time the worksheet is calculated. Guru Tip: Unlike RAND, this function returns integers. When I need to add some "noise" to data, I will add =RAND(-3,3) to subtract/add anywhere from 1 to 3 to each number in a range. If you want to select random items from a list, the RANDBETWEEN() is a perfect argument for INDEX: =INDEX(J1:J30,RANDBETWEEN(1,30)).

RANK(number,ref,order) [Category: Statistical]]

Returns the rank of a number in a list of numbers. The rank of a number is its size relative to other values in a list. (If you were to sort the list, the rank of the number would be its position.) Guru Tip: most people leave off the 3rd argument which means that the highest value receives a rank of 1. However, if you are ranking golf scores, put any non-zero value as the 3rd argument. Then the lowest score receives a rank of 1.

Rank deals with ties in the same way that the sporting pages would. In the example below, two scores are tied for second. Both of these scores receive a 2 and none of the scores receive a 3. The next score receives a 4. Similar ties at 5th and 7th mean that no one is ranked 6th or 8th.

=RANK(B10,$B$2:$B$11,1)

	A	B	C
1	Name	Score	Rank
2	David	72	7
3	Davis	70	4
4	Jack	71	5
5	Jim	72	7
6	K.J.	69	2
7	Luke	73	9
8	Phil	69	2
9	Rory	71	5
10	Tiger	67	1
11	Vijay	73	9

While the tie method is correct, you might be trying to sort with a formula. If subsequent VLOOKUP formulas will be attempting to pull every name from the list, those VLOOKUP formulas will be expecting there to be a #3 ranking. In this case, force the later occurrence of rank #2 to appear as #3 by adding a COUNTIF function to count how many times this score has previously appeared in the list. Note the severely mixed reference as the second argument of the COUNTIF: The row number of the heading is frozen with a dollar sign, but the last cell in the range is a relative reference pointing to the row above the current formula.

`=RANK(G18,$C$9:$C$18,1)+COUNTIF(G$8:G17,G18)`

	A	B	C	D	E	F	G
1	Leaderboard				Leaderboard		
2	1	Tiger	67		1	Tiger	67
3	2	K.J.	69		2	K.J.	69
4	3	#N/A	#N/A		3	Phil	69
5							
6	=VLOOKUP($A4,$A$9:$C$18,2,FALSE)						
7							
8	Rank	Name	Score		Rank	Name	Score
9	7	David	72		7	David	72
10	4	Davis	70		4	Davis	70
11	5	Jack	71		5	Jack	71
12	7	Jim	72		8	Jim	72
13	2	K.J.	69		2	K.J.	69
14	9	Luke	73		9	Luke	73
15	2	Phil	69		3	Phil	69
16	5	Rory	71		6	Rory	71
17	1	Tiger	67		1	Tiger	67
18	9	Vijay	73		10	Vijay	73

RATE(nper,pmt,pv,fv,type,guess) [Category: Financial]

Returns the interest rate per period of an annuity. RATE is calculated by iteration and can have zero or more solutions. If the successive results of RATE do not converge to within 0.0000001 after 20 iterations, RATE returns the #NUM! error value.

RECEIVED(settlement,maturity,investment,discount,basis) [Category: Financial]*

Returns the amount received at maturity for a fully invested security.

REGISTER.ID(file_text,resource,type_text)

Returns the register ID of the specified dynamic link library (DLL) or code resource that has been previously registered. If the DLL or code resource has not been registered, this function registers the DLL or code resource and then returns the register ID for the Macintosh.

REGISTER.ID(module_text,procedure,type_text)

Returns the register ID of the specified dynamic link library (DLL) or code resource that has been previously registered. If the DLL or code resource has not been registered, this function registers the DLL or code resource and then returns the register ID for Windows.

REPLACE(old_text,start_num,num_chars,new_text) [Category: Text]

REPLACE replaces part of a text string, based on the number of characters you specify, with a different text string. Guru Tip: I am betting you don't want REPLACE. You really want SUBSTITUTE. See SUBSTITUTE.

REPLACEB(old_text,start_num,num_bytes,new_text) [Category: Text]

REPLACEB replaces part of a text string, based on the number of bytes you specify, with a different text string. This function is for use with double-byte characters.

REPT(text,number_times) [Category: Text]

Repeats text a given number of times. Use REPT to fill a cell with a number of instances of a text string. Guru Tip: create in-cell bar charts using REPT and the pipe character as shown below:

=REPT("|",B2)		

	A	B	C
1	Category	Sales (000)	
2	A	25	|||||||||||||||||||
3	B	29	||||||||||||||||||||||
4	C	35	|||||||||||||||||||||||||
5	D	39	||||||||||||||||||||||||||||
6	E	43	|||||||||||||||||||||||||||||||
7	F	49	||||||||||||||||||||||||||||||||||
8	G	44	|||||||||||||||||||||||||||||||
9	H	32	||||||||||||||||||||||
10	I	26	|||||||||||||||||||
11	J	19	|||||||||||||

RIGHT(text,num_chars) [Category: Text]

RIGHT returns the last character or characters in a text string, based on the number of characters you specify. Guru Tip: See an example under LEFT where you can extract a specific number of characters from the right side of text. In many cases, you will have to use LEN and FIND to calculate the number of characters.

=RIGHT(F4,LEN(F4)-FIND("-",F4))		

	F	I	K
1		MID	RIGHT
3	Item #	Suffix	Suffix
4	U-2	2	2
5	CCNC-69	69	69

RIGHTB(text,num_bytes) [Category: Text]

RIGHTB returns the last character or characters in a text string, based on the number of bytes you specify. This function is for use with double-byte characters.

ROMAN(number,form) [Category: Math]

Converts an arabic numeral to roman, as text. Guru Tip: Great for presenting bad financial news. Convert your financial statements to Roman numerals using ROMAN. If you need to create an outline using Roman numerals, use =ROMAN(ROW(A1)) and copy down.

ROUND(number,num_digits) [Category: Math]

Rounds a number to a specified number of digits. Guru Tip: =ROUND(A1,2) will round to two decimal places. =ROUND(A2,-3) will round to the nearest thousand!

ROUNDDOWN(number,num_digits) [Category: Math]

Rounds a number down, toward zero.

ROUNDUP(number,num_digits) [Category: Math]

Rounds a number up, away from 0 (zero).

ROW(reference) [Category: Lookup & Reference]

Returns the row number of a reference. Guru Tip: =ROW(A1) is a clever way of writing the number 1, because as this formula is copied down a column, it will automatically point to ROW(A2) for 2, ROW(A3) for 3, and so on. In the image below, both IPMT and PPMT need payment numbers as the second argument. Rather than adding a new column with the numbers 1, 2, 3, ..., 180, the formula uses ROW(A1) as the second argument in row 8. As this gets copied down, the second argument will generate the numbers 1 through 180. See Page 11

=IPMT($B$3/12,ROW(A1),$B$2,-$B$1)

	A	B	C	D
1	Principal	175000		
2	Term	180		
3	Rate	6.5%		
4	Payment	1524.44		
5				
6				
7	Month	Interest	Principal	Balance
8	Aug-2008	$947.92	$576.52	174,423
9	Sep-2008	$944.79	$579.64	173,844
10	Oct-2008	$941.65	$582.78	173,261
185	May-2023	$24.51	$1,499.93	3,024
186	Jun-2023	$16.38	$1,508.06	1,516
187	Jul-2023	$8.21	$1,516.23	0

ROWS(array) [Category: Lookup & Reference]

Returns the number of rows in a reference or array. Guru Tip: You might use ROWS to figure out how many rows are returned by a dynamic range generated by OFFSET.

RSQ(known_y's,known_x's) [Category: Statistical]]

Returns the square of the Pearson product moment correlation coefficient through data points in known_y's and known_x's. The r-squared value can be interpreted as the proportion of the variance in y attributable to the variance in x.

RTD(ProgID,Server,Topic,[Topic2],…) [Category: Lookup & Reference]

New in Excel XP – Retrieves real-time data from a program that supports COM automation.

SEARCH(find_text,within_text,start_num) [Category: Text]

SEARCH returns the number of the character at which a specific character or text string is first found, beginning with start_num. Use SEARCH to determine the location of a character or text string within another text string so that you can use the MID or REPLACE functions to change the text. Guru Tip: SEARCH is more flexible than the more popular FIND function. SEARCH allows for wildcards in find_text. Also, SEACH is not case-sensitive, so there is no need to use LOWER to modify within_text as you might have to do with FIND.

SEARCHB(find_text,within_text,start_num) [Category: Text]

SEARCHB also finds one text string (find_text) within another text string (within_ text), and returns the number of the starting position of find_text. The result is based on the number of bytes each character uses, beginning with start_num. This function is for use with double-byte characters You can also use FINDB to find one text string within another.

SECOND(serial_number) [Category: Date & Time]

Returns the seconds of a time value. The second is given as an integer in the range 0 (zero) to 59.

SERIESSUM(x,n,m,coefficients) [Category: Math]*

Returns the sum of a power series based on the formula:

$SERIES(x,n,m,a) » a_1x^n + a_2x^{(n+m)} + a_3x^{(n+2m)} + ... + a_ix^{(n+(i-1)m)}$

SIGN(number) [Category: Math]

Determines the sign of a number. Returns 1 if the number is positive, zero (0) if the number is 0, and -1 if the number is negative.

SIN(number) [Category: Math]

Returns the sine of the given angle. Guru Tip: While the sine function that you learned about in geometry dealt with degrees, Excel's function needs a number of radians as an argument. To find the sine of 90 degrees, use =SIN(RADIANS(90)). In the figure below, three sine waves figure out the current day's biorhythm chart.

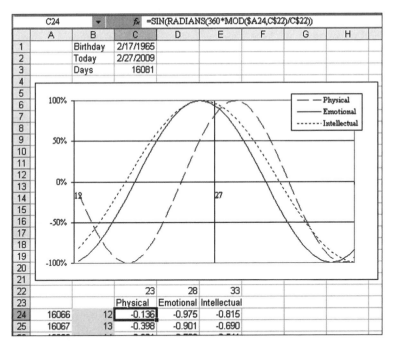

C24		*fx*	=SIN(RADIANS(360*MOD($A24,C$22)/C$22))				

SINH(number) [Category: Math]
Returns the hyperbolic sine of a number.

SKEW(number1,number2,...) [Category: Statistical]]
Returns the skewness of a distribution. Skewness characterizes the degree of asymmetry of a distribution around its mean. Positive skewness indicates a distribution with an asymmetric tail extending toward more positive values. Negative skewness indicates a distribution with an asymmetric tail extending toward more negative values.

SLN(cost,salvage,life) [Category: Financial]
Returns the straight-line depreciation of an asset for one period.

SLOPE(known_y's,known_x's) [Category: Statistical]]
Returns the slope of the linear regression line through data points in known_y's and known_x's. The slope is the vertical distance divided by the horizontal distance between any two points on the line, which is the rate of change along the regression line. Guru Tip: See image under FORECAST. Use with INTERCEPT to describe the linear regression line. The slope value is also the first value returned from the LINEST function.

SMALL(array,k) [Category: Statistical]]
Returns the k-th smallest value in a data set. Use this function to return values with a particular relative standing in a data set. Guru Tip: While you frequently use MIN to find the smallest value, =SMALL(A2:A1000,2) will return the 2nd smallest value. Great for eliminating outliers. See pages 46 & 49.

SQL.REQUEST(connection_string,output_ref,driver_prompt,query_text,col_names_logical)*

Connects with an external data source, and runs a query from a worksheet. SQL.REQUEST then returns the result as an array without the need for macro programming. If this function is not already available, install the Microsoft Excel ODBC add-in (XLODBC.XLA).

SQRT(number) [Category: Math]

Returns a positive square root. Guru Tip: Sure – it is nice of Microsoft to provide this function, but what if you need a cube root or a fifth root? To find a square root, raise a number to the (1/2) power. =25^(1/2). To find a cube root, raise the number to the (1/3) power: =125^(1/3).

SQRTPI(number) [Category: Math]*

Returns the square root of (number * pi). Guru Tip: This obscure function is used to convert round objects into equivalent sized square object. If you have a round pizza with a radius of 8", use =SQRTPI(8^2) to see that the equivalent sized square pizza is 14.18".

	E2			▼		*fx*	=SQRTPI(B2^2)
	A	B	C	D	E	F	
1	Pizza Diameter	Radius	Area		Equivalent Square Pizza Size	Area	
2	8"	4"	50.3		7.09"	50.3	
3	12"	6"	113.1		10.63"	113.1	
4	13"	7"	132.7		11.52"	132.7	
5	15"	8"	176.7		13.29"	176.7	
6	16"	8"	201.1		14.18"	201.1	

STANDARDIZE(x,mean,standard_dev) [Category: Statistical]]

Returns a normalized value from a distribution characterized by mean and standard_dev.

STDEV(number1,number2,...) [Category: Statistical]]

Estimates standard deviation based on a sample. The standard deviation is a measure of how widely values are dispersed from the average value (the mean).

STDEVA(value1,value2,...) [Category: Statistical]]

Estimates standard deviation based on a sample. The standard deviation is a measure of how widely values are dispersed from the average value (the mean). Text and logical values such as TRUE and FALSE are included in the calculation.

STDEVP(number1,number2,...) [Category: Statistical]]

Calculates standard deviation based on the entire population given as arguments. The standard deviation is a measure of how widely values are dispersed from the average value (the mean).

STDEVPA(value1,value2,...) [Category: Statistical]]

Calculates standard deviation based on the entire population given as arguments, including text and logical values. The standard deviation is a measure of how widely values are dispersed from the average value (the mean).

STEYX(known_y's,known_x's) [Category: Statistical]]

Returns the standard error of the predicted y-value for each x in the regression. The standard error is a measure of the amount of error in the prediction of y for an individual x.

SUBSTITUTE(text,old_text,new_text,instance_num) [Category: Text]

Substitutes new_text for old_text in a text string. Use SUBSTITUTE when you want to replace specific text in a text string; use REPLACE when you want to replace any text that occurs in a specific location in a text string. Guru Tip: This function is great for replacing a substring with another substring. Also great for getting rid of strange characters. =SUBSTITUTE(A2,CHAR(160),CHAR(32)) will replace all non-breaking spaces from web data with regular spaces. For another example, see CODE. Also see page 120.

SUBTOTAL(function_num,ref1,ref2,...) [Category: Math]

Returns a subtotal in a list or database. It is generally easier to create a list with subtotals using the Subtotals command (Data menu). Once the subtotal list is created, you can modify it by editing the SUBTOTAL function. Guru Tip: In layman's terms, the SUBTOTAL function will sum all entries in a range but will ignore other SUBTOTAL functions within the range. This allows you to add multiple levels of subtotals in a range without affecting the grand total. Microsoft figured this functionality would be useful for SUM and the 10 other standard calculation functions: AVERAGE, COUNT, COUNTA, MAX, MIN, PRODUCT, STDDEV, STDDEVP, VAR, and VARP. Rather than adding 11 new functions (such as SUBMAX, SUBAVERAGE...), they added a single function and allow you to specify the calculation using the function_num. If you ever wondered why the number 9 is used to represent the popular SUM function, it is because SUM falls 9th alphabetically in the list when you are using the English version of Excel. Function_num values from 1 to 11 perform the "classic" SUBTOTAL calculation which includes visible and hidden rows. Using 101 to 111 performs the "new" SUBTOTAL calculation which excludes hidden rows. Nothing you can do will make it exclude hidden columns. Also see page 41.

SUM(number1,number2, ...) [Category: Math]

Adds all the numbers in a range of cells. Guru Tip: a workhorse function that is probably the most used function in Excel. Use the Sigma icon or Alt+= to enter a sum function. If you replace the comma with a space, the SUM will add up the intersection of the ranges. For an example, see page 39.

SUMIF(range,criteria,sum_range) [Category: Math]

Adds the cells specified by a given criteria. Guru Tip: Added in Excel 97 to make simple conditional sums easier than using array formulas or SUMPRODUCT. To look through the items in B2:B20 for rows that match "ABC", then add up the corresponding revenue from column C, use =SUMIF($B$2:$B$20,"ABC",$C$2:$C$20). While most people will use a sum_range that is the same size and shape as the range, you can specify just the top left cell of the sum_range and Excel will expand the range to be the same size and shape as the range: =SUMIF($B$2:$B$20,"ABC",$C$2). In the unusual case where range and sum_range are the same, you can omit the third argument. This happens when you are testing if the numbers to be added are larger than a threshold as in cell F18 below. Also see page 12

=SUMIF($B$2:$B$20,E5,$C$2:$C$20)							
	A	B	C	D	E	F	G	H
1	Rep	Item	Sales					
2	Fred	DEF	4075		Sales by Item:			
3	Joe	ABC	4727		ABC	15314		
4	Bob	DEF	2842		DEF	32440		
5	Bob	DEF	3022		XYZ	10260		
6	Bob	XYZ	2361		Total	58014		
7	Bob	DEF	2798					
8	Joe	DEF	2114		=SUMIF($B$2:$B$20,E3,$C$2:$C$20)			
9	Fred	ABC	3901					
10	Bob	ABC	1778		Sales by Rep:			
11	Joe	ABC	1009		Bob	20975		
12	Fred	XYZ	2698		Fred	21822		
13	Joe	XYZ	1354		Joe	15217		
14	Bob	DEF	3940		Total	58014		
15	Fred	DEF	3423					
16	Joe	XYZ	3847		=SUMIF($A$2:$A$20,E11,$C$2)			
17	Joe	DEF	2166					
18	Bob	DEF	4234		>4000	13036		
19	Fred	DEF	3826					
20	Fred	ABC	3899		=SUMIF(C2:C20,E18)			

SUMIFS(sum_range,criteria_range1,criteria1,[criteria_range2,criteria2,…] [Category: Math]

Adds the cells in a range specified by multiple criteria. Guru Tip: New in Excel 2002. While SUMIF can only test for a single condition, SUMIFS can test for up to 127 pairs of criteria. Note that the argument order is rearranged from SUMIF. In the plural version of SUMIFS, the sum_range appears first, followed by a pair of arguments for each criteria. Using the same data set as shown in SUMIF, the following image shows how to find sales by sales rep and item using SUMIFS.

=SUMIFS($C$2:$C$20,$A$2:$A$20,F$2,$B$2:$B$20,$E3)

	E	F	G	H	I
2		Bob	Fred	Joe	Total
3	ABC	1778	7800	5736	15314
4	DEF	16836	11324	4280	32440
5	XYZ	2361	2698	5201	10260
6	Total	20975	21822	15217	58014

SUMPRODUCT(array1,array2,array3, ...) [Category: Math]
Multiplies corresponding components in the given arrays, and returns the sum of those products. Guru Tip: SUMPRODUCT allowed you to do SUMIF, COUNTIF, SUMIFS long before these functions existed. See numerous examples at the beginning of this book. To replace the SUMIFS in the image above, use the SUMPRODUCT in the image below. Also see page 15

=SUMPRODUCT(($A$2:$A$20=F$2)*($B$2:$B$20=$E3)*($C$2:$C$20))

	A	B	C	D	E	F	G	H	I
1	Rep	Item	Sales						
2	Fred	DEF	4075			Bob	Fred	Joe	Total
3	Joe	ABC	4727		ABC	1778	7800	5736	15314
4	Bob	DEF	2842		DEF	16836	11324	4280	32440
5	Bob	DEF	3022		XYZ	2361	2698	5201	10260
6	Bob	XYZ	2361		Total	20975	21822	15217	58014

SUMSQ(number1,number2, ...) [Category: Math]
Returns the sum of the squares of the arguments.

SUMX2MY2(array_x,array_y) [Category: Math]
Returns the sum of the difference of squares of corresponding values in two arrays.

SUMX2PY2(array_x,array_y) [Category: Math]
Returns the sum of the sum of squares of corresponding values in two arrays. The sum of the sum of squares is a common term in many statistical calculations.

SUMXMY2(array_x,array_y) [Category: Math]
Returns the sum of squares of differences of corresponding values in two arrays.

SYD(cost,salvage,life,per) [Category: Financial]
Returns the sum-of-years' digits depreciation of an asset for a specified period. Guru Tip: VDB is more flexible.

T(value) [Category: Text]
Returns the text referred to by value. Guru Tip: This is the corollary to the N function. =T of text is text. =T of number is nothing. While people have found

something actually useful for N, I am not sure why you would want to wipe out all the numbers in a range.

TAN(number) [Category: Math]

Returns the tangent of the given angle.

TANH(number) [Category: Math]

Returns the hyperbolic tangent of a number.

TBILLEQ(settlement,maturity,discount) [Category: Financial]*

Returns the bond-equivalent yield for a Treasury bill.

TBILLPRICE(settlement,maturity,discount) [Category: Financial]*

Returns the price per $100 face value for a Treasury bill.

TBILLYIELD(settlement,maturity,pr) [Category: Financial]*

Returns the yield for a Treasury bill.

TDIST(x,degrees_freedom,tails) [Category: Statistical]]

Returns the Percentage Points (probability) for the Student t-distribution where a numeric value (x) is a calculated value of t for which the Percentage Points are to be computed. The t-distribution is used in the hypothesis testing of small sample data sets. Use this function in place of a table of critical values for the t-distribution.

TEXT(value,format_text) [Category: Text]

Converts a value to text in a specific number format. Guru Tip: This is very useful when you are joining text and a date or text and currency. To ensure that the currency shows up with two decimal places and a comma, use ="Please remit "&TEXT(F20,"$#,##0.00"). See page 35

TIME(hour,minute,second) [Category: Date & Time]

Returns the decimal number for a particular time. The decimal number returned by TIME is a value ranging from 0 to 0.99999999, representing the times from 0:00:00 (12:00:00 A.M.) to 23:59:59 (11:59:59 P.M.). Guru Tip: Say that you have someone who entered a column of times. They entered 2:30 thinking that it meant 2 minutes and 30 seconds, but Excel interpreted it as 30 minutes past two o'clock. To convert that column back to something usable, the formula =TIME(0,HOUR(A2),MINUTE(A2)) would do the trick.

TIMEVALUE(time_text) [Category: Date & Time]

Returns the decimal number of the time represented by a text string. The decimal number is a value ranging from 0 (zero) to 0.99999999, representing the times from 0:00:00 (12:00:00 A.M.) to 23:59:59 (11:59:59 P.M.). Guru Tip: Like DATEVALUE, this function is used to convert a range of text that looks like times to real times. After converting the values, apply a time format to get the results to look like times instead of decimals. The advantage, of course, is that you can now do time calculations on the real times.

TINV(probability,degrees_freedom) [Category: Statistical]]

Returns the t-value of the Student's t-distribution as a function of the probability and the degrees of freedom.

TODAY( ) [Category: Date & Time]

Returns the serial number of the current date. The serial number is the date-time code used by Microsoft Excel for date and time calculations. Guru Tip: This is often better than the more popular =NOW() function, particularly if you are calculating the number of days between today and another date. With =NOW(), your date difference calculation will reflect decimal portions of a day as the workday elapses. With =TODAY(), the number of days will remain constant until midnight.

TRANSPOSE(array) [Category: Lookup & Reference]

Returns a vertical range of cells as a horizontal range, or vice versa. TRANSPOSE must be entered as an array formula in a range that has the same number of rows and columns, respectively, as array has columns and rows. Use TRANSPOSE to shift the vertical and horizontal orientation of an array on a worksheet. For example, some functions, such as LINEST, return horizontal arrays. LINEST returns a horizontal array of the slope and Y-intercept for a line. Guru Tip: In the image below, select blank cells A3:A7. Type =TRANSPOSE(A1:E1) and press Ctrl+Shift+Enter. To turn the vertical array back to horizontal, select five blank cells A12:E12. Type =TRANSPOSE(A3:A7) and press Ctrl+Shift+Enter. Note that you do not type the curly braces shown in the formula. Excel adds those when you press Ctrl+Shift+Enter to signify that this is an array formula.

=YEAR(A2)			
	A	B	C	D
1	Date	YEAR	MONTH	DAY
2	1/1/1930	1930	1	1
3	6/1/1950	1950	6	1
4	12/31/1999	1999	12	31
5	1/1/2000	2000	1	1
6	10/1/2010	2010	10	1

TREND(known_y's,known_x's,new_x's,const) [Category: Statistical]]

Returns values along a linear trend. Fits a straight line (using the method of least squares) to the arrays known_y's and known_x's. Returns the y-values along that line for the array of new_x's that you specify. Guru Tip: I usually use LINEST and then enter a range of formulas multiplying the slope and adding the constant. Instead, you could use TREND.

TRIM(text) [Category: Text]

Removes all spaces from text except for single spaces between words. Use TRIM on text that you have received from another application that may have irregular spacing. Guru Tip: If your VLOOKUP functions are not working, check to see if one list has extra spaces at the end of the value. =TRIM(" ABC   DEF ") will return "ABC DEF". TRIM removes leading spaces, trailing spaces and replaces multiple interior spaces with a single space. See page 120.

TRIMMEAN(array,percent) [Category: Statistical]]

Returns the mean of the interior of a data set. TRIMMEAN calculates the mean taken by excluding a percentage of data points from the top and bottom tails of a data set. You can use this function when you wish to exclude outlying data from your analysis.

TRUE( ) [Category: Logical]

Returns the logical value TRUE. Guru Tip: See FALSE().

TRUNC(number,num_digits) [Category: Math]

Truncates a number to an integer by removing the fractional part of the number. Guru Tip: For positive numbers, INT and TRUNC operate the same. However, for negative numbers, TRUNC will move towards zero and INT will move away from zero. As you see in this image, the INT(-1.6) is -2, while TRUNC(-1.6) is -1

=TRUNC(A6)			
	A	B	C
1			
2		INT	TRUNC
3	1.3	1	1
4	2.8	2	2
5	-1.6	-2	-1
6	-3.1	-4	-3
7			

TTEST(array1,array2,tails,type) [Category: Statistical]]

Returns the probability associated with a Student's t-Test. Use TTEST to determine whether two samples are likely to have come from the same two underlying populations that have the same mean.

TYPE(value) [Category: Information]

Returns the type of value. Use TYPE when the behavior of another function depends on the type of value in a particular cell. Guru Tip: Type returns 1 for numbers, 2 for text, 4 for TRUE and FALSE, 16 for errors, and 64 for an array.

UPPER(text) [Category: Text]

Converts text to uppercase. Guru Tip: Perfect for converting lower case text to upper case to facilitate matching two lists. Also see PROPER and LOWER.

VALUE(text) [Category: Text]

Converts a text string that represents a number to a number. Guru Tip: Guru Jonathon Broughton uses this function for all the times that others enter numbers as text indiscriminately. In the figure below, VALUE handles text, spaces, plus signs, minus signs, and even scientific notation. It will not work with the word "one", though.

fx =VALUE(D3)			
	C	D	E
1			
2		1	1
3		2	2
4		3	3
5		4	4
6		5	5
7	Total	6	15
8			
9		1	1
10		+1	1
11		2E3	2000
12		-3	-3
13		one	#VALUE!

VAR(number1,number2,...) [Category: Statistical]]

Estimates variance based on a sample.

VARA(value1,value2,...) [Category: Statistical]]

Estimates variance based on a sample. In addition to numbers, text and logical values such as TRUE and FALSE are included in the calculation.

VARP(number1,number2,...) [Category: Statistical]]

Calculates variance based on the entire population.

VARPA(value1,value2,...) [Category: Statistical]]

Calculates variance based on the entire population. In addition to numbers, text and logical values such as TRUE and FALSE are included in the calculation.

VDB(cost,salvage,life,start_period,end_period,factor,no_switch) [Category: Financial]

Returns the depreciation of an asset for any period you specify, including partial periods, using the double-declining balance method or some other method you specify. VDB stands for variable declining balance. Guru Tip: There are many depreciation functions in Excel: SLN, DB, DDB, SYD. The VDB method handles does SLN, DB, and DDB better than those individual functions do them. You can specify partial periods with VDB. If Factor is 1, then you are using DB. If factor is 2, then you are using DDB or double declining balance. If Factor is 4, then you are making stuff up and using a mythical QDB or quadruple declining balance. You could use a factor of 11 for HDB or Hendecuple Declining Balance but you might end up in tax court. (This is my 24th book that I've written but the first time I ever used the word Hendecuple). If switch is FALSE, then the calculation switches over to straight-line as soon as that method would yield a higher depreciation.

VLOOKUP(lookup_value,table_array,col_index_num,range_lookup) [Category: Lookup & Reference]

Searches for a value in the leftmost column of a table, and then returns a value in the same row from a column you specify in the table. Use VLOOKUP instead of HLOOKUP when your comparison values are located in a column to the left of the data you want to find. Guru Tip: VLOOKUP is the workhorse of Excel, says guru John Conmy. Use VLOOKUP to find the description for an item number as shown below.

D2				fx	=VLOOKUP(A2,$L$2:$M$29,2,FALSE)	
	A	C	D	K	L	M
1	Item	Qty	Description		SKU	Description
2	BG33-8	580	14K Gold Bangle Bracele		BG33-3	14K Gold Bar
3	Cross50-5	422			CR50-3	14K Gold Cro
4	RG78-25	638			RG75-3	14K Gold RA
5	BG33-8	775			RG78-25	14K Gold Bal
6	BG33-8	331			W25-6	18K Italian G
7	ER46-7	140			BR26-3	18K Italian G
8	RG75-3	231			BR15-3	14K Gold On
9	W25-6	878			BG33-8	14K Gold Bar
10	CR50-6	571			BG33-17	14K Gold Bar

WEEKDAY(serial_number,return_type) [Category: Date & Time]

Returns the day of the week corresponding to a date. The day is given as an integer, ranging from 1 (Sunday) to 7 (Saturday), by default. Guru Tip: The return_type argument controls the results. Use a return type of 1 and the days are numbered as 1 for Sunday, 2 for Monday, … 7 for Saturday. If you use a return type of 2, then Monday is 1 and Sunday is 7. If you use a return type of 3, then Monday is zero and Sunday is 6. Also see page 7.

=WEEKDAY($A9,D$2)				
	A	B	C	D
1		Return Type --->		
2		1	2	3
3	Sunday, July 04, 2010	1	7	6
4	Monday, July 05, 2010	2	1	0
5	Tuesday, July 06, 2010	3	2	1
6	Wednesday, July 07, 2010	4	3	2
7	Thursday, July 08, 2010	5	4	3
8	Friday, July 09, 2010	6	5	4
9	Saturday, July 10, 2010	7	6	5

WEEKNUM(serial_num,return_type) [Category: Date & Time]*

Returns a number that indicates where the week falls numerically within a year.

WEIBULL(x,alpha,beta,cumulative) [Category: Statistical]]

Returns the Weibull distribution. Use this distribution in reliability analysis, such as calculating a device's mean time to failure.

WORKDAY(start_date,days,holidays) [Category: Date & Time]*

Returns a number that represents a date that is the indicated number of working days before or after a date (the starting date). Working days exclude weekends and any dates identified as holidays. Use WORKDAY to exclude weekends or holidays when you calculate invoice due dates, expected delivery times, or the number of days of work performed. To view the number as a date, click Cells on the Format menu, click Date in the Category box, and then click a date format in the Type box. Guru Tip: Say that you hire an employee and need to know when a 60-workday probation period is over. Just as in the NETWORKDAYS example, you can specify a range of holidays as the third argument in the function. This function assumes that your workweek is the five days from Monday through Friday. If you work any other work week, see page 4.

XIRR(values,dates,guess) [Category: Financial]*

Returns the internal rate of return for a schedule of cash flows that is not necessarily periodic. To calculate the internal rate of return for a series of periodic cash flows, use the IRR function.

XNPV(rate,values,dates) [Category: Financial]*

Returns the net present value for a schedule of cash flows that is not necessarily periodic. To calculate the net present value for a series of cash flows that is periodic, use the NPV function.

YEAR(serial_number) [Category: Date & Time]

Returns the year corresponding to a date. The year is returned as an integer in the range 1900-9999. Guru Tip: Use YEAR, MONTH, DAY, HOUR, MINUTE, and SECOND to break a date and time into component parts. Join the component parts back into a date using DATE or TIME.

=YEAR(A2)

	A	B	C	D
1	Date	YEAR	MONTH	DAY
2	1/1/1930	1930	1	1
3	6/1/1950	1950	6	1
4	12/31/1999	1999	12	31
5	1/1/2000	2000	1	1
6	10/1/2010	2010	10	1

YEARFRAC(start_date,end_date,basis) [Category: Date & Time]*

Calculates the fraction of the year represented by the number of whole days between two dates (the start_date and the end_date). Use the YEARFRAC worksheet function to identify the proportion of a whole year's benefits or obligations to assign to a specific term.

YEN(number,decimals) [Category: Text]

Converts a number to text, using the ¥ (yen) currency format, with the number **rounded to a specified place.**

YIELD(settlement,maturity,rate,pr,redemption,frequency,basis) [Category: Financial]*

Returns the yield on a security that pays periodic interest. Use YIELD to calculate bond yield.

YIELDDISC(settlement,maturity,pr,redemption,basis) [Category: Financial]*

Returns the annual yield for a discounted security.

YIELDMAT(settlement,maturity,issue,rate,pr,basis) [Category: Financial]*

Returns the annual yield of a security that pays interest at maturity.

ZTEST(array,x,sigma) [Category: Statistical]]

Returns the two-tailed P-value of a z-test. The z-test generates a standard score for x with respect to the data set, array, and returns the two-tailed probability for the normal distribution. You can use this function to assess the likelihood that a particular observation is drawn from a particular population.

INDEX